Whose World Order?

WHOSE WORLD ORDER?

*Uneven Globalization
and the
End of the Cold War*

Hans-Henrik Holm and
Georg Sørensen

Westview Press

Boulder • San Francisco • Oxford

Copyright © 1995 by Westview Press, Inc.

Published in 1995 in the United States of America by Westview Press, Inc., 5500 Central Avenue, Boulder, Colorado 80301-2877, and in the United Kingdom by Westview Press, 36 Lonsdale Road, Summertown, Oxford OX2 7EW

Library of Congress Cataloging-in-Publication Data
Holm, Hans Henrik, 1951–
    Whose world order? : uneven globalization and the end of the Cold
  War / Hans-Henrik Holm and Georg Sørensen.
      p.   cm.
  Includes bibliographical references and index.
  ISBN 0-8133-2186-7. — ISBN 0-8133-2187-5 (pbk.)
    1. World politics—1989–   2. Equality.   I. Sørensen, Georg, 1948– .
II. Title.
D860.H65   1995
327'.09'94—dc20

94-24014
CIP

Printed and bound in the United States of America

The paper used in this publication meets the requirements
of the American National Standard for Permanence of Paper
for Printed Library Materials Z39.48-1984.

10   9   8   7   6   5   4   3   2

Contents

Illustrations

Tables

Figures

Maps

Preface and Acknowledgments

The idea for this book took shape in 1992 when we were working on an analysis of the post–Cold War world from the European point of view.[1] One of our colleagues who reviewed our work commented on our Eurocentrism. Reluctantly, we had to agree. Even if there are uniform global trends, the world seen from Europe is different from the world seen from Pacific Asia, from China, from Africa, from South Asia, from Latin America, and from the United States. The second source of inspiration for the book was the confusion and perplexity that sometimes results when international relations (IR) scholars meet to discuss the future of international relations theory.

We decided to ask eight prominent IR scholars from eight different parts of the world to contribute to a book on the new world order. It was important to us that the authors were actually rooted in the country or region on which they were asked to contribute. If there were any potential clashes among different cultures and perceptions, we wanted them to surface. We gave the contributors our original analysis and asked them to address two questions: (1) What has changed, in political, ideological, and economic terms, as seen from your part of the world? Is there a new world order? (2) Reflect briefly on consequences of the changes for theorizing in international relations.

Collective deliberations on these initial contributions provided the framework for the analysis set forth in Chapter 1. The authors then rewrote their contributions in accordance with the common framework. Drawing on the revised contributions, but also on our own ideas, we wrote the final chapter on international relations theory.

Our first thanks, and deep gratitude, go to our fellow authors who took time away from many other urgent tasks to participate in the project. We have had the good fortune of developing new friendships in a context of stimulating and efficient cooperation. Jennifer Knerr and Eric Wright from Westview were highly positive and forthcoming about the project from the very beginning. It was a great advantage to have publication plans settled at a very early stage. We are also grateful to Nancy Graham Holm for providing the book title and generous help. Our secretary in Aarhus, Jonna Kjær, has handled both manuscript revisions and communications among participants across the globe most efficiently. Diane Hess has done a marvelous job editing the manuscript, and Libby Barstow has guided it safely through the production process.

We are grateful for financial support from the Aarhus University Research Foundation, Danish Institute of International Studies, Danish Social Science Research Council, Danish Commission on Security and Disarmament, and Danish Council for Development Research.

Our own friendship and cooperation go back many years. We use the method for sustained cooperation recommended by Robert Keohane and Joseph Nye: swallowing our pride while we tear apart each other's drafts. We have swallowed and torn in the hope that what's left makes for worthwhile reading.

We would like to dedicate this book to our youngest children, Hannah Marina and Sebastian. We cannot promise them a better world, merely a small contribution to an improved understanding of the world we have.

Hans-Henrik Holm
Georg Sørensen

❧ 1 ❧

Introduction: What Has Changed?

HANS-HENRIK HOLM AND GEORG SØRENSEN

What has changed in international relations? Answering this question has become one of the central issues in the international relations (IR) debate. There is no accepted set of overall theoretical paradigms to guide our questions and quest for answers. The usefulness of the realist, liberalist, and Marxist paradigms appears to have decreased significantly. Too many relevant questions appear to fall outside the frameworks suggested by these dominant traditions. If there is a consensus in the present debate, it is this: In a world of variation and differentiation we are left without a firm theoretical compass to guide us.

Starting from this world of variation, our argument is simple: Globalization and the end of the Cold War are the two main expressions of change in the international system. Globalization is, briefly, the intensification of economic, political, social, and cultural relations across borders. The process is uneven in terms of cross-national intensity, geographical scope, and national and local depth. In Ferdinand Braudel's terminology it is a *longue durée* variable, expressing accumulated social change over time.[1] The second variable is *événementielle,* as Braudel would call the end of the Cold War.

Throughout the book, we analyze the combined effects of these two variables when they are simultaneously "filtered through" different types of societal structures and different geographical regions. We distinguish between two types of societal structures: (1) core-type, industrialized countries with consolidated liberal democracies involving a high degree of both internal and external institutionalization; and (2) periphery-type, semi- or nonindustrialized, authoritarian or semidemocratic areas with a relatively low degree of internal and external institutionalization.

In the case of Pacific Asia, the regional perspective employed cuts across the distinction between core-type, industrialized areas with consolidated liberal democracies and periphery-type, semi- or nonindustrialized, authoritarian or semidemocratic areas. The other regions belong either to the core

(Western Europe, the United States) or to the periphery-semiperiphery (Africa, Latin America, South Asia) category. Finally, the changes in the former eastern bloc have created a "gray zone" (or semiperipheral area) in which a number of countries clearly resemble periphery-type societies (Azerbaijan, Turkmenia, Uzbekistan, and others). The most advanced countries (Hungary, the Czech and Slovak Republics, Poland, and also Russia) struggle for membership in the core. The notion of different societal structures is especially important for our analysis of the consequences of uneven globalization. In order to study the consequences of globalization, it is necessary to take the diverging societal structures of the affected units into account.

The regions of the world have gained increased prominence in the present international system.[2] The concept of region is multidimensional. Regions can be defined as geographical units with natural barriers—North America, Africa, Europe—or as social or cultural entities. Regions in the latter sense are identified through their closeness and links in language, culture, and historical roots: South Asia, Pacific Asia. Some of these regions also have clear geographical boundaries (e.g., Africa); others do not. Regions may also be defined as organized political units. They may be highly organized with powerful regional structures (e.g., the European Community), or they may be more loosely organized (e.g., the North American Free Trade Agreement [NAFTA]). Finally, regions may be seen as regions of identity. Where lines of communication are highly developed and where values converge toward common identities, regions are created. The Nordic countries (and also to some extent Latin America) are examples of regions in this sense.

In pursuing our analysis, we employ a geographically based concept of region to explore changes in three dimensions: (1) a security-conflict dimension, (2) an economic growth–welfare dimension, and (3) a domestic politics–democracy–civil society dimension. Thus, we emphasize variation in regional outcomes.

Yet the "Whose world order?" question stresses that the present international system is characterized by new and old patterns of hierarchy and dominance. And the processes of change we analyze point not only to the mutual existence of various types of regions but also to the fact that in some cases states are more important units. The United States, Russia, and China are still in a category by themselves. Indeed, some states dominate regions to such an extent that the regional perspective becomes one of analyzing a dominant state and its surroundings (e.g., India and South Asia).

Chapters 2–9 contain analyses reflecting perspectives of Africa, Latin America, South Asia, China, Russia, Japan (in the context of Pacific Asia), (Western) Europe, and the United States. The contributions combine more general reflections on changes with analyses of specific regions or countries. We have allowed variation in relative emphasis on either one of these aspects (see Figure 1.1).

FIGURE 1.1   Changes and Outcomes: The Structure of the Argument

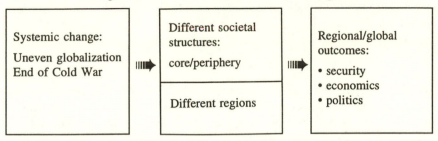

Have uneven globalization and the end of the Cold War produced a new world order? Our answer is no. Certainly there is not a new world order in the normative sense of the term. An international order built on ideas of justice, freedom, and peace has served as reference point for much of the debate on the so-called new world order. Emerging initially as a political justification for drawing a line in the sand during the Gulf War, it became a one-dimensional catchall phrase that is not analytically very helpful.[3] What we see instead is a world characterized by regional variation and transitional change, not by one particular order.

Hedley Bull defined international order as "a pattern of activity that sustains the elementary or primary goals of the society of states, or international society."[4] His focus is on states and the order between them. It is clear that in the post–Cold War world, the bipolar order has been replaced by something else. But what new order has taken its place? Some argue that multipolarity has been reinstated in the international system. Charles Krauthammer claimed that we live in a unipolar world dominated by the last remaining superpower, the United States.[5] Perhaps the most innovative view argues that the international system has become bifurcated into a "zone of peace" encompassing the developed industrialized North and a "zone of conflict" in the rest of the system.[6] In the zone of peace, war has become unthinkable as an instrument of interstate conflict. The combination of developed democratic structures and economically advanced, highly interdependent societies ties these states together. In the zone of conflict, democracy is frail or absent, and the economies are less developed. Ethnic, religious, economic, and ideological conflict is frequent both within and between states.[7]

In the zone of conflict, there is disorder rather than order in Bull's sense. Instead of trying to chart the post–Cold War order, we therefore need to focus on the nature of the changes we are witnessing in the global system. We thus start somewhere else, namely with the attempt to identify change. The changes in patterns of hierarchy and dominance brought about by globalization and the end of the Cold War have produced a changing international system. We see a changed role for the state in this system. We see new forms of sovereignty and changes in the relationship between politics and economics. This leads us in the direction of searching for new and different types of states.

WHAT HAS CHANGED?

What is it exactly that has changed? A good part of the disagreement about the scope and significance of change derives from an imprecise identification of sources of change. It is clear that the end of the Cold War is of crucial importance; yet this event alone cannot explain the novel developments in the international system. Our analysis is premised on the view that the end of the Cold War needs to be considered along with the concept of accumulated social change in the *longue dureé*. It is this blend of accumulated change and a dramatic event that "produces" the transformations in the international system that we are currently witnessing.

UNEVEN GLOBALIZATION

There are several possible ways of conceptualizing accumulated social change. We look for a combination of parsimony with sufficient respect for diversity. Our suggestion is the concept of "uneven globalization." The task in what follows is to define this concept in a way that allows different variations and nuances of globalization to come forward. Globalization can be briefly defined as the intensification of economic, political, social, and cultural relations across borders. Globalization is pushed by several factors; the most important is technological change. By "uneven" we intend to emphasize that the process of globalization is uneven in both intensity and geographical scope, in both the international and the domestic dimension. Behind this seemingly innocent definition is a wide-ranging debate about the real content of the globalization processes and the degree of change they invoke in the international system.

First, we may distinguish between globalization as increased internationalization of economic intercourse, on the one hand, and the emergence of a qualitatively new global economy, on the other. A contribution by Paul Hirst and Grahame Thompson is helpful in this regard. They identified two ideal types of international economic exchange. One is called "a world-wide international economy" and is described as follows:

> The world-wide international economy is one in which the principal entities are nation-states, and involves the growing interconnection between national economies. It involves the increasing integration of more and more nations and economic actors into market relationships. ... The form of interdependence between nations remains, however, of the "strategic" kind. That is, it implies the

continued relative separation of the domestic and the international frameworks for policy making and the management of economic affairs. ... Interactions are of the "billiard ball" type; international events do not directly penetrate or permeate the domestic economy but are refracted through national policies and processes.[8]

This is the less dramatic and more narrow type of economic globalization. We might call it "intensified interdependence" between national economies.

The contrasting ideal type involves qualitative change toward a system in which "distinct national economies are subsumed and rearticulated into the system by essentially international processes and transactions. ... The international system becomes autonomized, as markets and production become truly global. Domestic politics, whether of private corporations or public regulators, now have routinely to take account of the international determinants of their sphere of operations. ... the national level is permeated by and transformed by the international."[9] Whereas intensified economic interdependence involves more of the same in the sense that economic intercourse between national economies increases, true economic globalization invokes a qualitative shift toward a global economic system that is no longer based on autonomous national economies but on a consolidated global marketplace for production, distribution, and consumption. Here the "global economy dominates the national economies existing within it."[10]

Both of these meanings of globalization focus on economic processes. But globalization involves more than merely economics. Globalization can indeed be said to include "every aspect of social activity—be it communication, ecological matters, commerce, regulation, ideology or whatever."[11] Globalization in this sense may also be interpreted in two different ways. On the one hand, it can be seen as a somewhat trivial trend toward increasing interconnectedness between peoples and between individuals. It is, moreover, identified by some observers as a cyclical trend, and it is not immediately clear that interconnectedness (including economic interdependence) has increased unremittingly over time.[12]

On the other hand, globalization in the broad sense can be interpreted as leading toward a fundamental, qualitative shift in the conditions of people's lives. Globalization increases risks and opportunities for individuals, who become both objects of and participants in global processes, and individual actions may have dramatic consequences for international relations. This is the view adopted by Anthony Giddens, James Rosenau, and many others. The life conditions of peoples and communities are changed through globalization; local traditions and modes of behavior are being transformed or challenged; distant events have immediate consequences not only for states but for individuals' daily lives. For example, ordinary individual or family decisions about savings and investment require complicated analysis that involves forecasting interest rates; interest rates are determined by global cur-

TABLE 1.1   Dimensions of Globalization

| | Range/Scope of Change | |
Type/Scope of Processes	Quantitative (More of the same)	Qualitative (Epochal shift)
Narrow: Economics	Intensified interdependence	Economic globalization
Comprehensive: Social change	Increasing interconnectedness	Globalized societies

rency markets, which are in turn affected by global economic and political developments. The Chernobyl disaster threatened Brazilian children via the distribution of possibly contaminated European milk powder donations to Brazilian schools. Anthony Giddens has made a penetrating analysis of these "consequences of modernity," and James Rosenau has argued that these processes lead to dramatic consequences for international relations.[13]

In sum, these considerations provide us with four dimensions of globalization, as shown in Table 1.1. It is important to emphasize that we employ the concept of globalization in all of the four meanings in the table. The point is that all four aspects of globalization can be found in the real world. It cannot be decided beforehand which kind of globalization is the more important or predominant. This is a case for empirical analysis and underlines our previously stated premise: The process of globalization is uneven both in intensity and in geographical scope and depth.

Furthermore, unevenness entails the possibility of fragmentation. Globalization has meant increased integration for the Organization for Economic Cooperation and Development (OECD) countries, yet this process has also involved increasing marginalization of a number of Third World countries or parts of countries. Integration in the core and fragmentation of large parts of the periphery have gone hand in hand. At the same time, there are other reasons for fragmentation. In the former Soviet Union, fragmentation takes place because of a failed attempt at (Soviet communist) nation-building. In former Yugoslavia and elsewhere, ethnonationalist movements push fragmentation in a context of local or regional core-periphery relationships.[14] In sum, uneven globalization is best conceived as a dialectical process, stimulating integration as well as fragmentation, universalism as well as particularism, and cultural differentiation as well as homogenization.[15]

The notion of unevenness also implies that globalization may unfold in processes that are less than geographically global in scope. The predominant mode of globalization may be regionalization, that is, "the intensification of patterns of interconnectedness that define the contours of a regional sub-system."[16] Therefore, the regions need to be studied and analyzed specifically so that we may be clear about similarities and differences. We need to study the effects of uneven globalization and the end of the Cold War as they are "filtered through" different regions. It is a central thesis of this book that the combined effect of uneven globalization and the end of the Cold War is increased variation, not only between North and South but also among different regions of the world.

It is misleading to suggest that states are merely passive objects exposed to the swell of globalization. States are active players and their policies are probably the single most important determinant of the scope and direction of globalization, although some states have more capacity to act than others. There is an interplay, in other words, between the globalizing forces of modernity and the policies undertaken by states. Globalization may be said to entail a movement toward a single, unified global economy; states may push, resist, attempt to circumscribe or twist, this process to their own advantage. We do not accept the view that globalization more or less automatically leads to the demise of the state. At the same time, globalization is not a process that may simply be brought under the control of states.[17] Our premise is that globalization presents a number of serious challenges to the ways in which states have traditionally pursued economic, political, and social goals. In response to these challenges, basic features of state structures and state behavior are undergoing dramatic change. The scope and significance of these changes should be explored in empirical analysis.

THE END OF THE COLD WAR

The Cold War was based on the nuclear military competition between the two superpowers. This created a bipolar international system that constituted the decisive framework for all states' security concerns for 45 years. It involved a large network of defense alliances, the considerable presence of superpower military forces in Europe and elsewhere, and a system of economic and other commitments between states based on specific patterns of Cold War amity and enmity. Far from all of these different underpinnings of the Cold War are gone; yet the Cold War has ended in the sense that the bipolar rivalry is gone. A smooth process of liberal democratization and transition to a market economy in Eastern Europe and the former Soviet Union cannot be taken for granted. Yet the changes that have already taken place, including the demise of the Soviet Union, are so profound that a return to the Cold War is inconceivable. When the end of the Cold War is combined with accumulated effects of globalization, we arrive at the debate about the wider significance of what has happened. Are we witnessing, as some have argued, one of history's big punctuation marks: a watershed event that falls in line with other historical watersheds such as 1789, 1917, and 1945?[18] Is the end of the Cold War the beginning of peaceful relations among states? Is it the successful attempt to create effective international governance and solve the security dilemma inherent in the old international system?

Or are we exaggerating its importance? Was the Cold War merely a brief historical interlude when we saw bipolar confrontation structuring the international system, and does its demise mark the return to business as usual in international relations?[19] Is the anarchic structure of the international system returning in force rather than diminishing in importance? And are we, consequently, on the road toward more violent conflict between and within states in the post–Cold War system?

The present international system contains elements that can support both of these viewpoints, and yet in part, they are mutually exclusive. On the one hand, a change of the international system that eliminates the risk of war between core states is a fundamental qualitative shift in international relations. The international system of the last some 400 years was based on sovereign and independent states that ultimately could choose to fight rather than to cooperate with each other. When the interstate war option is no longer a policy instrument in large parts of the international system in the post–Cold War world, then the system has changed in a qualitative way.[20] On the other hand, most realists and neorealists see the changes marking the end of the Cold War as a much less dramatic issue concerning changes in alliance patterns and power relations in terms of the relative distribution of capabilities in the system. The shift is from a bipolar to a multipolar, or perhaps to a unipolar, system.[21] But this is not a fundamental change in the international system—only a change in the structure of polarity.[22]

To the realist the consequences of the end of the Cold War are therefore minor, at least in theoretical terms. As concerns the stability of the system, however, there may be dire consequences. The stability based on nuclear deterrence and superpower balancing in the bipolar confrontation is gone, and instead conflicts between states and within states will reappear. The anarchy of the international system is revealing itself—states have to fend for themselves, security alliances like the North Atlantic Treaty Organization (NATO) and the Warsaw Pact are transformed or break up, and states have to reconsider their security priorities and obligations. One realist's prediction is that larger states will turn inward in their security concerns and smaller states will be left to support themselves in a new and insecure environment.[23] The end of the Cold War is not the "end of history" but the "return of history."

Others have argued that this is a much too pessimistic and shortsighted view of what the end of the Cold War means.[24] The end of the Cold War is a fundamental event, coming at a time in history when the international system was already ripe with change due to forces of globalization. The breakdown of bipolarity has unleashed forces that have fundamentally changed the nature of international relations. The foundations of state power have changed. The Cold War was also a battle of ideas, and the "losers" have experienced immense domestic turbulence as a result of the breakdown of the traditional foundations of state power. "The victory of liberalism and democracy also brought the war in Yugoslavia, for democracy requires the definition of a political community: liberalism and nationalism go together."[25]

Power was always both a fundamental and a troublesome concept in international relations. Realists stress the importance of military power because violent conflict is always a possibility: "All history shows that nations active in international politics are continuously preparing for, actively involved in, or recovering from organized violence in the form of war."[26]

Even when realists expanded the notion of power to include economic and technological capabilities as well as less tangible elements such as prestige and leadership qualities, power was always power of the state. The end of the Cold War invokes change of power in a double sense. On the one hand, nonmilitary forms of power become much more important, including "soft power." The importance, for example, of television and new information technology has dramatically increased.[27] On the other hand, power is becoming more dispersed among actors both within states and in the international system. The building of the European Union with new powers to different European regions, to trade unions, to social groups, is a case in point.

These processes dramatically increase the influence of nonstate actors. One scholar claimed that a global civil society "is being constructed before our eyes."[28] In other words, the end of the Cold War signals a profound transformation of the role of the state in international society.

Furthermore, there is the claim that the end of the Cold War signals the end of war. The prevalence of liberal democracy in the great contest with authoritarianism means a change of international relations in the direction of peace.[29] Even if the entire world has not become democratic, the number of democracies is increasing, and there is a zone of peace with the consolidated democracies as the core.[30]

We thus have two competing interpretations of the end of the Cold War. On the one hand, it is seen as a qualitative change of international relations with fundamental consequences for the nature and the understanding of international politics. War is much less likely and there are increasing prospects for international governance. On the other hand, there is the argument that the end of the Cold War merely meant changes in the distribution of power within an anarchic system of states, a system that retained its ancient features of state units facing a security dilemma. In summary, a distinction between quantitative and qualitative change and between relations among states and global processes in a wider sense is helpful. We thus end up with the four categories shown in Table 1.2.

The qualitative-quantitative distinction brings out the debate between a "back to the future"–oriented realism, according to which changes in the

TABLE 1.2   End of the Cold War: Dimensions of Change

| *Locus of Change* | *Range/Scope of Change* | |
	Quantitative	*Qualitative*
State	Polarity in international systems	End of war
	Balance of power	
Global processes	Fragmentation and integration	Globalized societies without war

balance of power are the major event after the Cold War, and a view based on liberalism, according to which a possibility exists for the end of war between states, at least in some parts of the international system; the major reason for such optimism is the advance of liberal democracy.

The distinction between global processes and states emphasizes that the changes taking place are not necessarily confined to states as we knew them during the Cold War. New political forces surface: Ethnic and regionally based groups lay claim to independence or autonomy and thereby threaten the traditional understandings of sovereignty and statehood. Nonstate actors may gain access to weapons of mass destruction and undermine the entire concept of national security (see Chapter 8). Fragmentation of states is taking place together with attempts at integration and the creation of new institutions at the supranational level.

If we combine the most radical interpretations on both of these dimensions, we arrive at the vision of a globalized society without war: In a liberal democratic world, violent struggle between competing states will disappear. States will indeed cease to be repositories of the loyalties and cravings of groups of individuals. A power structure in the traditional sense can no longer be identified because power is diffused to different levels, from the individual microlevel to the global governance macrolevel. There is a wide variety of power resources, or means of influence, and concrete resources are much less fungible across issue areas.

We have described different aspects of globalization and of deliberations concerning the effects of the end of the Cold War. Taken together, they present us with quite different possibilities of interpreting current events. On the one hand, we have a not very dramatic prospect of increased interdependence as a result of globalization together with modifications in the balance of power after the end of the Cold War. On the other hand, we have the more dramatic notion of globalized societies in a world without violent struggles between states. It is a world where states to an increasing degree are enmeshed in structures in which both individuals and nonstate institutions are of importance, a world where notions of hegemony and uni- or multipolarity become increasingly irrelevant because globalization and the end of the Cold War have invoked a system in which states have ceased to be the privileged actors of special importance that they were in the old order. This radical vision is the ultimate expression of the direction of change taking place. We do not deny that elements corresponding to this vision exist or are in the making in the real world. But it is not a valid picture of the actual state of affairs and of the dominant trends in major regions. This will be demonstrated in the analyses of regional variation that make up the bulk of this book.

INSTEAD OF THE GRAND VISION:
REGIONAL VARIATION

In what follows, we briefly summarize the chapters in this volume. Instead of the grand vision just recognized of globalized, peaceful societies, the contributors present a picture of great regional variation. Out of these analyses of specific regions, combined with general reflections on changes in the international system, discernible patterns may be identified. We start with the chapters on core regions and countries, then move on to the periphery and, finally, to Russia.

Speaking from Europe, Michael Zürn traces in Chapter 8 a complex process of historical development in which processes of globalization pushed by earlier state measures have created a present situation where national policies of welfare, culture, communication, and security are increasingly ineffective. The result in the political sphere is attempts at further integration combined with subnational tendencies toward fragmentation. The end of the Cold War produced new types of conflict in the former communist countries, and the speed of European integration appears to be locked in battle with the increases in fragmentation in Europe. It is this twin process of fragmentation and integration that has created the current turbulence.

The acute problem seen from Western Europe is one of "uneven denationalization": On the one hand, the rise in international governance is slower than the process of globalization, which means that the loss of national policy effectiveness is not recaptured at a supranational level, resulting in a "deficit in the capacity to govern." On the other hand, the existing institutions of international governance are not equipped with mechanisms for democratic control and as a result, people tend to become "alienated from the remote political process."

Robert Keohane, in Chapter 9, is less pessimistic about the capacities of states to govern. Although it is true that globalization has increased the demand for international governance, advanced liberal democracies have, in general, been able to meet this demand, even if this will not necessarily be the case in the future. In response to globalization among industrialized liberal democracies, the institution of sovereignty is changing. "Rather than connoting the exercise of supremacy within a given territory, sovereignty provides the state with a legal grip on an aspect of a transnational process, whether involving multinational investment, the world's ecology, or the movement of migrants, drug dealers, and terrorists. *Sovereignty is less a territorially defined barrier than a bargaining resource for a politics characterized by complex transnational networks.*" Yet institutions of international governance continue to basically reflect national interests of dominant domestic coalitions in participating states. States bargain away elements of sovereignty in pursuance of their own interests. What they get in return is influence on developments of their concern through "partial authority over others' policies." At the same time, such procedures have stringent domestic preconditions, with constitutional democracy as the most important factor. It is the presence or absence of pluralist democratic institutions that determines to what extent the end of the Cold War will place us in a renewed situation of anarchy and conflict or in a changed, more cooperative and institutionalized international system. There will thus be great variation among the different regions of the world. In major parts of the world preconditions for democracy are lacking and sovereignty will continue to function in traditional ways. What role will the United States play in these developments? According to Robert Keohane, U.S. policy is turning inward, focusing on economic considerations. U.S. willingness to provide leadership in shaping international institutions of a global nature will therefore depend on the extent to which these institutions are seen to serve national economic interests.

In Pacific Asia, the end of the Cold War has produced few dramatic changes. In Chapter 7, Takashi Inoguchi points to three major reasons for this. First, no all-encompassing military security arrangements existed in the region during the Cold War. Second, the region is the economic powerhouse of the world in terms of rapid growth, thus creating rising military expenditures while the dependence on outside powers is being reduced. Finally, traditional rivalries have always been strong in the region, and the lack of regionwide political institutions both reflect and reinforce this. The end of the Cold War has localized politics in Pacific Asia even more than was the case earlier, and the state is still more firmly in control here than in other regions. The lack of common institutions could lead one to worry about stability, but this lack is to some extent compensated for by the cultural and ethnic networks that permeate the region.

Furthermore, Inoguchi notes how the economic forces of globalization tend to call forward defensive responses from many states, such as protectionism, new regulations, and cartelization. In this context, there is a tendency for regional bloc formation, which poses special problems for Pacific Asia because there is a demand for more regional cooperation at the same time that such cooperation must avoid taking on the form of a regional protectionist umbrella. Pacific Asian countries depend on global market access for their rapid economic development, so regional economic cooperation in Pacific Asia takes place through channels such as corporate networks, the Chinese community in Asian countries, and market mechanisms.

From a Chinese perspective, Zhang Yunling stresses, in Chapter 5, that globalization has primarily meant integration among the developed countries—the triad of the United States (North America), the European Community (Western Europe), and Japan—whereas the former eastern bloc and countries in the South have been largely excluded. Yet China vigorously pursues economic modernization and seeks further economic integration with developed countries for that purpose. In Zhang's opinion, hardly anything can divert Chinese attention from the top-priority aim of economic modernization and growth. For this reason, China will seek international stability and economic cooperation with developed countries and refrain from a position of radical leader of the South, struggling for a more equal world order. Furthermore, China will seek regional economic cooperation instead of power-oriented policies toward regional hegemony. The end of the Cold War refocused China's attention on the regional power situation. In security terms, the regional perspective has become much more important for China, as concerns both risks and new possibilities for cooperation.

Osvaldo Sunkel clearly conveys in Chapter 3 that Latin American countries are also following global trends and pressures toward additional economic cooperation and integration in the world market, after a long period of protectionist policies of import substitution. Sunkel interprets the current phase of economic globalization in a historical perspective; economic growth has proceeded in long, Kondratieff-like cycles of upswings and downturns combined with superstructures of political order (or hegemony) in upturns and political disorder in downswings. The worldwide postwar growth phase was combined with a vastly expanding role of the states in economic regulation and welfare. The present phase of economic globalization is market-driven, led by the large transnational corporations, and in both national and international contexts, state regulation of economic activity is being rolled back. Although the end of the Cold War has fewer consequences in Latin America than elsewhere because the region was less of a battleground between East and West, it does contribute to reinforce reductions in the role of the state and thereby exacerbate the effects of globalization. The overall consequence is a process of globalization that is largely hierarchical, both among countries globally and within domestic societies in Latin America and elsewhere. Cores of advanced economic activity are surrounded by peripheries of economic stagnation and crisis; transnational economic integration is accompanied by national disintegration, albeit with significant variation in relative intensity among countries. Sunkel emphasizes that in order to mitigate these developments, the states must be brought back in, not to repeat the same kind of activities as in the past but to strike a new balance, more appropriate to contemporary conditions, between market dynamics and state policies in order to secure a measure of equality and welfare. However, for this to take place, the frail, elite-dominated democracies in Latin America need to establish wider social roots in order to secure a more solid, popular basis; this is happening only slowly.

In South Asia the end of the Cold War has created an opportunity to solve old problems of confrontation between the major players, India and Pakistan. There is no longer a great-power confrontation to bolster tension between India, Pakistan, and China. In Chapter 4, Gowher Rizvi emphasizes the marginalizing aspects of current processes of economic globalization. The triad (United States, European Community, and Japan) of developed countries has turned its attention to its own problems and to the former planned economies. Aid and investments will increasingly go to these latter countries, which are competitive in areas that challenge South Asia. In effect, South Asian countries may be increasingly left to their own devices, that is, to regional cooperation, in their pursuit of economic development. Rizvi is highly skeptical, as in Sunkel, about the rollback of the state that took place in South Asia during the 1980s, and he also stresses the need for more democracy in order to pave the way for improved state performance: "The solution to the economic problems of the Third World is not to unleash the market by emaciating the government but to ensure good governance and strengthen the capability of the people so that they can realize their entitlement." Success in regional cooperation also depends on stronger democracies; with continued elite dominance, the respective national bourgeoisies will seek to preserve their privileges.

Claude Ake takes on the African perspective in Chapter 2. The end of the Cold War has produced an identity crisis: "Those who believed so passionately have very little now to believe in. Ideological solidarity and the discipline that came from soldiering in the Cold War crumble, leaving in their wake a confusing freedom and a blurring of self-definition." Ake points to the homogenizing effects of globalization in a process that also increases hierarchization. The division between North and South, between rich and poor, is larger than ever and the gap is growing. Yet globalization pushes the "theology" of market forces, as well as liberal democracy, across the world. But this has not been helpful in Africa. The concrete shape of market forces in Africa is structural adjustment programs (SAPs) launched by the International Monetary Fund (IMF) and the World Bank; so far they cannot claim "a single case of unambiguous success." Liberal democracy in Africa has meant a "formal minimalist democracy" of low-quality multiparty elections. People are allowed to "choose between oppressors and by the appearance of choice legitimize what is really their disempowerment." There are no clear-cut solutions. Africa is now forced to attempt the option of self-reliance, which is by no means a sure key to improvement. At the same time, democracy needs to be promoted in its original meaning, popular power, not only in the South but also in the North. "The ordinary people of Africa are supporting democracy as 'a second independence.' This time they want independence not from the colonial masters but from indigenous leaders. They want independence from leaders whose misrule has intensified their poverty and exploitation to the point of being life-threatening. And they are convinced that they cannot now get material improvement without securing political empowerment and being better placed to bring public policy closer to social needs."

Finally, there is Russia. If the Soviet Union went under because of its inability to successfully complete a process of modernization, Russia's journey toward the same goal will be a difficult and unsafe one. Vladislav Zubok, in Chapter 6, sees Russia as being in a precarious position in the international economic system with chances both of graduating to the core and of sinking into the periphery. The short-term prospects are disastrous; Russia's links to the world economy consist mainly of three elements: import of consumer goods from the West, export of raw materials, and sales of arms. The president has not so far been able to formulate a coherent policy for economic development. The private sector, however, expands rapidly, and there are success stories from some of the regions. Even under present hardships, only a small minority supports the idea of the "restoration of the Union." Russia may yet succeed. What is clear from Zubok's analysis is that domestic factors will be the principal determinants of the outcome. The international system may have set the stage for present struggles for modernization, but the international system is not of decisive importance for the end result in Russia. The region that was the Soviet Union is immersed in the struggle to gain sovereignty in the traditional sense and to build national institutions. Building international institutions and employing sovereignty as a bargaining chip is not relevant in the midst of the extreme fragmentation process taking place.

In conclusion, what emerges from these analyses is not a grand vision of globalized, peaceful societies but great diversity, not only between North and South but also among and within the different regions and countries of the world. New zones of peace and new zones of conflict exist alongside each other, all in the same "world order." Instead of seeing a generally peaceful world, we see numerous different ways of trying to achieve security in the face of several types of risk. Some of these attempts are global, but the major ones appear to be regional. Thus security is becoming increasingly regionalized, and the variations among regions change the global security debate. Global peace is hardly on the agenda. There is a zone of peace among the consolidated liberal democracies of the North, but even here there are old and new risks, brought about by processes of fragmentation and by the deficit in the capacity to govern caused by uneven denationalization.

Pacific Asia and South Asia have specific regional security problems that have not gone away with the ending of the Cold War; they are simply cast in a new light. The region has new opportunities for peaceful solutions but also faces possible new conflicts fueled by increased military spending and based on old hostilities no longer kept in check by the bipolar confrontation. In Africa, the end of the Cold War has not resolved the security problems caused by the grip of personal rulers on their respective populations and by autonomous military apparatuses outside constitutional control.

Regarding economic matters, the globalization of finance, production, and communication is creating a more unified world market. The lifting away of the Cold War overlay has drawn increasing attention to the importance of economic growth strategies within states and in regions. Two problems emerge as a consequence: The autonomy of national governments to undertake national macroeconomic strategies has become seriously eroded. And the globalization of the world economy pushes the issues of income inequality and the growth differential among regions into center stage in both international and national politics in the South and the North. Globalization prompts economic integration as well as fragmentation. Defensive responses to globalization of protectionism and new regulations tend to foster the creation of regional economic blocs.

The basis for such measures of regional self-reliance are dramatically different as we move from the North to the South, and variation inside the South is also considerable: It is clear that the world emerging from the end of the Cold War is marked by globalization that is uneven to an unseen extent and has economic and social differences of immense proportions. The contributors speaking from Africa, Latin America, South Asia, and even from China all stress this point. A new system of dominance is in the making. It consists of the conventional element of economic dominance of a center over a periphery, perhaps with a new twist added: The centers in the triad have less economic need for large parts of the periphery; less need for raw materials because they are increasingly insignificant for advanced economic growth; less need for cheap labor outside a small number of countries in the "near peripheries" of South Asia, Eastern Europe, Mexico, Central America, and the Caribbean; and a lack of interest in large parts of the periphery as concerns direct investment because the markets are uninteresting, undynamic, with no purchasing power and high political risks.[31] This creates the prospect of "self-reliance by default," which Ake mentions for Africa. Ironically, this prospect comes at a time when current economic wisdom in the North is recommending world market integration more than ever and when countries of the periphery are eagerly seeking such integration.

But the structure of dominance contains a novel element: the renewed prominence of the political and ideological dimensions—the dominant notion of global liberal democracy sustained by an economy controlled by market forces. Although there is nothing wrong with this notion as a general principle, it creates severe problems in several parts of the periphery when translated into concrete measures of rollback of the state and structural adjustment programs. Claude Ake, Osvaldo Sunkel, and Gowher Rizvi present a concept of more genuine popular democracy as the road to avoiding the replacement of market failure with state failure, but this is a longer-term prospect and might not succeed. Yet they point to the fact that a more or less "standard liberal democracy plus market" may in the short and medium term create at least as many problems as it solves and might even undermine the democracy it is supposed to build.

These conclusions present new challenges to a theorizing in international relations that aspires to take the end of the Cold War and uneven globalization seriously. Mere adaptation of existing theories based on concepts of sovereign states in an anarchic international system is insufficient. In the final chapter we address the implications of our results for international relations theory.

❧ 2 ❧

The New World Order: A View from Africa

CLAUDE AKE

If academic writings are any guide, there are not many who believe that a new world order has emerged or that it is even in the making. This skepticism may have less to do with the reality than the image of the person who coined the term. For a new world order is indeed emerging, constituted by the process of globalization and the winding down of the Cold War. Both events reinforce each other in reconstituting the world and the way we relate to it. They have created a phenomenal orientational upheaval and a frantic search for collective identity framed by what I may call, for lack of a better term, political ethnicity. Political ethnicity is the politically articulated insistence by a social group on its historical uniqueness and its prerogatives. What makes the group ethnic is that it defines membership categorically in terms of some attributes that are essentially primordial in the sense that the question of their historicity does not arise.

THE COLD WAR

The Cold War, arguably the greatest war of the modern world in terms of its reach, impact, and intensity, is over, but its influence was so pervasive and profound that its passing away can be expected to be in its own right a momentous event in world history. It is proving to be just that. Already, it is restructuring the world and our consciousness of it. The new world order is indeed an objective necessity. The winding down of the Cold War has given tremendous impetus to a severe identity crisis and, increasingly, to political ethnicity as the epic confrontation of the two great ideological camps has yielded to a bland pragmatism. Both winners and losers seem bewildered; the one for fighting so fanatically an enemy whose celebrated strength and malevolence appears to have been largely a figment of the imagination, the

Africa

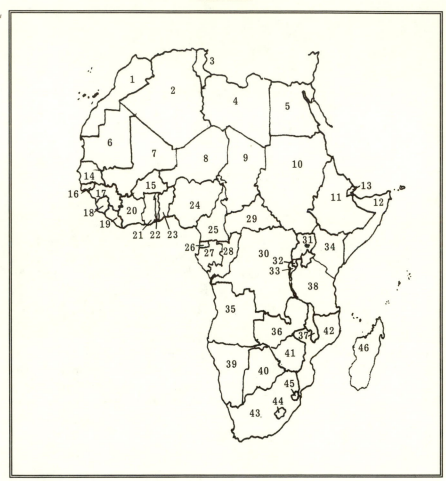

1. Morocco
2. Algeria
3. Tunisia
4. Libya
5. Egypt
6. Mauretania
7. Mali
8. Niger
9. Chad
10. Sudan
11. Ethiopia
12. Somalia
13. Djibouti
14. Senegal
15. Burkina

16. Guinea Bissau
17. Guinea
18. Sierra Leone
19. Liberia
20. Ivory Coast
21. Ghana
22. Togo
23. Benin
24. Nigeria
25. Cameroon
26. Guinea
27. Gabon
28. Congo
29. Central African Rep.

30. Zaire
31. Uganda
32. Rwanda
33. Burundi
34. Kenya
35. Angola
36. Zambia
37. Malawi
38. Tanzania
39. Namibia
40. Botswana
41. Zimbabwe
42. Mozambique
43. South Africa
44. Lesotho

45. Swaziland
46. Madagascar

other for defending vehemently, at inestimable cost, what it should have recognized all along as a fake substitute for its cherished model of society. Those who believed so passionately have very little now to believe in. Ideological solidarity and the discipline that came from soldiering in the Cold War crumble, leaving in their wake a confusing freedom and a blurring of self-definition.

Contemporary society appears to be in the grip of a postmodern consciousness that eschews all epiphanies and sees no faith, only pluralities, differences, contradictions, and archaeologies of knowledge that validate themselves rather arbitrarily. In the context of this epistemology, politics becomes unprincipled and the validity of seeking ends such as peaceful coexistence and development partnership is exposed to doubt. At the same time self-definition is blurred, for there is no clarity in indeterminacy.

The lack of belief is compounded by the lack of a great cause or a great enemy, which has made the search for collective identity more frantic. The end of the Cold War is revealing how far political identity depends on these factors. After the Cold War, Europe is less coherent, less keen on integration even though it also recognizes that it is too late to turn back or even stand still. The United States has frankly recognized the need to redefine itself. So has Japan, and Germany too. The Soviet Union fell apart before the question became pressing, but its components have not escaped it. The Cold War alliances in the South have largely collapsed, leaving many worried about regional security and searching frantically for new alliances and identities. Everyone recognizes that new causes and new enemies are critical for this quest. But they are hard to come by. Gypsies, immigrants, indigenous peoples, homosexuals, and minorities are not really the stuff of heroic causes, but some are making do with them. "Third World chaos" and "terrorist Third World countries" are emerging as prime candidates of military threat to the North, but they are not so convincing. The poor countries are luckier. Development remains a plausible cause and poverty a great enemy.

The North's image of itself (at any rate, the image of its leadership) has contributed to the identity crisis and to political ethnicity. The North has always conflated its own model of society with the ideal state of being. In the 1960s, this was epitomized in the rather premature proclamation of the end of ideology. That this turned out to be a costly mistake did not apparently matter. For in the heady triumphalism of the post–Cold War era the claim has been revived, and it is more dogmatic and grander: The real and the ideal have become one in the contemporary North; history is over. Not many will say it with the audacity of Francis Fukuyama, but it would appear that many in the North feel that way and think that way. That is the rub. If history is over, where are we? The end of history is not a cry of triumph but an ac-

knowledgment of dark despair. If the presumption of perfection is a problem, so are the realities that keep breaking through this presumption. In the
best of all possible worlds, many are puzzled to find themselves powerless,
unemployed, poor, and deprived. And such a state cannot be caused by the
good society.

In short order, this translates to paranoia, irredentism, ethnic conflict, and
racism. In the South, the surge of political ethnicity mainly expresses the
multiple crisis of economy, polity, and identity. Ethnic identity offers a way
of coping, a highly desirable replacement of present realities such as the hu-
miliations of being underdeveloped in a world in which rich and poor, weak
and strong alike worship technological progress, wealth, and power. It offers some comfort in the face of cultural extinction and a great deal of comfort in a world of increasing complexity, change, and strangers that one neither comprehends nor controls. Ethnicity offers an alternative map of a
community that is intimate, predictable, caring, and privileged in its exclu-
sivity.

UNEVEN GLOBALIZATION

It is increasingly difficult to agree on a definition of globalization; as studies
of the process proliferate, so does the problem of defining it. But there is
some agreement of what some of its elements are. Among other things, globalization is the march of capital all over the world in search of profit, a process reflected in the reach and power of the multinational corporation. It is
about growing structural differentiation and functional integration in the
world economy; it is about growing interdependence across the globe; it is
about the nation-state coming under pressure from the surge of transnational phenomena, about the emergence of a global mass culture driven by
mass advertising and technical advances in mass communication. Globalization is a very complex process. It is by no means unidirectional and it is quite
contradictory. It uniformizes and diversifies, concentrates and decenters; it
universalizes but also engenders particularities; it complexifies and
simplifies. Always, it is mediated and differentiated in form and content by
historical specificities.

For all its complexities, ambiguities, contradictions, and historical specificities, globalization has an overriding trend, namely homogenization. Indeed, it is the thrust of homogenization that gives a dialectical unity to the
singularities, ambiguities, and contradictions of the process. But something
even more important hides behind the homogenization. Globalization is not
just an abstract process of homogenization: There are identifiable centers
from which it draws its impetus, notably New York, Tokyo, Frankfurt, London, Paris. It is not an abstract universal that is magically emerging everywhere; it is concrete particulars that are being globalized. What is globalized

is not Yoruba but English, not Turkish pop culture but American, not Senegalese technology but Japanese and German. The geometry and trajectories of globalization are clear enough. Globalization articulates the structuration and dynamics of power. It is a complicated process of hegemonization in which the hegemon is not often in control and is at once dominant and subjected. As a process of hegemonization, globalization uniformizes and hierarchizes. Hegemony does not entail the eradication of diversity; it articulates and relates the differences without eliminating them.

In its effects, the process of globalization is much like the winding down of the Cold War. To begin with, it causes orientational upheaval, anxiety, and identity crisis. It is producing changes on a monumental scale, changes that represent drastically different ways of being and thinking; for instance, globalization is challenging the much-cherished idea of national sovereignty and the organization of the world into nation-states. Much of the impetus of globalization comes from the accumulation of capital; it is a by-product of the drive for competitive efficiency, an effort to create, control, and profit from a global mass market. The stakes are high, the demands on the competitors get ever more strenuous, there is no respite from anxiety. Globalization produces many losers and many more who worry about losing. It alters economic and political relations in the local space, it threatens cultures. Some are universalized, but even this is a threat, for in universalizing, it also transforms. It eradicates some, museumizes others. It collapses distance and conjures proximity that can be discomforting. In universalizing certain values, globalization can exacerbate scarcity, competition, and conflict.

Uneven globalization is not only a process but also an ongoing structuration of power. The popular notion of the world becoming one is more than anything else perhaps a description of hegemonization. Globalization is the hierarchization of the world—economically, politically, and culturally—and the crystallizing of a domination. It is a domination constituted essentially by economic power. To the extent that globalization is so driven by economic forces, it represents the triumph of materialism and its ultimate triumph in mastering the world.

Here again, globalization and the winding down of the Cold War interface. There is some truth in the popular notion that the Soviet empire collapsed and put an end to the Cold War because it was too tyrannical and because the surge of democracy proved irresistible, but these were relatively minor contributory factors. The collapse came mainly because the Soviet Union failed to prosper economically, and the main lesson of this great historical event is the centrality of economic management performance in the determination of the feasibility of regimes. It would appear that the lesson of the Cold War is well taken in the primacy that is now accorded by everyone to economic growth and the prevailing theology of the market.

WHAT HAS CHANGED?

Uneven globalization and the winding down of the Cold War have unleashed forces that are reshaping the world and our consciousness. The changes they are introducing are so far reaching that we can properly speak of the constitution of a new world order. In the African's view, the fundamental feature of the new world order is the radical division of the world into rich and poor nations, aggregations usually referred to in geopolitical terms as North and South.

This division existed in the era of the Cold War. But it was obscured by "the second world," the ideological struggle between capitalism and socialism and the hegemonic contest between East and West. Indeed, there were always two basic cleavages, North-South and East-West. Now the East-West cleavage has virtually disappeared, leaving only North-South, which is all the more conspicuous now for having the field alone and all the more important for being reconstituted by the peculiar dynamics of the post–Cold War world. The term North-South does not accurately describe these polarized formations, for it is only shorthand for a plurality of highly asymmetrical relations of power, especially economic, technological, political, and military. But it will suffice.

The disparity in means and power is stunning by any conventional measure of economic and technological distance and military capability. For instance, in a rough estimate, 75 percent of the world's population lives in the South but accounts for less than 25 percent of the world's productive output and less than 15 percent of global trade. By all indications, the poor world's share of the world's population is still increasing, and its share of the world's output is diminishing. The ratio will approach 80 percent of the world's population having less than 20 percent of its resources by the year 2000.

To all appearances the gap between the rich and the poor world is growing. According to the United Nations Development Programme (UNDP), the income of the richest 20 percent of the world's population was 30 times that of the poorest 20 percent by 1960; by 1990, it was 60 times more.[1] And it is not difficult to see why the gap remains and grows. Per capita, the North has 9 times the number of scientists and technical personnel in the South and 24 times more investment in technological research.[2]

The saliency of the North-South dichotomy does not underplay the contradictory and even conflictual plurality of each of these formations. Cultural differences have survived the uniformizing effect of capitalism even in the North, where it has been most successful. The cultural differences among France, Britain, and Germany are considerable. Between the United States and Japan, they are immense. Another source of diversity and conflict is that these countries are highly nationalistic and this nationalism will likely turn aggressive in the present surge of ultraconservatism and increasing economic competition. The growth of German power has already ruptured the balance of the European Community (EC), and it begins to look as though, in spite of its modesty, it is Germany rather than the EC that will emerge as the European power; this will be highly stressful for Europe. The alienation between Japan and the United States continues to grow despite every effort to contain it. The question now is not whether it will lead to conflict but how serious a conflict. Those who won the world wars so decisively, have lost the peace just as decisively, setting the arena for the renewal of political, economic, and hegemonic competition.

In the South, the divisions are more numerous and deeper still. Most countries of the South are plural societies in the grip of strong centrifugal forces, including secessionism. The South is deeply divided by religious differences that are often politicized. It is prone to violent, atavistic nationalism, territorial disputes, and struggle over natural resources. The satellization of the South by the wealthier nations of the North is another source of division and conflict in the South; now and then it leads to proxy wars.

And yet in the North, as well as the South, solidarity exists amidst these substantial differences. As is to be expected, the North is more conscious and more solidary, a fact readily discerned in the Group of Seven's (G-7) keen defense of member countries' collective interests and its tendency to conflate them with those of humankind, its constant striving for more unity within its ranks, and its members' ready consensus on North-South issues. This consensus is discernible even in academic theories of the world order.

As for the South, solidarity is still rudimentary because it is more numerous, more complex, more diverse, heavily dependent, and easily divided. However, southern solidarity has grown considerably from the futile battle of the 1970s for a new international economic order. By the early 1980s, the assertiveness of the South was muted by economic crisis. However, it is on the upsurge again, this time precisely because of the South's economic marginality, now greatly increased. The solidarity of the South was evident during the Gulf War in the ambiguity of most countries who were outraged by Iraqi aggression but felt nonetheless that the war was essentially about the North monopolizing the control of essential commodities and putting upstart poor countries in their place.

Significantly, the end of the Cold War, which might have been expected to enhance global peace and security, appears to have increased the insecurity of the South and sent it scrambling for means of shoring up its security. This prospect was a main concern at the thirtieth anniversary meeting of the Nonaligned Movement in Accra (September 2 to 8, 1991). The conference attendees paid a great ideal of attention to the solidarity of the South in the struggle against political marginality and oppressive poverty, which was proclaimed as a necessary step in the building of a truly new world order in which cooperation replaces conflict. One specific aspect of the political struggle mentioned was the democratization of the international political system, especially the United Nations, including a shift in decisionmaking from the Security Council to the General Assembly and in trade negotiating from GATT (General Agreement on Tariffs and Trade) to UNCTAD (UN Conference on Trade and Development).

The North-South divide is arguably more threatening to the safety and well-being of humankind than the old ideological bipolarity, whose main threat, a superpower nuclear war, was never really more than a theoretical possibility. Whereas the bipolarity of the Cold War was characterized by equality, the new one is characterized by gross inequality that is destabilizing on account of its association with extreme poverty. Moreover, "the end of ideology," which is always acclaimed as an asset to peace, will accentuate the bitterness of this contestation. As the bonds of principle and political morality come loose and yield to pragmatism, the struggling national entities, absorbed in their self-aggrandizement, confront each other merely as powers whose conflicting claims resolve into a calculus of strength; the end of ideology, which is also the end of innocence, "de-moralizes" international politics, transforming it into a Hobbesian struggle not in the sense that there is no order or hierarchy but in the structuration of order, hierarchy, status, and value as functions of mere power. In this sense, the world is nastier.

The consequences of the reconstitution of the world in terms of the primacy of the economic are interesting. Economic forces are constituting the world into one economy and, to a lesser extent, one political society. Nations participate in global governance according to their economic power, which is coextensive with their rights. This global order is ruled by an informal cabinet of the world's economically most powerful countries; its law is the logic of the market, and status in this new order is a function of economic performance.

What this means for the poorest regions of the world, notably Africa, is easy enough to see. The logic of this new world effectively disenfranchises the poorest regions such as Africa and tends to disallow concessions to their weaknesses. Africa's share of every major world economic indicator, marginal to begin with, has been declining. According to *World Development Report* Africa's percentage share of global GNP (gross national product) was 1.9 percent in 1960 and 1.2 percent in 1989; its share of global trade, 3.8 percent in 1970, was down to 1.0 percent in 1989; Africa's share of global commercial bank lending was 0.3 percent in 1970 and 0.3 percent in 1989; foreign private investment was 24.8 percent in 1970 and 15.0 percent in 1989.[3] These statistics have not even registered the declining strategic significance of the region and its economic consequences and the preoccupation of the rich countries with the liberalizing former socialist states. The prospects of Africa coming out of its current crisis are poor; those of accelerated development are poorer still.

The response of the agents of development to the African crisis is a typical new world order response, namely the liberation of market forces through structural adjustment programs (SAPs). Since 1982–1983, over 30 African countries have been obliged to adopt International Monetary Fund–type SAPs. But so far, there is not a single case of unambiguous success. Economic regression continues with growth rates lagging well behind population growth.

But in a world in which the market is a theology, it has been impossible to accept that SAPS are not working and probably cannot work in Africa. More and more SAPs continue to be conducted amidst growing poverty, growing disenchantment, and collapsing consensus while the IMF pleads for greater political will. Here is another problem of the ideological catholicity of the new world order. It is the poor and the weak who bear the burden of this catholicity; generally it does not reflect their interests and they cannot change it, nor can they afford to indicate that they dislike it.

SECURITY ISSUES: THREATS TO THE SOUTH

For the South, especially Africa, one major source of threat is the North's open contempt and the presumption that the South's interests do not matter. The attitude is inflammatory and seriously constrains the realization of Africa's interests. A U.S. scholar of the South has given us some telling examples of this attitude. In a famous lecture, Hugh Trevor-Regius, professor of modern history at Oxford University, said, "Perhaps in the future, there will be some African history. But at present there is none; there is only the History of Europeans in Africa. The rest is darkness ... and darkness is not a subject of history." In a similar vein, the American media icon Eric Severeid declared: "There is very little in most of the new African and Asian nations worth anything in twentieth century terms that was not put there by Westerners."[4] Then there is the famous encounter of Henry Kissinger and Gabriel Valdes, the Chilean foreign minister under the government of Eduardo Frei. Valdes had told President Richard Nixon that for every dollar of U.S. aid, Latin America was sending back $3.80 to the United States. Questioned about his facts, he added that his statistics came from a study conducted by a U.S. bank. That did not stop Kissinger from summoning Valdes for a reprimand. Kissinger said to Valdes: "Mr Minister, you made a strange speech. You come here speaking of Latin America, but this is not important. Nothing important can come from the South. History has never been produced in the South. The axis of history starts in Moscow, goes to Bonn, crosses over to Washington, and then goes to Tokyo. What happens in the South is of no importance. You're wasting your time."[5]

The South is also threatened by the perception, now widely prevalent in the North, that the military superiority of the North is partly redundant, that too many southern nations are acquiring weapons of mass destruction and their delivery systems for Northern comfort. Charles Krauthammer argues that one consequence of a world shrunk by technology is the narrowing of the divide between great powers and regional powers, who increasingly have access to relatively crude but highly destructive weapons. Citing the case of Iraq, he laments that "relatively small peripheral and backward states will be able to emerge rapidly as threats not only to regional, but also world security." In the face of this reality, "there is no alternative to confronting, deterring and if necessary, disarming states that brandish and use weapons of mass destruction."[6]

Despite their vastly different visions of the new order, William Pfaff comes to much the same conclusion as Charles Krauthammer. He argues that one novel feature of the contemporary world is "the proportionate weakening of the military advantage enjoyed until now by the advanced industrial countries, as industrializing nations—Iraq, China, India and others—acquired the ability to produce weapons of mass destruction. This obviously is what has given such significance and emotional weight to the Gulf crisis. Iraq is a metaphor for a Third World that can attack the wealthy nations that dominate the international system, and so avenge the poverty of the South."[7]

Sergei Rogov offers another version of the increasingly popular notion of a threatening South: "With regard to North-South relations, there is a real possibility that the post–Cold War order will be characterized by competition rather than co-operation. The arms race may shift its center of gravity to countries of the South, some of which have become recipients of significant arms flows if not weapons producers in their own right. The proliferation of nuclear, chemical and biological weapons and the means of their delivery, and of sophisticated conventional armaments and military technology, creates a serious threat to international security."[8]

In the same vein, David Rothkopf argues that technology has disarmed the great powers by making them too strong to risk a fight while giving disproportionate powers to lesser players who can dare to fight because they have too little to lose.[9] Some have gone so far as to present the South as the new enemy to replace the Soviet Union. For instance, Charles Krauthammer argued recently that the new enemy of the United States and the West is "the small outlaw states, the Iraqs of the future."[10] The emergence of these small outlaw states, which he calls "weapon states," are for Krauthammer the "most crucial new element in the post–Cold War world." Specifically, the weapon states are dangerous because they "have deep grievances against the West and the world order that it has established and enforces. They are therefore subversive of the international status quo, which they see as a residue of colonialism. These resentments fuel an obsessive drive to hightech military development as the only way to leapfrog history and to place themselves on a footing from which to challenge a Western-imposed order."[11]

Apparently the danger from the South is taken seriously enough to elicit changes in northern defense strategies in the direction of orientation toward the South. In a speech delivered on August 2, 1990, President George Bush outlined a post–Cold War defense strategy that shifted attention from major global conflicts, particularly the Soviet threat, which had been drastically reduced by the end of the Cold War, and the decomposition of the Soviet Union. Defense policy was now oriented to "the rise of would-be regional hegemons such as Iraq and to global issues such as shifting demographic, ethnic and religious problems, economic stagnation, and sharp differences in living standards and humanitarian conditions that would be likely to fuel old conflicts or give rise to new ones," in short, to the South. The purpose of military power was to be seen as "a stabilizing factor in key regions by deterring conflicts, dampening local arms races, and protecting U.S. interests and allies, should conflicts occur."[12]

This purpose was to be accomplished by a base force made up of four units, Pacific, Atlantic, Strategic, and Contingency, drawing on four types of military capabilities, space, research and development, transport, and reconstitution. The capabilities and the organization of the base force were intended to maximize deterrence, forward presence, crisis response, and reconstitution. All these characteristics profiled a force posture for low-intensity conflicts so characteristic of the South. The turning of defense strategy to focus on the South underscored the security threat of the South in the new world order.

Finally and most important, the South, especially Africa, is threatened by its economic plight. Indeed, the security threat to Africa has always been primarily economic because economic weakness fed the other weaknesses—military, political, and technological. Now Africa is weaker than ever thanks to the dismal economic performance of the 1980s. Since 1970 some parts of Africa have declined so decisively that they have established once and for all the notion of the reversibility of development.

Africa is more conscious than ever of the economic underpinning of its security and marginality in an age when economic power has come in to its own and when the tragic consequences of its perennial economic crisis are all too evident. The problem is to go beyond this consciousness and effectively overcome underdevelopment and poverty. This problem remains intractable.

DEMOCRACY, SECURITY, AND DEVELOPMENT

It would appear that the most important condition for the health of the new world order is that everybody take democracy seriously. And we speak of democracy in the broadest sense of respecting the rule of law, working on the basis of negotiated consensus, broadening and deepening participation, cultivating tolerance and acceptance of the equality of all humankind, sharing the burdens and rewards of our common humanity with equity, and building peace on justice. For the moment, there is no part of the world where democracy comes remotely close to being taken seriously.

Even conceptions of the new world order illustrate our failure to take democracy seriously. These conceptions are so ethnocentric that they do not even frame a discourse about the world. For example, one familiar view of the new world order characterizes it as unipolar. Charles Krauthammer, who is a proponent of this view, argues that although there is a multiplicity of world powers, they are all second-rate powers relative to the United States, which is the only first-rate power. This unipolar world, some time in the making, is immediately constituted by the disintegration of the Soviet Empire and the fact of an "ideologically pacified North" submitting to the leadership of the United States; it is expressed with forceful clarity by the Gulf War.[13] Krauthammer argues that for all the celebration of the Gulf War as a triumph of multilateralism, it is actually notable for revealing the unipolarity of the new order and exploding the myth of multilateralism. Multilateralism entails a coalition of equals, but the multilateralism of the Gulf War was more apparent than real because it was not a coalition of equals, not even an expression of collective security.

Krauthammer raises the question of the feasibility of the U.S. unipolar status in apparent reference to those who argue that resource constraints and global overreach do not allow the United States to take on a unipolar status. He argues that the economic decline of the United States is overplayed, that the U.S. share of world GNP has remained roughly the same through this century. For good measure, he adds that the economic problems of the United States, including its indebtedness, arise from domestic failures rather than global overreach. For him, the more interesting and problematic issue is whether the people of the United States will support a unipolar status. He has doubts about their support on account of the tradition of isolationism, popular disenchantment with the heroic role of the United States, and mistaken beliefs about the extent of the threat to national and international security. He insists that only political will stops the United States from seizing the "unipolar moment," imposing its vision and bestowing peace on the world.[14] This view runs against the widely held belief that ours is increasingly a world of transnational phenomena in which the significance of state power is reduced and the question of world domination by a single state cannot arise. Some, such as David Gergen, argue that if there was ever a unipolar moment, it was too fleeting and its opportunities could not be seized.[15]

Zbigniew Brzezinski thinks of the new world order very much in terms of the leadership role of the United States. However, his concerns are much broader because he devotes a great deal of attention to emerging strategic issues and because it is these issues that define the role of the United States.

He sees two elements to the present global transformation: the collapse and disintegration of the Soviet bloc and the ascendancy of the "Western concepts of democracy and the free market." In the course of hegemonic and ideological struggles, a broad Western coalition extending from Europe to Japan has been forged as a "functionally pragmatic transnationalism" with a shared interest in collective security and free trade. One important effect of this is that international politics (among the coalition members) has become organic as distinctions between the domestic and external realms blur. Since the members of the Western coalition are too interdependent and too well armed to fight each other, global politics is becoming in some ways similar to U.S. urban centers, where violence is concentrated in the poorer segments of society. "Today, on a global scale, war has become a luxury that only poor nations can afford. ... While morally unpalatable, this reality nonetheless does somewhat enhance global security."[16]

The new world order has framed a new geostrategic agenda, and it is on the resolution of this agenda that the prospects of peace and stability depend. Brzezinski says that the geostrategic agenda can be thought of as a triangle drawn from Brussels to Tokyo, Tokyo to Cairo, and Cairo to Brussels. The Brussels axis is the European project of economic and political unification, which will supposedly lead to a more stable world by terminating intra-European power conflicts. The Tokyo axis is the Far East Regional Security project. The concern here is that in the interest of peace and security, Japan, China, South Korea, and Taiwan could be brought into some structure of regional cooperation with the help of the leverage provided by the paramountcy of U.S. power in the region. The Cairo axis is the Middle East project, where the end of the Gulf War and the end of the Cold War have created unprecedented opportunities for a settlement, not only to bring peace but to check the proliferation of weapons of mass destruction. Here, as in the other two axes, the willingness of the United States to use its leverage will be decisive.[17]

Like Krauthammer, Brzezinski sees that from a global perspective the threat to peace lies in the South. He quotes with approval the address of President Jacques Delors to the International Institute for Strategic Studies in March 1991: "All around us, naked ambition, lust for power, national uprisings and underdevelopment are combining to create potentially dangerous situations containing the seeds of destabilization and conflict, aggravated by the proliferation of weapons of mass destruction.[18]

How are these threats to be managed? As far as the more remote geostrategic threats are concerned, four kinds of initiatives are necessary. The first is to deepen the political and military unity of Europe as a partner of the United States. The second is "the progressive strengthening of the political and economic power of the various Soviet national republics," that is, advancing the decomposition of the Soviet Union. The third is to engage the

United States, Japan, and China in a regional security arrangement in the Far East. The fourth and final initiative is "to push through peace settlement in the Middle East." All these geostrategic objectives depend on the United States for the simple reason that "no other power currently possesses the attributes needed for effective global leverage; military reach, political clout, economic impact as well as social and cultural appeal."[19]

As far as the immediate danger of threats emanating specifically from the South is concerned, the response—direct police action—is not discussed but taken for granted. What is discussed is the expected objection to imperialist violation of the sovereignty of weaker nations: "In determining when and how to address such problems the international community may have to be guided less by traditional notions of sovereignty (i.e. one state violating the sovereignty of another) and more by the scope of the threat itself. In other words, there may develop situations in which external intervention in the seemingly internal affairs of the state—as in Yugoslavia yesterday and perhaps elsewhere tomorrow—may be necessary and justified by the potential consequences of activities that are otherwise of internal character and that do not, of themselves, involve inter-state collision."[20]

William Pfaff's conception of the new world order is markedly different. In sharp opposition to the unipolarity thesis, he argues that the very category of superpower has vanished with the Cold War rivalry. It has vanished because it was constituted by the possession of a nuclear arsenal and by competition over a model of humankind's future. According to Pfaff, not only is the United States no longer a superpower but it is left in a situation of having to consider what it must do and even to define what it is.

That is not to deny that the United States remains phenomenally powerful, easily the world's most formidable military power. However, power itself has become, in the context of world politics, an immensely complicated fact because of the growing need to differentiate between proliferating categories of significant power—political, military, economic, technological, and so on. Pfaff argues that although the United States excels in military power, it is heavily indebted and its military power is partly redundant relative to its security needs. Moreover, its ability to mobilize consensus for public policy is less than adequate and it is beset with social tension. For these reasons, Pfaff concludes that despite the power of the United States, "the international prospect today is not so much a world dominated by a single super power as it is one lacking even great powers that meet the traditional definition of invulnerability."[21]

Nonetheless, he raises the question of the role of the United States in the face of threats to international security such as the proliferation of weapons of mass destruction and the mutual alienation of North and South. He challenges those who see U.S. intervention in the Persian Gulf as a model of determined activism in the interest of world peace. Like Kissinger, Pfaff insists that the impressive global coalition the United States put together does not herald a new era of multilateralism led by the United States. Indeed, according to Pfaff, a new world order maintained by a U.S.-led global coalition presupposes that the interests of the United States will coincide with the opinions at the United Nations on virtually every major issue. To police the world through a U.S.-led global coalition would entail using the permanent members of the Security Council against the South, which is purportedly the primary source of threat. This would, Pfaff argues, effectively institutionalize "what in the past has proven the principal source of grief for the United States in the post-war policy; its attempt to suppress radical movements of indigenous origin and native energy in the Third World."[22]

These conceptions of the new world order underline the perspectivism of this discourse. Although the diversity of these conceptions is striking, the underlying unity is more striking still. To begin with, all of them are preoccupied with the role of the United States in the new world order, particularly in underwriting its collective security. Whether they are celebrating the unipolar moment, articulating a geostrategic agenda, or arguing the vulnerabilities that have banished all hope of domination by the United States, always the preoccupation is the role of the United States; to talk of the new world order is to define the changing role of the United States in collective security.

Also, these conceptions of world order, old or new, are about the fate of a part of the world, the grand northern coalition against Soviet socialism. The strategic agenda of these conceptions of the world order is also focused on the peace and security of the grand coalition, this very important but nonetheless small part of the world. Consider, for instance, the objectives of Brzezinski's geostrategic agenda. The project of the first axis—the Brussels axis—is the consolidation of the grand alliance. That of the Tokyo axis is to bring a potentially powerful competitor, China, into a cooperative arrangement dominated by a powerful member of the grand coalition, Japan. The strategic objective of the Cairo axis is to protect access to an essential raw material and pacify a potentially hostile region with weapons of mass destruction. The rest of the world, the South, is not entirely irrelevant. But its relevance lies essentially in its nuisance potential.

No view of the world order presented here reveals serious interest in the collective security of the entire world system, only in the collaboration of the entire world system in securing the favored subsystem. And collaboration entails, among other things, the willingness to accept punishment, including violation of national sovereignty in the interest of a collective security arrangement whose collectivity is more apparent than real. No leading policymaker sees the world as a universe of actors, each with its own authenticity and interest. All of them see only a world of subjects and objects, respective bearers of relevant and irrelevant interests. All of them dichotomize the world without appearing to be aware that their analysis constitutes this dichotomy as the basic feature of the world order. Collective security depends on arming one side and disarming the other, by violent means if necessary. All serious threats are from one side; only the strong on the other side will be secure.

There are similar concerns in regard to solutions to the security problems of the new world order. Solutions become nonsolutions because they are so ethnocentric and so insensitive to the rights of others that they do not address the world. For instance, one view frequently put forward is that the powerful nations of the North should police the world firmly and disarm by every means necessary those who threaten world peace."First, we will have to develop a new regime similar to COCOM (Coordination Committee on Export Controls) to deny yet more high technology to such states. Second, those states that acquire such weapons anyway will have to submit to strict outside control, or risk being physically disarmed. A final element must be the development of antiballistic missiles and air defense systems to defend against those weapons that do escape Western control or pre-emption."[23]

This is such a recurrent theme, it is virtually common sense. Recent events in the United Nations and the impressive international coalition that President George Bush put together during the Gulf War suggest that this model of collective security, which rests on international sanctions or coercion to bring delinquent countries who threaten the peace into line, has an appeal that reaches beyond the North. However, it has many problems. Apart from the considerable problems of putting together acceptable, sustainable, and effective apparatuses of coercion, there is a problem of applying the model evenhandedly, if at all. The application of coercion against a major military country is highly unlikely. If coercion was threatened against Great Britain, for instance, the threat would be ignored, leaving only the impossible option of going into a major war; and that would be the end of collective security. Such logic will make coercion applicable only to weaker countries, who are by virtue of their weakness in no position to influence the determination of where, when, and how sanctions may be applied in the name of collective security. That will leave us with a collective security arrangement for the rich and powerful against the poor and weak. Even when coercion can be applied in the interest of collective security, its consequences are likely to be extremely costly and self-defeating. Invariably, the innocent are punished severely and tragically while the guilty go free. The source of delinquency is unlikely to be the ordinary people of the country but its leader or a handful of its leaders, those who are well protected in the event of war and unlikely to be exposed to death or severe deprivation. In all probability, as in Iraq, hundreds of thousands of largely innocent people die. There has to be a better way. The prospect of mounting periodic Desert Storms against countries such as Nigeria, China, India, Pakistan, Egypt, and South Africa looks like a recipe for the end of civilization.

LIBERAL DEMOCRACY:
THE ROAD TO PEACE AND SECURITY?

The crux of the problem of our search for international peace and security is easy enough to see. It inheres in a failure to see that collective security must be truly collective to hold, that an order in which the majority of members have no stake and see no justice is ultimately unviable. In the present historical conjuncture, collective security on a global scale is impossible as long as we are dominated by realist Hobbism instead of taking democracy seriously and basing order on justice.

It is paradoxical that the issue of taking democracy seriously should arise, for the West appears to believe that it was democracy that conquered communist Europe and ended the Cold War in the final process of consummating its mastery of the world. As William Pfaff argues, it is the democracies of the West, whatever their imperfections, that are the success stories of the day.[24] According to him, they triumphed not by virtue of their science and technology, not only by military power, but because of the organizing values of their society. The United States, despite a highly activist policy of confronting communism worldwide in order to contain it, was in the end only a spectator to the collapse and the decomposition of the Soviet Empire. As the "democratic revolution swept through Eastern Europe, Bush and his government were more spectators than participants—a bit confused, generally approving but above all, passive."[25]

In the aftermath of the Cold War there is no alternative legitimacy to democracy, and it does not look as though there is any chance that the surge of democracy can be resisted in any part of the world. It is entirely understandable that many believe we are witnessing the final triumph of democracy in the world.

So it appears. The reality may be more complicated. It is not clear whether we are witnessing the universalization of democracy or its final demise. The West, the bastion of democracy, has had democracy under unrelenting pressure for centuries, pressure for the reconstruction of the meaning and practice of democracy in consonance with the rejection of popular sovereignty and an increasingly trivial notion of popular participation. The seeming universalization of democracy appears to be the consummation of this process. Democracy has been trivialized to the point that it is no longer threatening to power elites, who are all too pleased now to proclaim their democratic commitment, knowing that it demands very little of them. Democracy is universalized in a highly devalued form that is largely irrelevant to the new political realities of the West except as an ideological representation and that is quite dangerous to the Third World countries, especially Africa, who are obliged to take it seriously and run the risk of performing delicate operations with blunt instruments.

But what is democracy? This looks like a very difficult question, for democracy has been given a profusion of meanings that verges on anarchy. Libraries have been written on the theory and practice of democracy, and more will surely be written, for every attempt to bring clarity invariably compounds the richness of meaning and the confusion.

Nonetheless, the question is not so difficult. For a political concept, democracy has an uncharacteristically precise meaning. The question is not and never has been a matter of determining what democracy means or what it is supposed to mean but rather involves navigating the tangled web of contradictions arising from how different social forces perceive the implications of democracy for their interests. The apparent confusion over the meaning of democracy is politically induced. It is not even really a confusion over meaning but a confusion of the multiplicity of alternatives offered by those who are uncomfortable with democracy or who reject it entirely. In fairness to them, those who have been trying to replace democracy are not in the least confused about what it means. It is precisely because they know its classical meaning only too well that they are trying to replace it.

The Greeks, who invented democracy, defined it precisely. And they were agreed on its meaning across the ideological spectrum of Athenian politics. They left us not only a precise and noncontroversial definition but also a historical practice of democratic governance complete with institutions. Democracy for the Greeks meant rule by the demos, or popular power.

They dispelled the ambiguity that might have arisen from the concept of people by specifying it in sociological and economic terms. The people were not just seen in numerical terms; they were also to be understood in class terms. The demos who rule can be seen at one level as the whole people, but at another level when the necessity for sociological specificity, especially class character, is called for. Then they can be seen as the masses as opposed to the elite, as a numerical majority who are also the lower stratum economically. Aristotle insisted that in the final analysis the real basis for the classification of the people is not number but social class. Democracy presupposes that sovereign authority is vested in the poorer classes, not in the owners of property.

The history of democracy is a history of resistance to its essence, popular power. Democracy was even blamed for the ascendancy of Sparta over Athens. The ideal of "homo politics," which was associated with the direct democracy of Athens, was quickly replaced by "homo militants," its very negation, and this was what prevailed through the long Roman interregnum.

The centuries of *respublica Christiana* do not appear to have helped a return to Athenian democracy. If anything, they may have rendered it more difficult. The values of *respublica Christiana* framed a new ideal being, *homo credens*, in an age of faith, authority, and hierarchy. The Athenians tried to realize the good life in the polis. Christians sought it in the afterlife and were encouraged to see themselves as pilgrims just passing through human society; the apoliticism this bred was a far cry from the overcharged political activism that nourished Athenian democracy.

The French Revolution was a watershed in the attempt to reach back to the Athenian idea of democracy as popular power, an idea that was expressed in its theory of popular sovereignty and its practice of political participation. In waging the Revolution, the French created a formidable, implacable army not only against themselves but also against democracy. The rising European bourgeoisie welcomed the French Revolution in its hostility to the economic and political institutions and values of feudalism. However, they were appalled by the possibilities of popular sovereignty as reflected in the radical egalitarianism of the French Revolution. They understood only too well the threat this posed to their right of property and the privileges they enjoyed by virtue of their social and economic status. Expectedly, they undertook to wage war against these tendencies.

In the end they succeeded in replacing democracy with liberal democracy. Liberal democracy is different from democracy even though it has significant affinities to it, such as government by the consent of the governed, formal political equality, and inalienable human rights including the right to political participation. However, it is markedly different. Instead of emphasizing the collectivity, liberal democracy focuses on the individual and her inalienable rights; it substitutes government by the people with government by consent of the people. For the sovereignty of the people it substitutes the sovereignty of the law. Instead of emphasizing universality, it celebrates specificity, even placing its claims above those of the collectivity.

In the final analysis, liberal democracy repudiates the very essence of democracy, namely popular power. It is not really a political morality in the sense that democracy was to the Athenian, but a political convenience, for its appeal to the European bourgeoisie was that it is the political correlate of the market, that is, the political condition for maximizing its efficiency and sustainability. Also, it was appealing to the privileged by virtue of the fact that it guaranteed the rights, most significantly the property rights, of the individual against even the will of the majority.

Liberal democracy has not stood still. It has been evolving continuously, and nothing useful about the meaning of democracy or about the democratic status of contemporary society can be said without taking account of this development. Among those who made important contributions to democratic theory since the nineteenth century are Max Weber, Joseph Schumpeter,

Robert Michels, Vilfredo Pareto, Robert Dahl, David Truman, Henry Mayo, and Seymour M. Lipset.

Max Weber's work was particularly useful in placing democracy in the context of industrial capitalism, which he portrayed in *The Protestant Ethic and the Spirit of Capitalism* as uniquely different from other kinds of societal structures. It is particularly so in its use of calculation in a technical sense, calculation whose quintessential expression is the scientific method. But the calculative attitude goes beyond the realm of science into production, culture, institutions, and values—for instance, it drives capitalist production in considerations regarding technical improvement, minimum input, and maximum output, efficiency, predictability, information, knowledge, and predictability.

The calculative attitude is a departure from the theological and metaphysical consciousness of the past, and it has weakened the appeal of the grand moralities and ideologies, fostering social atomization and throwing people back to themselves and their preoccupation with their value-maximizing strategies. Following Joseph Schumpeter, the pluralists dismissed the feasibility and even the desirability of classical democracy as well as the nineteenth-century theories of representative democracy, notably that of John Stuart Mill. They held that ordinary people never really exercise any decisive influence in politics, being as they are ignorant, apathetic, and disempowered by bureaucratization; nor do the representatives of the people really ever represent them. More often than not, they lead, manipulate, or dominate them.

Like Schumpeter, the pluralists accepted that the essence of democracy was not participation in rule but the choices of those who rule. These affinities reflected the fact that the pluralists largely shared Schumpeter's prejudices regarding the moral, psychological, and intellectual limitations of the masses.

Liberal democracy was further devalued by the interventions of Robert Michels, Vilfredo Pareto, Robert Dahl, David Truman, and others. But these details will not detain us here. Suffice it to say that as capitalism took hold, developed into monopoly capitalism, and constituted what may be called, following Foucault, a highly complex disciplinary society, the theory of democracy abandoned, in turn, popular sovereignty, political participation, and representation. It subsequently embraced competitive elitism and then degenerated to the apoliticism of the group theory of politics and social movement theory, which claimed that what we may reasonably expect is to be able to pursue some of our interests through groups of like-minded people in some local social pace. And now, the appellation of democracy refers to the formality of multiparty electoral competition.

Democracy has been displaced by something else that has assumed its name while largely dispensing with its content. In a formal sense what appears to have won is not democracy but liberal democracy. But this is misleading too. For liberal democracy has atrophied in a long process of devaluation and political reaction, in the course of which it has largely lost its redeeming democratic elements. Liberal values have lost ground under pressure. In most of the countries of the West, liberal is now a term of abuse, a label to be avoided by all means by any person who wants to win an election.

DEMOCRACY IN AFRICA

The failure to take democracy seriously poses special problems for Africa. But before going into this, let us be clear why democratization is important for Africa. Political independence in Africa was not the heroic event it was made out to be. The nationalists inherited the colonial state instead of transforming it in accordance with the democratic aspirations of the nationalist movement. When their frustrated followers began to turn against them, they resorted to repression, which only caused more resentment, more alienation, and still greater repression. Political legitimacy largely disappeared, as did constitutionalism and the rule of law. The rulers hung on grimly to the enormous power of the colonial state by all means, and those who were excluded from this power and exploited by it used every means to get it. Politics was no longer a contest over who should rule and how, but by virtue of the mutual alienation of government and the opposition and also the character of the inherited colonial state, politics became a contest of exclusive claims to legitimacy, a deadly zero-sum game that inevitably degenerated into warfare. As is to be expected, this Hobbesian politics could only throw up Leviathans in the form of personal rule, single-party regimes, and military regimes, the last being the quintessential expression of a politics, which having become warfare, propelled specialists of war to the forefront of politics. In this Hobbesian world, leaders struggle to survive in a siege mentality, and the ruled struggle against a powerful state they see as a hostile force to be evaded, cheated, or captured.

It is not possible to pursue development in these circumstances. Libraries have been written to record, lament, and explain the failure of the development project in Africa. But it has not failed. It never began because the political conditions were lacking. The process of democratization in Africa offers, for once, the prospect of creating the political environment conducive to development. But these prospects are now endangered because the African elite and the international community are giving the wrong type of support to the wrong type of democracy.

The ordinary people of Africa are supporting democracy as "a second independence." This time they want independence not from the colonial masters but from indigenous leaders. They want independence from leaders whose misrule has intensified their poverty and exploitation to the point of being life-threatening. And they are convinced that they cannot now get material improvement without securing political empowerment and being better placed to bring public policy closer to social needs.

Democracy is being interpreted and supported in ways that defeat these aspirations and manifest no sensitivity to the social conditions of the ordinary people of Africa. Generally the political elites who support democratization are those with no access to power, and they invariably have no feeling for democratic values. They support democratization largely as a strategy of power. The influential international development agencies, especially the International Monetary Fund and the World Bank, lend subversive support to democratization with an apolitical concept of democracy as accountability, transparency, and competitive efficiency, mere technical correlates of policy reform. The West, through political conditionality, lends ambiguous support to democratization in order to seize an unexpected opportunity for consummating Western hegemony. What it is supporting is a formal minimalist democracy as multiparty elections without being fussy about the quality of the elections. Democratic elections can only decide who control, to their own benefit, an unreformed and inherently oppressive colonial state. The people can chose between oppressors and by the appearance of choice legitimize what is really their disempowerment.

The idea of the powerful nations of the world on how democracy and economic development relate in Africa is epitomized by the IMF-type SAPs. The West and its development agents are convinced that SAPs will optimize democratization and economic growth, thus solving Africa's major problems in one fell swoop. SAPs enhance democratization by destatization, pluralizing decisionmaking centers, encouraging individualism, predictability, and the rule of law; economic liberalization will give impetus to political liberalization, which will be all the more enduring for having an economic base. It is no wonder the West has such abiding faith in SAPs. To call policy reform an orthodoxy is perhaps an understatement; it is for all African ailing economies a necessity because all the major industrialized countries as well as the international development agencies insist that it is the solution and will not cooperate with anyone who rejects it.

The standard policy reform package of any SAP entails the reduction of public expenditure, privatization, devaluation for a more "realistic" exchange rate, export promotion, and import restriction. There is a case for reform along these lines, but what is not so clear is the particular form that these reforms have taken in Africa. The distinctive feature of the African SAPs is their rigorous austerity: an outright ban on essential commodities where no local substitutes exist; a precipitate rollback of subsidies, which may quadruple prices overnight; a steep rise in unemployment from massive privatization and destatization associated with steep rises in unemployment, devaluation, and a wage freeze. Two relatively mild cases illustrate the rigor of adjustment. In 1989, when the first wave of reform in Gabon occurred, government expenditure was cut by 50 percent. The Nigerian naira, which was roughly at par with the U.S. dollar before the adjustment programs, exchanged at 20 to 1 U.S. dollar in 1993. It is not difficult to imagine the effects of these phenomenal increases in unemployment, inflation in combination with a wage freeze, and the withdrawal of subsidies in economies where as many as 40 percent of the population might be living below the poverty line. SAPs are not a mere inconvenience: They generally cause deep despair, widespread malnutrition, and premature death; and as the United Nations Children's Fund (UNICEF) reports show, much of the burden falls on children.

In every case the regimes implementing SAPs had been in power and were bitterly resented for creating the conditions that necessitated SAPs in the first place. The vehement opposition to SAPs in Africa, misunderstood by the international community, is directed not against the rationale of the SAP but against the regimes that were so discredited that their people distrusted their competence and good intentions and tended to think that they were more likely to make things worse than better. In Nigeria, the only place where an SAP was subjected to a public debate, it was overwhelmingly rejected on the basis that the loans for the program would be corruptly appropriated. The adoption of the SAP itself is a conspicuous acknowledgment of failures; it further erodes regime legitimacy and increases the alienation of the political leadership.

In these circumstances the political leadership in Africa was not in a position for consensus-building. Neither was consensus-building encouraged by the international situation. The industrialized countries were left in no doubt that it was up to them to find ways of effecting policy reform. IMF and the World Bank are adamant that SAPs are inevitable and nonnegotiable and urge African leaders constantly to muster the political will to effect them, "will" being a euphemism for ruthlessness. Not only were the circumstances unfavorable for consultation and consensus-building but there was a strong presumption to the effect that it was highly undesirable to debate the SAP or seek a mandate for it because people would not willingly accept its rigors. Thus it came about that policy reform was put beyond democratic legitimation and regarded as something that had to be imposed. And so it was. The very implementation of the SAP has been a setback for democracy, its rigors even more so. The African SAPs often break down existing social consensus, and they always require a strong dose of authoritarianism.

The strategy that the logic of the new world order and the powerful players in the world prescribe for democratization and economic growth in Africa does not look promising. The one thing that looks promising in all this is that Africa no longer has the choice of not taking self-reliance seriously, an option it should have taken all along. It is a very difficult option and is likely to make things a lot worse before they get better, if they improve at all.

CONCLUSION: WHOSE WORLD ORDER?

The new world order is still forming, and it is yet unclear what its final shape will be. What is clear already is that its moral and political quality as well as its viability will depend a great deal on a deeper commitment to democracy. In the South, such commitment will bring public policy to the service of social needs; it will facilitate the mobilization of everyone in the interest of development; and it will place emphasis on negotiated consensus, which will reduce conflict. In the North commitment will reduce the internal tensions arising from inequality, social pluralism, xenophobia, and economic competition and will restrain them from causing serious ruptures or proxy wars in the South.

A deeper commitment to democracy will encourage even development. The experience of the 1990s has shown that any form of government that cannot eradicate hunger and severe deprivation cannot avoid violence and cannot survive. Similarly, no peaceful and secure world is going to be possible without solving the problem of uneven development and the poverty of much of the world's population. The North would do well to resist the temptation that it can appropriate at will and pay no heed to even development and the rule of law in global governance. The ghetto is too large and the haven it inhabits is small and shrinking. A policy of policing the status quo is feasible, but only in circumstances that effectively repudiate civilization. If the new world order is to be an improvement on its predecessor, it has to place the highest priority on democracy and even development. This is a tall order.

❧ 3 ❧

Uneven Globalization, Economic Reform, and Democracy: A View from Latin America

OSVALDO SUNKEL

The international relations literature is overwhelmingly concerned with the multiple consequences of the end of the Cold War. The same is true, but to a much lesser extent, in Latin America. In this region the most important changes that have been taking place for over a decade are basically of a domestic nature: the adoption of sweeping neoliberal economic reform packages on the one hand, and on the other the political transition from authoritarian governments to democratic regimes.

Both processes started in this area long before the sudden and earthshaking changes in international relations that began at the end of 1989 with the fall of the Berlin Wall, the ensuing collapse of the Soviet Union and the socialist bloc, and the end of the Cold War. In comparison to most other regions of the world, Latin America has not been noticeably impacted by these momentous historical events. But significant consequences will no doubt arise in the near future, especially regarding national and international security matters but also in political, ideological, and economic affairs.

Socialist Cuba, heavily dependent on the former Soviet bloc, has of course suffered a deadly blow, and profound changes with unpredictable consequences are bound to happen sooner rather than later. With some exceptions in Central America, where Cuban influence used to be important, the immediate effects in Latin America of the collapse of "real socialism" are so far secondary. This is true both compared to other world regions and regarding the profound changes taking place in the region itself.

Economic reform in Latin America began in the Southern Cone in the mid-1970s, with results that ranged from the disastrous in Argentina—trying yet again in 1994—to the highly successful in Chile, but at enormous

43

Latin America

1. Mexico	9. Cuba	17. Peru
2. Guatemala	10. Haiti	18. Brazil
3. Belize	11. Dominican Rep.	19. Bolivia
4. Honduras	12. Colombia	20. Paraguay
5. El Salvador	13. Venezuela	21. Chile
6. Nicaragua	14. Guyana	22. Argentina
7. Costa Rica	15. Surinam	23. Uruguay
8. Panama	16. Equador	

costs. Almost a decade later, with the unfolding of the debt crisis, which exploded in 1982, and the implementation of internationally backed economic adjustment and restructuring policies, economic reform programs had spread all over the region.

In a radical departure from the state-led, protectionist development strategies and policies of the postwar era, the aim of contemporary economic reform is to liberalize and deregulate national and international markets of goods, services, finance, and factors of production, forcing the Latin American economies to engage in worldwide competition. In order to achieve this objective, policymakers have considerably reduced and changed the state's role in socioeconomic development. The assumption is that national and foreign private enterprise, operating in an environment of free markets, will become the new engine of growth and development.

Regarding the recovery or initiation of *democratic regimes,* it may be convenient to recall that the military dictatorships and authoritarian regimes that prevailed during the 1970s started to fall one after another at the end of that decade. The immediate causes were of a very diverse nature. But one precipitating underlying factor was undoubtedly the social and economic crises gaining momentum under the veil of an apparent prosperity financed by increasing foreign indebtedness. This came to an abrupt end when the debt bomb exploded in 1982 and severe economic adjustments became inevitable. These created serious political tensions and conflicts that helped to bring about the transition to democratic regimes.

But there are other elements of a longer-term nature that have to be taken into account, among them the increasing "demand for democracy" among growing sectors of the population in Latin America. By this I mean the increasingly generalized aspirations and demands for greater participation in the economic realm (ownership, incomes, consumption, jobs); in the social arena (human rights, social mobility, grass-roots organizations); in political activity and power (elections, citizenship, participation in decisionmaking); and in cultural life (access to education, information, the media, and cultural goods and services generally). These demands have spread and become particularly strong among former relatively excluded sectors such as women, youth, religious minorities, regional groups, and ethnic minorities and majorities.

Prior to the economic crisis, the contrast was already increasing between these demands for democracy and the capacity of the authoritarian political systems to deliver political participation and economic and social well-being. Because popular support was predicated precisely on leaders' claims to economic superiority over democratic regimes, these conditions, particularly the following debt crisis, undermined the regimes' credibility.

Paradoxically, just over a decade later the region may again be facing a similar contradiction, but in the reverse order. Latin America's fledgling political democracies are struggling to survive the heavy social costs inherited from the debt and development crises and from the economic reforms that they were forced to introduce in their wake during the so-called lost decade of the 1980s. Will these forces now contribute to wrecking incipient democratic political systems as they struggle with a deteriorated social situation in circumstances of a heightened democratic demand and fewer economic resources? The ominous political crises in Peru, Venezuela, and other countries in the early 1990s are sounding the alarm bells.

These profound structural, institutional, and ideological changes, and their socioeconomic and political consequences and dilemmas, are the key contemporary issues in the region. They constitute the most pervasive problem and the central concern all over Latin America.

This trend toward an increasing prominence of economic, social, and political issues is likely to be further strengthened as a consequence of the decline that *security considerations* had in the region and in U.S.–Latin American relations during the Cold War period. In the post–Cold War era, security remains a minor issue in the region, and the profound change in international relations is giving rise to the renewed importance of concerns such as the environment, migration, civil-military relations, human rights, drug trafficking, technology transfer, and trade. But given the aforementioned contradiction between social and economic trends, questions concerned with poverty alleviation, increased equity, and sustainable development strategies and policies will probably become of central concern.

UNEVEN GLOBALIZATION AND ECONOMIC REFORM

Economic reform became generalized in Latin America after the initiation of the debt crisis in 1982. But such reforms had already been initiated in the countries of the Southern Cone and are now of worldwide scope, suggesting that pressures in that direction were profound and had existed for a long time.[1]

My basic argument, from a substantial perspective of world order, is that during these last decades of the twentieth century, we are in the midst of a period of epochal civilizational transformation, a sea change in the sociocultural affairs and arrangements of humanity, within and among societies and their environmental life-support systems. The wave of economic and political reforms that has been and is sweeping Latin America somewhat belatedly is part and parcel of this wider process and is largely conditioned by it. In order to grasp the vast and profound nature of the changes in this period, I find it convenient to compare it to another such phase of systemic transformation: the interwar period during the first half of this century, about which we have sufficient historical perspective.

Capitalist development over the last century or so has gone through four clearly distinct phases. From around 1870 to 1913 there was a period of intense and sustained growth and low unemployment. This was followed by a phase of slow growth, high unemployment, and considerable instability during the interwar period, conditions that continued through World War II until around 1950. From 1950 until 1973 capitalist growth and development achieved historically unprecedented levels of dynamism, full employment and social progress, but since then growth has been slow, stagnant, or highly unstable; unemployment is high and rising, and social conditions are deteriorating.[2]

The phases of rapid economic growth and development, sometimes labeled respectively as pax Britannica and pax Americana, seem to have been associated with periods of relatively stable national power structures and international geopolitical arrangements, dominant ideologies, waves of diffusion of major technological innovations, and new forms of business organization and financial expansion, all of which have tended to generate a stimulating and confident business and investment climate. I would like to suggest that in these cases or periods a relatively lasting and stable world order or system came into existence.

In contrast, the periods of slow and unstable growth or relative stagnation, for example, the interwar period and the early 1990s, are characterized by several kinds of severe shocks, acute crises, and abrupt transformations in national and international sociopolitical structures and institutions. The profound transformations in the ideological, technological, institutional, and cultural realms, as well as in the geopolitical situation and international relations, particularly regarding hegemonic powers, was and is creating an atmosphere of uncertainty.[3] These phases of profound transformation may have transitional periods that can be relatively short and give rise to a new world order, or they may drag on for a rather long period of instability.

Since we seem to be immersed in one of these latter transitional periods of disorder, it is instructive to go beyond economic trends in order to look into some of the more profound changes in several related fields that characterized the interwar period.

The period comprising World War I, the turbulent decade of the 1920s, the Great Depression, World War II, and the beginnings of the Cold War was a period of profound crises in the capitalist system: runaway inflations, huge and prolonged unemployment, boom and bust in the U.S. economy during the 1920s while stagnation prevailed in Europe, and the total collapse of the international trading and financial system. Moreover, it was characterized by a transition from one epoch to another in the realms of ideology, values, social and political organization, culture, technology, and international relations.

Some of the changes during that period that are more relevant to our concerns were the following: The British Empire gave way to U.S. hegemony in international affairs; other nineteenth-century empires also collapsed and decolonization led to the creation of numerous new states in Africa, Asia, the Caribbean, and elsewhere; fascist authoritarian regimes rose to prominence and were eventually defeated in World War II; a new era of cheap energy based on oil and electricity allowed a technological and organizational revolution in industry, transportation, and communications; socialism took hold initially in Russia and eventually spread over a large part of the world, becoming a powerful historical reality that threatened the very existence of capitalism; within capitalism itself the persistent and severe economic and social crises of the period, and the socialist challenge, led to profound institutional transformations, including a complete change in economic policies that gave an expanded and crucial role to the state.

All these aspects are illustrative of the qualitative changes in this period. I believe it is most important to pursue the latter aspect in more detail as an important and convenient thread to bring us up to the present phase.

THE STATE AS THE ORGANIZER
OF NATIONAL DEVELOPMENT

For the following several decades and all over the world, the state emerged from this period as the most powerful institutional actor. It expanded the traditional political role of governments to include economic, social, and cultural activities. The state became the savior of the capitalist system through the creation and activities of what was to become known as *the public sector*. It was also the crucial institution in leading the way to the establishment of an alternative socialist system in the Soviet Union and later in other countries.

In the newly established socialist economies the state became the owner of the means of production. It organized a centralized planning system in order to impose profound structural and institutional transformations and force accelerated processes of modernization, particularly as regards industrialization and social services.

What is seldom explicitly recognized is that the phenomenon of a vastly expanded and strongly interventionist state, though in a far less radical fashion than in the socialist countries, swept the whole of the capitalist world as well. In the industrialized capitalist world, several European countries with national-socialist or corporatist-fascist regimes emerged as the more extreme cases of the state as an overpowering economic and political entity. These regimes were followed, after their defeat in Germany and Italy, by social-market or mixed economies, where a democratic state played a different but also significant and growing role. In the Scandinavian countries and the United Kingdom the welfare state was established, and in the United States the New Deal and full employment policies took hold.[4] In Japan a state-organized and managed market economy had been created long ago, after the *Meiji Restoration* in 1868, in order to modernize society, industrialize, and catch up with Western industrial countries. This state-run market economy was largely recreated after Japan's defeat in World War II and was taken as a model by other very successful Asian countries.

Inspired by the aforementioned models, underdeveloped countries all over the world adopted various mixtures of state-led economic and social development strategies and policies. The aim was to overcome their backwardness and their skewed economic structure, which was characterized in most cases by a specialized commodity export sector and a primitive domestic productive structure, particularly regarding the manufacturing sector. Policies took different shapes according to the prevailing ideologies, power configurations, and other initial conditions such as resource bases, cultural and institutional characteristics, and stages of development.

In most Latin American countries, the main new functions of the state were *intervention in goods and factor markets* to shift resources to industrialization and modernization generally; *financing of long-term projects and programs* to overcome the lack of private national and international long-term financial markets; *redistribution of income* through the enactment of social legislation and the creation of infrastructure and services in the social sectors: health, education and culture, housing and urban development, social security; *public investments in infrastructure* in order to provide physical support for the creation and integration of the internal market by means of transportation, communication, and energy facilities; *creation of public enterprises* in activities that did not interest or were beyond the capabilities of private entrepreneurs; *generation of employment opportunities* in the aforementioned activities, which contributed substantially to the development of universities and higher education, responsible for the training of the qualified human resources needed in all these new activities.[5]

One consequence and indicator of the newly found prominence of the state and the *public sector* everywhere was a substantial increase in the share of government expenditures in GDP (gross domestic product). The increase was particularly strong during the decades of the 1960s and 1970s but then tended to level off and decline in several cases in the 1980s.

THE STATE AND THE POSTWAR WORLD ORDER

The collapse of the international economic and financial systems during the Great Depression of the 1930s produced a catastrophic reduction in trade flows, a strong increase in protectionism, and the disappearance of private international finance and investments. The state thus became the central institutional actor within the confines of the national economies of most countries in Latin America and elsewhere. The need to reconstruct war-devastated Europe and the international economy at the end of World War II led respectively to the Marshall Plan and the organization of a multilateral system of international institutions (the United Nations, the IMF, the World Bank, and GATT). Developed-country governments also created public bilateral international mechanisms to foster exports and multilateral and bilateral aid and technical assistance institutions to cooperate in the development of underdeveloped countries. In a way, these measures were the seeds of a "global state" and the establishment of an *international public sector.*

In these different ways, during the postwar decades, both at the national and international levels, in the North and in the South, as well as in the East and in the West, the state supported and promoted capitalist development and became the central pillar of socialist development, giving rise to an unprecedented phase of worldwide economic growth that has been labeled the "Golden Age"[6] or the "Golden Years."[7]

Due in large part to the new role of the state, average social conditions as expressed in indicators such as life expectancy, child mortality, literacy, and so on also improved substantially during the postwar period. Developing countries reduced their average infant mortality from nearly 200 deaths per 1,000 live births to about 80 in about four decades (1950–1988), "a feat that took industrial countries nearly a century to accomplish."[8] The portion of families living in conditions of poverty in Latin America declined substantially during the postwar period from 51 percent in 1960 to 35 percent in 1980, when it started to increase again to 37 percent in 1986 as a consequence of the debt crisis and the adjustment and restructuring policies that followed. Absolute poverty followed a similar path, declining sharply from 26 percent to 15 percent between 1960 and 1980 and then increasing again to 17 percent in 1986.[9]

Although it may sound bizarre in the light of present circumstances, the improvement in social conditions also applies to the centrally planned economies of Eastern Europe and the USSR. For one, economic growth was similarly fast, and at least *until the 1970s* did not exhibit the gross inequality and widespread poverty of the underdeveloped capitalist world.[10] Moreover, most socialist bloc countries are classified among the "high human development" countries as measured by the UNDP Human Development Index. Cuba could also be mentioned. Its rapid economic growth and especially the

TABLE 3.1   Long-Term Trends in the International Economy
Before and After the 1970s

	Between 1950 and 1970	After 1980
World economy	Exceptionally rapid and sustained growth	Slow and unstable growth
International trade	Great expansion	Slow growth, instability
Terms of trade	Relatively low and stable (in relation to early 1950s)	Severe deterioration (in relation to 1980)
Public international financing	Rapid and sustained increase	Very limited
Direct foreign financing	Rapid and sustained expansion	Strong increase among developed countries, very scarce for underdeveloped countries
Private financing	Exceptional expansion after the mid-1960s	Scarce, decreasing and substantial negative net flow (debt servicing)
Interest rates	Very low	Very high during most of 1980s
Protectionism	Decreasing	Strong increase
International cooperation	Very favorable attitude	Very negative attitude
External conditionality in economic policy matters	Short-term IMF	Short-term: IMF, international banks, U.S. government Long-term: World Bank, U.S. government

SOURCE: Osvaldo Sunkel, "Del desarrollo hacia dentro al desarrollo desde dentro," in O. Sunkel, ed., *El desarrollo desde dentro: Un enfoque neoestructuralista para America Latina* (Mexico City: Fondo de Cultura Económica, 1991), p. 80.

substantial social improvements that took place, in this case *until the mid-1980s*, contrast dramatically with the rest of Latin America.

As shown in the first column of Table 3.1, it is striking how favorable the global economic environment was in the 1950s and 1960s in almost all crucial aspects: an exceptionally rapid overall rate of sustained expansion of the world economy; even faster growth of international trade; a considerable reduction in protectionism; increasing public international finance, both multi- and bilateral; substantial international technical cooperation and aid;

small but growing private direct investment and the emergence of the multi-national corporation; and a very low rate of interest.

THE CONTEMPORARY TRANSITIONAL PHASE

Seen in historical context and from the perspective of the 1990s, the "golden" postwar years, the "old world order," were a considerable success in most countries. The contrast between this positive global postwar picture, which lasted *until the 1970s,* and the dismal decade of the 1980s is quite remarkable. Moreover, the postwar years are generally overlooked, lumped into one single (and supposedly disastrous) period. As illustrated in the second column of Table 3.1, after 1980 all the variables mentioned before lost their positive momentum and influence or became acutely negative. This situation became particularly grave for Latin America, most countries of the developing world, and several countries of the socialist bloc after the debt crisis erupted in 1982.

During the critical decade of the 1970s a considerable part of the national and international institutional setup that had emerged out of World War II was substantially transformed. The worldwide process of socioeconomic and political reforms that we are witnessing in the 1990s started in the late 1960s with the collapse of the Bretton Woods system of international economic relations around 1970, the two oil shocks of 1973 and 1979, and the adoption of radical neoliberal economic policies by the Margaret Thatcher and Ronald Reagan governments. These eventually became the central ideological backbone of the overall transformation process.

But the stunning events of the early 1990s, particularly those that erupted suddenly and unexpectedly in the former Soviet bloc countries and that gave rise initially to the optimistic expectation of a new word order, have been obscuring these and other more fundamental forces at work—both in those countries and in most parts of the world—over several decades. Some of the most relevant and profound phenomena, as seen from Latin America, are briefly mentioned here.

A profound scientific and technological revolution has taken place that has shifted the earlier concentration on the physical sciences to the biological disciplines. The development of microelectronics and the information and telematic revolution, robotics, biotechnology, and new materials has produced fundamental changes throughout the economic, social, and political systems, including the nature of interfirm and labor relations, the work process, and traditional international and locational comparative advantages. These changes entail potentially damaging consequences for underdeveloped primary commodity–exporting countries. But they could also open new opportunities, provided Latin American countries can marshal the will and capacity to face in a creative manner the challenges of technological innovation adoption and adaptation.[11]

Moreover, environmental degradation, natural resource exhaustion, and threats to local, regional, and global ecosystems have introduced a whole new dimension into human affairs and international relations. It has become apparent that there is an urgent need for a shift to sustainable development, as proclaimed at the 1992 Rio de Janeiro Earth Summit. The alternative is to face increasingly serious challenges to humanity's life-support systems. This is another heavy burden for underdeveloped countries in general and Latin America in particular. But the region may have certain advantages over other heavily populated and resource-scarce regions given its relative abundance of natural resources.

Worldwide, the United States has lost some of its earlier overwhelming economic predominance, although retaining and exercising its uncontested military might. Europe, and especially reunited Germany, together with Japan, are emerging as comparable economic powers and beginning to exercise the corresponding political clout. The core of the world economy is being reorganized around three closely interrelated main blocs led respectively by the United States of America, Japan, and the European Community (EC), with Germany becoming the predominant economic actor in the latter case. Some see in this trend the emergence of a "new mercantilism," which evolves as the powers of the nation-state erode and multinational blocs develop to pursue the national interests of the dominant powers of each bloc.[12] This new triad of economic power, made up of a fifth of the world population, concentrates two-thirds of world GDP, four-fifths of outward stocks of foreign direct investment, and one-half of world trade.[13] With the exception of the NICs (newly industrializing countries) and a few other countries, most of the countries in the periphery of the world economy and the vast majority of the population of the former Third World are linked to this process by means of the increasing transnationalization of more or less significant segments of their economies and societies.

Latin America is undoubtedly the region of the Third World where this process of transnationalization has been taking place for a longer time and has penetrated further and deeper. Although European countries and Japan and other Asian countries have an increased presence in the region, the United States continues to be the overwhelming hegemonic power in economic, political, military, ideological, and cultural affairs. Therefore, the nature of the evolution of U.S.–Latin American relations will continue to be of central importance in shaping this region's future, notwithstanding the eventual consolidations of a trilateral system of world power blocs.

The former *public* multilateral system of international economic relations among nation-states that emerged after World War II has been substantially eroded by the expansion of the multinational enterprise sector and the emergence of the global corporation. This process, coupled with international financial deregulation and the successive Eurodollar, petrodollar, and foreign direct investment booms has generated a closely integrated and concentrated *private* transnational corporate core of the world economy. This corporate core is particularly powerful in the investment, financial, and other telecommunications and information-related services spheres, which have taken advantage of the technological revolution. International financial capital has vastly outgrown productive capital in importance and power, and therefore the interests related to worldwide financial transactions tend to prevail over concerns with national economic growth, full employment, and social welfare.

Consequently, the main former international *public* concerns with world economic growth and development receive negligible attention in the rather weak, informal, highly elitist, and ineffectual mechanisms of *public* international economic and financial management. This is particularly true as far as Latin America is concerned. Since the region was classified as a middle-income area in relation to its needs for technical assistance and development aid, it has practically disappeared from the international cooperation scene. Moreover, once it ceased to be a threat to the international financial system as a consequence of its huge indebtedness, developed-country governments lost all interest in the region even though the debt crisis continues to plague many of its countries. Meanwhile, the international institutions that were supposed to fulfill those public international roles, principally the IMF and the World Bank, have become engaged mainly in the implementation of neoliberal economic reform packages in the former socialist bloc countries and particularly in Latin America.

A new economic world order is emerging that is reaching an advanced stage of globalization. One of the consequences is a generalized worldwide economic reform trend toward the dismantling of the public sector, which led economic growth and social development in the postwar period. But some economic reform processes are more generalized than others. The change is of a relatively mild variety in the powerful industrial economies that constitute the core of the global economy and certainly does not touch their import-substituting protectionist practices and barriers. The peripheral economies and former socialist countries, as well as those that still cling to socialism, are undergoing more or less intense processes of wholesale economic reform. The starting point of this process is precisely the elimination of barriers to international trade, investment, finance, transportation, and communications. This economic reform is followed by the abolition of government interventions in the internal economy through deregulation, liberalization, and privatization; a reduction in the size of the state apparatus; and the adoption of policies to promote private enterprise, free markets, and international competition.

One major economic consequence has been the relative contraction of the industrial sector that was built up during the import-substituting period. In a few cases this seems to have had the salutary effect of eliminating the clearly uncompetitive enterprises while stimulating restructurization, innovation, and increased productivity and competitiveness in the industrial sector and the economy as a whole. But in many cases the industrial sector has suffered a serious reduction and the economies have once again become natural resource–based exporting economies. In the more successful cases the export base has been diversified into higher technology and value-added products. Even if during an initial period these new, more efficient and diversified export sectors have been quite dynamic, signs of increasing difficulties regarding market access and declining international prices have already become apparent. The old and well-known dilemma of how to become an exporter of more dynamic manufactures and other goods and services is therefore back. This will undoubtedly become a central issue in the debate about development strategies and policies.

Uneven Globalization:
Transnational Integration and National Disintegration

The dialectics of transnational integration, although modernizing segments and aspects of peripheral countries, may also generate conditions of social segregation, fragmentation, and disintegration.[14] This may be seen in the various sectors of economic activity where new enterprises are set up and those of the greatest innovative capacity are restructured to compete in international and domestic markets. This means new and well-paid jobs of high productivity for some. But many workers are displaced in the process of privatization and reduction of government services and enterprises, in the restructuring of private firms, and in those businesses that are not able to stand up to the increased international competition.

Divergent trends are thus generated between those who enter the expanding modern sector of high productivity, which is in the process of internationalization, and those who sink to an inferior level of employment in low-productivity jobs in conditions of underemployment or self-employment, swelling the ranks of the informal economy and the poor. Frequently, the former tend to be fewer than the latter, at least during a rather long transition period, depending on the population growth rate and the labor force; the possibilities of emigration; the intensity of the restructuring process; the incorporation of capital-intensive technology; the level of savings and investments; and the skills, education, and work habits of the active population.

The process of creation and displacement of jobs is bound to add, for some time to come, to the existing conditions of structural heterogeneity. This process discriminates against older persons, the big contingents of young people without work experience, and women. In contrast, it favors urban adults with better qualifications and skills, greater initiative, and the ability to gain access to the higher segments of the labor markets.

Thus, in the different productive sectors, in the regions, in urban and rural areas, and among the different social strata, we see in unequal proportions, modernity and backwardness in production activities and affluence and poverty, as well as sharp contrasts in the physical environment, a basic factor that determines the quality of life. This gives rise to large cultural, institutional, political, and demographic differences, which tend to be self-reproducing. Consequently, the new generations living in a state of poverty have few possibilities of escaping from it. Economic growth, although without doubt an indispensable condition for tackling this situation, is not in itself the solution. Without institutional changes and effective economic and social policies, it may even accentuate inequalities and contribute to discrimination and social conflict, criminal behavior, political confrontation, and dissatisfaction, instability, and social violence in general.[15]

Liberal Democracy in Latin America Today

The late 1990s wave of democratization that has been sweeping Latin America since has important antecedents in a few well-established democratic regimes that were in existence since before World War II and in the growing number of countries that became democracies in the favorable developmental conditions of the postwar period until the mid-1960s. These antecedents, together with several fundamental social changes experienced in the postwar period, explain the large expansion in the contemporary demand for democracy.

Among these changes are the rapid and extensive processes of urbanization and industrialization, which have transformed Latin America into an area with a majority of urban populations and with several semi-industrialized countries. There has also been at least partial modernization of substantial rural areas. Primary education and literacy have become almost universal in many countries, and secondary and higher education has advanced considerably. There has been a true revolution regarding the scope and reach of the mass media and the diffusion of information to all sectors of society. In addition, the revolutionary struggles of the late 1960s and early 1970s and the political and economic survival strategies adopted by the popular classes during the authoritarian period and during the economic crisis and reform policies of the 1980s have strengthened civil society. We now see a great variety and diversity of grassroots and community organizations in the social, economic, political, and cultural realms at all levels of society.

Among the more recent causes of the increased demand for democracy, the most important are probably related to the very experience of living under particularly vicious military dictatorships characterized by brutal and wholesale violations of human rights and justified in the name of the national security doctrine, the notion that there was an "enemy within" the nation that had to be exterminated. Even if democracies are undergoing very hard economic times in the region, few are willing to risk another go at military governments.

Most in the military are of the same opinion. With the exception of Chile, military governments were rather unsuccessful and unpopular, particularly as they were unable to deal with an economic and social crisis that is still largely present. Furthermore, the "enemy within" has largely disappeared both ideologically and in reality at the national and international levels. The exceptions are the Shining Path in Peru and some guerrilla movements in Colombia. The complete change in U.S. diplomacy with its new emphasis on the support of democratic regimes and human rights and on the reduction of military expenditures is another important influence in the same direction.

Another important and relatively recent factor is the process of intellectual and ideological renewal and increased moderation and convergence of the principal left-wing political parties, movements, and currents of opinion. They have become increasingly characterized by a new sense of realism and pragmatism, facilitating the configuration of wider-based progressive movements that are in favor of the democratic process.

This development, to some extent, has been the consequence of the defeats suffered by the left-wing governments and movements of the early 1970s, the terrible repression under the military dictatorships, and the hard but highly positive learning experience of living in exile both in communist and democratic countries. The experience of the social democratic and socialist governments in several European countries faced with economic difficulties that in turn caused limitations in their political options and the widespread internationalization of their economies and societies has also been an important lesson.

The international environment also experienced changes that supported the democratization process in the region. Portugal and particularly Spain exercised a strong intellectual influence. The European Social Democratic and Christian Democratic Parties and governments have been lending a helping hand to those struggling to establish democratic regimes in Latin America. The adoption by the United States under the Carter administration of a foreign policy stand in favor of the defense of human rights, including specifically the support of democratic regimes, notwithstanding their contradictions and ambiguities, signaled a very important and positive change.

More recently, it is of course obvious that the spectacular crisis and definitive collapse of the Soviet bloc, and the terminal effect this has had on Cuba, have weakened even further all parties and movements formerly linked to communism. They have lost not only ideological credibility and political legitimacy but also vital concrete means of financial, logistical, and material support. In some cases the material and financial sources of support have been replaced by deals with the drug trade, but this will certainly not contribute to the recovery of their political legitimacy.

It is important to point out that this historic collapse of the extreme left has had a very salutary effect on the extreme political right in Latin America, including certain of its local and foreign supporters among the business classes and the military. The rightists in Latin America used to define their positions, policies, and activities mainly in terms of their anticommunism, of the "enemy within," but this danger having disappeared, they were mostly left without a cause.

There is, thus, a powerful set of profound changes, experiences, and trends, both social and political, domestic and international, that have favored the adoption and hopefully the consolidation of democratic regimes in Latin America. But there are also serious obstacles, among them the persistence of strong strains of antidemocratic cultures and institutions characterized by behavioral features such as paternalism, clientelism, intolerance, and authoritarianism. Furthermore, querrilla movements persist, though at a reduced level. The most worrying phenomenon is the expanding scourge represented by the drug trade in some of the Andean countries. It extends its tentacles throughout national and international society and is particularly damaging in those cases where it supports guerrilla movements. In these cases it contributes to a vicious circle of crime and violence with the consequent militarization of governments and civil society. These negative forces continue to aim at limiting the democratization process to restricted, elitist, and oligarchical regimes supported and infiltrated by the armed forces.

There is the danger that these forces may combine in a negative way with the transnationalization process, which is much more advanced and intense in Latin America than in any other underdeveloped region. There is a tendency for the business and technocratic segments of the local middle and upper classes to become intimately related to transnational networks in the economic, financial, communications, mass media, and military circles, constituting rather homogeneous nuclei of similar income levels, consumption patterns and lifestyles, including ideological, political, and cultural affinities.

When these privileged classes are faced with a choice between policies favoring the working classes and the informal and poor sectors—which would imply sacrificing to some extent their own insatiable consumerist aspirations—and policies that would favor these inclinations while sacrificing the lower classes even further, they might very well prefer the latter. But in the longer term, the former might provide stronger support for sustainable development and the consolidation of democracy. This is one of the critical dilemmas facing Latin America at present.

Uneven Globalization and the End of the Cold War: Opportunities and Constraints for Latin America

One fundamental consequence of the abrupt disappearance of the Soviet bloc is a profound change in world governance. The Cold War scenario provided for two superpowers to share the governance of world society in open but limited conflict and implicit cooperation. This resulted for several decades in the freezing of all internal and international conflicts affecting the stability of the bipolar Cold War situation. The collapse of the Soviet bloc has opened up Pandora's box, allowing all kinds of latent conflicts to surface and predominate and producing a dominolike process of increasing fragmentation of apparently long-consolidated nation-states.[16] Latin America and the United States stand out as a significant exception to this trend.

Nevertheless, although the United States has experienced a relative economic decline, it still has an overwhelmingly powerful military. This fact, coupled with the economic ascendancy of a militarily weak Europe and Japan has placed the United States in a strange situation as a sort of de facto but socially reluctant, financially feeble, and politically illegitimate world police force incapable of providing a new alternative structure of world governance to a highly unstable post–Cold War era.

The predominant role of the state that emerged after World War II under various socioeconomic and political guises has been giving way to a renovated and strengthened civil society in the social, political, and cultural realms, strengthening the trend toward democracy.[17] It could be argued that the events of May 1968 and the Prague Spring that followed were early warnings, in the capitalist and socialist worlds, of the social movements that were gaining strength and momentum. These movements championed minorities, youth, women, green power, decentralization, participatory democracy, and human rights, leading to the corresponding proliferation of grassroots and nongovernmental organizations and contributing to the retrenchment of the state.

This has also been the case in the economic field. Most prominent are the increased role of the market and the strengthening of private enterprise, particularly transnational corporations. Public expenditure in GDP has declined, public enterprises and services have been massively privatized and denationalized, and there has been a shift from public to private investments, both national and foreign.[18] This process has been reinforced by and is closely linked to the dynamic expansion of transnational corporations, giving rise to an unprecedented globalization process and to the reorganization of the relations between them, the state, and local capital. All this is leading to a profound reorganization of public- and private-sector relations, both national and international.[19]

With globalization and more complex forms of private international economic interpenetration of national markets, the aforementioned phenomena generate new problems, for instance, those associated with different national practices that affect international competitiveness. This becomes part of the increasingly stronger and wider conditionality under which economic reforms are pursued in Latin America. Therefore, the agendas of international—and also regional—negotiations are at a turning point: The focus is shifting from the similar treatment of *products* in international trade to the achievement of uniformity of *national institutions and policies*. This is the reason, for instance, for the search for a wider mandate for GATT in the direction of assessing policy and institutional differences as sources of "distortions," which contributes further to state loss of control over national economic policies.[20]

Latin America is therefore faced with several fundamental changes in its structure of production, international relations, and income and wealth distribution that affect the nature of national development possibilities, including, most importantly, the survival and consolidation of democratic regimes. Simultaneously, it is undergoing economic, ideological, and political reforms that weaken the capacity of society and the state to adopt explicit development policies—except policies that support free markets and private enterprise and measures to support them.

Nevertheless, postwar economic development strategies and policies based on Keynesian theories of full employment and an active role of the state, Marxist and Harrod-Domar theories of capital accumulation, Prebisch-Singer and ECLAC (UN Economic Commission for Latin America and the Caribbean) theories of protected industrialization, Rosenstein-Rodan cum Nurkse and Hirschman theories of balanced or unbalanced public investment and planning, Schultz's theory of human resource development, and so forth, were rather successful influences in the expansionary postwar period. To be sure, there was a growing gap between expectations and reality because in spite of the previously described successes, there were also great disappointments: Social, sectoral, and spatial progress was very uneven; inequality, underemployment, and poverty, although diminished, remained widespread; and a new and then-unrecognized scourge—environmental degradation—increased exponentially.

Consequently, the prevailing wholesale condemnation of earlier development theories, strategies, and policies and of government intervention and planning is based on ideologically biased historical interpretation. It is therefore mostly unwarranted, vastly exaggerated, and in need of serious and unbiased reconsideration. Fortunately, this begins to be recognized even in U.S. academic circles. "This paper argues that in the light of new developments in industrial organization, international economics, and growth theory, the old development economics now looks much more sensible than it seemed during the 'counter-revolution' against interventionist development models. ... Thus this paper calls for a 'counter-counter-revolution' that restores some of the distinctive focus that characterized development economics before 1960."[21]

As mentioned, one of the consequences of the crisis of capitalism in the interwar period was the worldwide emergence of the state as the most powerful institutional economic actor. This had rather positive effects on development during the postwar period until the mid-1970s. Therefore, there is urgent need to replace the prevailing view of the role of the state in that period with one less ideological. A more objective critical revision is required both to revalue the state's positive role during that historical phase and to examine the reasons for its decline or even reversal since the early 1980s or so, and the consequences thereof. The role of the state seems to have gone through a cycle of increasing and then declining returns. In the earlier phase the state was looked to as a *solution* in times of crises. More recently it has been looked at as the very *problem* causing the crisis. This is an interesting reversal of opinion.

In the economic sphere, the state has undertaken increasingly wider and less justifiable intervention in the functioning of markets. In this way it has hindered the market's function as *complementary* to that of the state in the allocation of productive resources. This has had increasingly negative effects on resource utilization, efficiency, productivity, competitiveness, and growth. Because of its insatiable thirst for fiscal revenues with its increased role, the state has faced accentuating problems in raising further taxes. This has led to growing deficits, inflationary pressures, and wage increases.

In the case of underdeveloped countries that specialized in commodity exports, including Latin America, the earlier "easy" and abundant tax and foreign exchange revenues from those exports shrunk in relative and sometimes in absolute terms. Over time the public sector and import needs grew much faster than the income derived from the commodity export sector. The ruling elites were thus faced with the very serious and difficult political task of establishing an effective tax system and promoting exports. This could be postponed during the 1970s as abundant and cheap foreign borrowing became available, but it had to be faced inevitably after the debt crisis.[22]

From an institutional point of view, the state was the source of an excessive bureaucratization of society, increasing administrative abuse, and interference and control of private life and economic activities and was increasingly arbitrary, rigid, incompetent, and corrupt. At the socioeconomic level, there was a heightened conflict between the increasingly overbearing state apparatus and the strengthening of citizens' aspirations to more participation, decentralization, and greater freedom for individual and social organizations. Furthermore, regarding international relations, there appeared to be a growing mismatch between the transnationalization processes of the economic and financial systems, including social and cultural life, and the attempts of the national state to regulate them. All of these processes contributed to questioning the political legitimacy of the state.

It does not follow from the recognition of these negative consequences of excessive state expansion that countries should reduce the state's importance to the bare minimum. It seems important to set the historical record straight with respect to the role of the state and the development experience more generally. In this age of a rather naive belief in laissez-faire, it is crucial to distinguish the rights from the wrongs in that experience instead of condemning and burying them wholesale under the prevailing ideological mantle. More unbiased research is urgently needed on comparative development experiences, not only for theoretical but also for very urgent and practical policy reasons.

Several recent neoliberal experiments have had seriously negative consequences regarding the concentration of wealth and income, inequality, poverty, unemployment and underemployment, the decay of inner cities, the abuse of the environment, and the threat posed to democratic institutions without having achieved the spectacular growth records of the postwar period. There is dire need for an alternative—or at least for strong qualifications—to the simplistic current prescription of privatization, deregulation, and liberalization as the cure-all for earlier statism. To rely entirely on private-sector dynamism under an impartial regulatory institutional framework without any guiding development strategy and principles does not seem advisable.

The dramatic socioeconomic reality of Latin America and most Third World countries today is not only or even predominantly the consequence of the internal development policies of the 1950s and 1960s. It is also, to an important extent, the consequence of the severe external shocks of the 1970s, of the profound transformations in the structure and dynamics of the privatized and globalized world economy, and of the nature as well as the overwhelming financial and institutional power of neoliberal economic doctrines.

I submit that these latter shocks and changes compounded and aggravated the defects of the earlier phase. Moreover, the handling of the external shocks and new conditions by the elites of most developing countries has been as abysmally inept when they were riding the debt boom as when they were collapsing under the debt burden. The overall historical picture looks to me like a premature interruption of vigorous but flawed development processes that needed to be and could have been corrected, and in some instances were in fact being reoriented by the end of the 1960s and then pursued with great success, as in the NICs, ASEAN (Association of Southeast Asian Nations) countries, and China.

Most other countries abandoned their efforts at reorienting development strategies influenced by financial permissiveness and shortsightedness and fostered nationally and internationally by neoliberal policies of liberalization and deregulation. In a climate of U.S. and international financial liberalization, U.S. banks were recklessly expanding their lending to undeveloped countries. These countries lacked international experience at the same time that their increasingly transnationalized elites sought to protect their vested interests. Thus unprecedentedly abundant resources—which could have been used in the national and international *public* interest to redress the accumulating economic and social development problems of the late 1960s—were wasted.

In this sense, the so-called lost development decade was not that of the 1980s but rather that of the 1970s, when both the need for adjustment and restructuring and the resources to carry them out were present. And the opportunity, mostly based on targeting investment toward and trade expansion in the microelectronics and semiconductor revolution, was also there. This was understood and acted upon by several Asian countries, who subsequently experienced growth, but was missed by Latin America, the socialist countries of the Soviet bloc, and Africa.

Understanding this historical process—the new internal circumstances and the changed international context, as well as the relations between them—is of the utmost importance. This is particularly true because of the implications of the highly transnationalized nature of the world economy and society, the profound changes taking place in technology, the reorganization of the institutional structures and international arrangements of the emerging major world geopolitical and economic areas, and the radically new conditions for world development posed by the environment, none of which are addressed by the neoliberal economic reform processes that are taking place in Latin America or by the international institutions that are promoting them.

CONCLUSION: A MORE DEMOCRATIC ORDER?

Recognizing and attempting to understand these and other overall trends as well as possible future scenarios and present options is crucially important for development strategies and policies and should be taken into account in the processes of economic reform. For the shape of the future will depend not only on these and other tendencies and forces at work but also, and very critically at this stage when the situation is still in a state of flux, on the wider and longer-term strategic visions and concrete institutional proposals that can be put forward both at the global and at the national levels to confront, adapt, or otherwise react to them.

Some *public issues* concerned with poverty, equity, the environment, and longer-term growth and development strategies urgently require consideration, both at the national and international levels. For example, at the international level, will the three emerging blocs develop in collaboration or conflict, and what will either scenario mean for their mutual relations and those with the existing and former socialist blocs and the underdeveloped world? Will this large group of latter countries have some say in international economic governance? Will it be possible to reverse the net capital flows from debtor to creditor countries, provide access to the highly protected markets of the OECD countries, share or otherwise take advantage of the rapidly changing technological know-how concentrated in global firms? Will there be new and more appropriate cooperation and aid to underdeveloped and existing or former socialist countries, and if so, in what sort of way: negotiation or imposition through various kinds of conditionalities? Moreover, how will we share and protect the increasingly limited environmental life-support systems of the world? How will individual firms, groups of enterprises, industries, individual nations, and groups of nations respond to these challenges? Should they just trust the market to work it all out?

Similar kinds of questions need to be posed at the national level. If one were to believe the world financial press and what is published by the main international economic institutions and mainstream economic journals, after having arrived at "the end of history," we would also seem to have reached the end of economics, especially the "economics of development."[23] Neoclassical economics and the more extreme neoliberal economic policy menu derived thereof—deregulation, liberalization, openness, minimal state, correct prices, reliance on the market and the instincts of private entrepreneurs, and so on—are being pushed with little variation everywhere, regardless of the country's initial conditions: size, resource base, location, culture, social structure, institutions, international relations, and historical evolution. Neoliberal economics is presented as constituting the ultimate wisdom, a generalized consensus from the right to the left.

Although there is undoubtedly much more agreement, or at least convergence, than in the past on several main issues of economic policy, there is also a lot of confusion regarding the prevailing neoliberal view. Far from having also reached "the end of ideology," another contemporary catchphrase, we are in danger of becoming locked into an unprecedented ideological monopoly, a sort of unidimensional ideology, to paraphrase Marcuse, or "monoeconomics" in Hirschman's characterization. To cut through this intellectually stifling ideologism, it is necessary to have a closer look at the convergencies but also the divergences that in fact exist about several critical issues of economic policy, particularly from the development perspective.[24] The latter consideration is crucially important because economic reform programs may create an institutional setup with lasting effects that may not be conducive to longer-term growth and particularly development.

It is necessary to take into account the experience of those countries that have been able to organize cooperative or corporative managerial capitalism, such as Germany, Austria, Japan, Korea, Taiwan.[25] "The new interventionism seeks to guide, not replace, the market. It uses price and non price methods to channel investment away from unproductive uses, expand technological capacity, strengthen links with foreign firms and give a directional thrust to selected industries. These interventions need to be based on a plan for the pattern of trade and industry over time, and this plan must be open to feedback from the market. ... That is ... assistance ... must be made conditional on performance."[26] An interactive government-business-finance interface seems to be crucial to produce national strategies of international market penetration. This is quite different from the individualistic neoliberal model pursued by the U.S. or UK economies, which is nevertheless the one that prevails in the economics profession and the one that inspires economic reform programs everywhere.

There is another rather formidable subject that will have to be incorporated as a central concern in discussions about economic reform in this age of democracy in Latin America. I have already referred to the themes of social participation, decentralization, social movements, strengthening of civil society, and nongovernmental organizations as a challenge to the old state. But this rise in civil society and organization also poses a challenge for the new state. This is an ample and complex field that seems to deal in essence with what I would call the "widening and deepening" of democracy, an area in which some Asian countries have not been nearly as effective as in the economic field. One way of interpreting the present transitional historical period would be to recognize that development has been sacrificed to growth and to contrast "the irrationality of capitalism with the inviability of socialism."[27]

How can we impregnate capitalism with the public and social concerns of socialism without frightening the capitalist entrepreneur and at the same time avoid militarized bureaucratic authoritarianism of the right or the left and strive for more individual and social freedom? How can we achieve a synthesis of the capitalist engine of growth with the socialist concern for the improvement of the oppressed, exploited, marginalized, and discriminated majorities and minorities? How can we avoid that the process toward transnational integration and the pressure for increased competitiveness lead to further national economic, social and cultural disintegration? How can we protect public goods such as the environment, human rights, and justice from private, bureaucratic and technocratic assault?

Perhaps the common thread of concern and proposals around these issues is the search for a more radical conception of democracy: stronger and wider-structured participation through a strengthened civil society; less big-state and big-business power and closer democratic social control of both by a denser, stronger network of private citizens' organizations to fulfill public functions and represent, in particular, the weaker groups and sectors of society. One implication is more support for building and reforming such organizations. Another is that developed countries should support underdeveloped countries committed to democracy with increased access to their markets, decreased debt service, easier terms for technology transfer, and so on rather than by imposing neoliberal economic reform conditionality.

Still another implication is the need to explicitly reconsider the role of the state. To put the debate in terms of more or less state or to see the state either as the solution or the problem is to miss the real issues. It is clear that the state has to fulfill certain basic overall functions to make the market work. The point here is to clarify what works and what doesn't and how to go about making changes. Furthermore, it is also accepted by neoclassical theory that the state has certain functions to perform in cases of recognized market failure. The point is to find ways to perform those functions efficiently without incurring government failure. Finally, it is widely recognized that underdeveloped countries have special characteristics and that several of the assumptions of neoclassical economics do not pertain or do so only slightly. There is a strong case for government interventions to foster development, provided of course that government institutions have a minimum operational capability. And this is a big proviso, but the way forward is not to ignore the need for state action but to engage very actively and decisively in the reform and reconstruction of a modern state in Latin America. The state must perform regulatory and strategic coordination and guidance functions in interaction with the private sector. Sometimes it may have to enter into the production sphere, provided these interventions are temporary and made conditional on performance. When effective private groups eventually emerge, they can successfully take over; the state can then regulate them and move on to other strategic areas in need of development. A dialectical, mutually reinforcing process between the state and the private sector must be worked out, its nature highly dependent on the concrete circumstances of each country, including in particular the strengths and weaknesses of the state apparatus.

The same strategy should be followed with transnational corporations so that national producers can enter into some form of association with them and gradually seek greater autonomy as national learning and growth processes give them sufficient strength. There are several examples indicating that such a strategy is feasible, provided, of course, that the national power, institutional capabilities, and the political will exist.

These and other forms of public and state action are required for practical, not ideological, reasons to face up to the new conditions prevailing at present: the critical importance of knowledge and education; the changed and rapidly evolving nature of technology; the reorganization of the work process, business organization, and labor relations; heightened environmental awareness and restrictions; the increasing competitiveness in the world economy due to the advanced degree of transnationalization and global interconnectedness and integration; the growing inequality within and among countries; and the universal aspiration to have democratic societies.

The big challenge that Latin American countries face, given the present phase of national and international disorder, is to find out whether and how to get public institutions able to adopt the right kind of longer-term policies, rather than to accept the comfortable short-term position of reducing government intervention to the bare minimum on the assumption that this is the best that can be done. Only a more democratic state, controlled by civil society, can promote the longer-term national interest, which obviously requires stabilization, adjustment, and restructuring but also the recovery of economic growth, the alleviation of poverty and the reduction of inequality, the preservation of the environment, and a dynamic integration into the world economy. All of these requirements involve the need for determined public strategies, policies, and action at the national, international, and global levels.

4

South Asia and
the New World Order

GOWHER RIZVI

The momentous changes that have taken place in the international system since 1988 are transforming the familiar contours of the international order. Many of the assumptions upon which the postwar global alignment was based have virtually disappeared. The end of the Cold War, the virtual breakup of the Soviet Union and the abdication of Russia's claim to the status of a superpower, and the emergence of three economic blocs—the United States, the European Community, and Japan—have signaled the demise of the postwar bipolar international order. The Gulf crisis heightened the prospect of a unipolar world order dominated by the United States, even though then-president Bush's promise of a new world order turned out to be cynically self-serving.

The end of the Cold War and the lifting of the iron curtain led not only to the virtual collapse of the communist regimes in Eastern Europe but also to the disappearance of the East-West dividing line. The great schism is gone and Europe is once again Europe: Eastern Europe no longer exists as a separate socioeconomic entity, Germany is already reunited, and in time parts of Eastern Europe will probably also become a part of the extended European Community. All this is bound to have a profound impact on the global security alignment, on regional conflicts, on North-South relations, and on the pattern of international economic linkages and world trade. There are fears that in the new order the Third World may be further marginalized and radical Islam may replace communism as the main threat to Western security.

The Third World is inextricably linked to the international system and will also inescapably experience the trickle-down impact of the global transformation resulting from the end of the Cold War rivalry. It is no coincidence that in 1988, when the superpowers began to build bridges, there was a profound impact on numerous conflicts in the Third World. The Iran-Iraq

South Asia

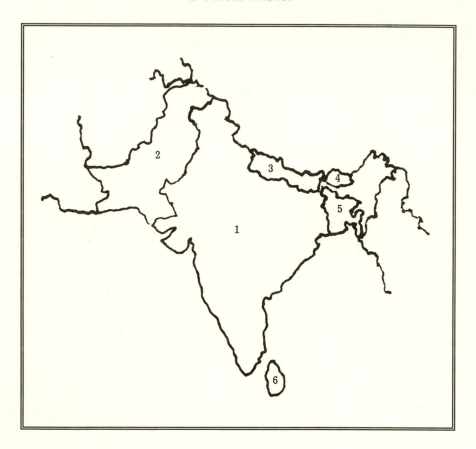

1. India
2. Pakistan
3. Nepal
4. Bhutan
5. Bangladesh
6. Sri Lanka

War ended after eight years, Soviet troops were pulled out of Afghanistan after nine years of bloodletting, Vietnam began a process of disengagement of troops from Cambodia, and the People's Republic of China's hostility toward Vietnam began to be toned down. In other areas the Palestinians accepted UN Resolutions 242 and 338 and implicitly recognized the existence of Israel, Morocco and the Polisario Front began working their way to a negotiated settlement, the Soviets persuaded the Cubans to withdraw from Angola, South Africa was compelled to withdraw its forces from Angola and Namibia, Sino-Soviet and Sino-Indian relations seemed to be on the mend, and even the North and South Koreans began talking of reunion.

The purpose of this chapter is to examine the impact of the end of the Cold War and the changes in Europe on South Asian security, domestic politics, and economy and finally to examine the compulsions toward regional integration. The impact of superpower détente is not immediately visible in South Asia even though there is already evidence to suggest that changes of far-reaching significance are imminent in the 1990s.

SOUTH ASIA IN A CHANGING WORLD ORDER

The changes in South Asia may not be as dramatic as in Eastern Europe, but the ramifications for the region will nonetheless be quite considerable. The superpowers' disengagement from the subcontinent could bring about a decisive change in the military balance and might also inject a new realism into the region. Global changes, together with domestic compulsion, on all sides of the borders could make old policies of confrontation untenable or at least obviously anachronistic.

The end of the Cold War has already unleashed profound changes in the international system. As the two superpowers and their allies cast aside their global rivalry, visualized as a zero-sum game in which the gain of one was invariably the loss of the other, the so-called policy of containment and countercontainment must also become obsolete. The deescalation in numerous regional wars following the move toward the superpowers' détente clearly suggests that conflicts in the Third World, even though they have their own dynamics, cannot be sustained at the same level once their external backers decide to end their support. This would appear to be particularly true in South Asia.

Neither of the two superpowers had any direct stake in the Indo-Pakistan rivalry; nor was South Asia ever an area of high priority for either of them.[1] The geostrategic significance of the region is due only to its location between West Asia and Southeast Asia, the two areas of concern to the superpowers. The intervention of the United States, the Soviet Union, and China in the region arose, however, not from an intrinsic interest in the subcontinent but principally from their concern about each other. The region was sucked into global rivalries of the Cold War in the 1950s as each of the superpowers sought to check the influence of the other through the so-called policy of containment and countercontainment. With the superpowers lined up behind each of the belligerents, political and military stalemate became entrenched. Since the main purpose of the two superpowers was to limit the influence of the other in the region, neither had any incentive to resolve the conflict or risk its escalation. At the same time India could not compel Paki-

stan, which had been greatly bolstered by its external ally, into an acquiescence of the status quo in Kashmir. Pakistan remained committed to reversing Kashmir's "accession" to India, but its enhanced military prowess was
more than off-set by Soviet support for India. As long as the superpowers' rivalries endured, the status quo in the subcontinent was virtually assured.[2]

Three external powers—the United States of America, the former USSR,
and China—have intervened in the conflict in this region before. But none of
them actually have an intrinsic stake in South Asia: Their interest in the region stemmed primarily from their concern with each other. Or put differently, South Asia merely became a key strategic arena in which to pursue
their global rivalries. It therefore followed that although each external
power was concerned to strengthen its protégé to contain the influence of its
rival, neither of their commitments extended to resolving the regional conflict, since that would have involved the risk of their getting directly entan-
gled. It could also be argued that it would have been against the interests of
the external powers to resolve the conflicts because that would have mini-
mized the dependence of the regional states on their external patrons.

Thus a fierce arms race started between India and Pakistan in which each
side was sufficiently armed to deter the other but neither could achieve the
decisive advantage to tilt the regional balance in its favor. A lopsided balance
of power was created in South Asia that made it impossible to alter the status
quo and that also queered the possibility of a political settlement. Four decades later—after three major wars and an economically ruinous arms
race—neither side has been able to achieve its objective. India has failed to
play the role of a dominant power in the region, which its superior size and
resources would have entitled it to; and Pakistan has been unable either to
alter the status quo in Kashmir or even to protect its territorial integrity.

It might even be argued that because the central concern of the outside
powers was more with each other than with the local states, their involvement in South Asia proved more durable than any particular form of alignment. There were no ideological underpinnings of significance to any of
these alliances between the South Asian states and the outside powers. To
that extent they were all alliances of convenience, reflecting classical bal-
ance-of-power behavior. If we follow that classical logic, keeping in mind
the motives of both the local and external states, the alliances were shifting
and interchangeable.[3] In 1962, following the Sino-Indian conflict, the
United States and Britain rushed to India's assistance notwithstanding that
India was allied to the Soviet Union. The threat of communist China to India
was considered sufficient to reverse the U.S. policy of hostility to India. And
again when Sino-Soviet relations deteriorated, the United States began to
view Pakistan's improved relations with China with approval, since in the
higher level of conflict China and Pakistan would be useful allies against the
Soviet Union. The essence of that logic is also that once the higher level of ri-

valry between the external powers was much reduced or eliminated, the compulsion to intervene in the region was greatly weakened.

It follows, therefore, that with the end of the Cold War the superpower policy of global containment has virtually become obsolete. Both the Warsaw Pact and NATO have become virtually obsolete and in search of a new role. The European schism has also ended, and the former European adversaries are now set to evolve a European security community. They no longer perceive each other as a threat but actually see the need for collective security to keep away threats from outside Europe and North America. The possible rapprochement between the Russian Federation and China and between China and India will further remove the incentive for superpower intervention in the region. At the same time as the utility of the South Asian states to their patrons diminishes, the ability of these states to draw the superpowers into their conflicts, or play one against the other, will correspondingly decline. The most dramatic evidence of the end of the Cold War can be seen in Afghanistan. Both superpowers have dropped their erstwhile protégés and Afghanistan has disappeared from the front pages.[4]

The ability of India and Pakistan to enlist the support of external powers in their local rivalry appears to have been drastically reduced in the changed international environment. Without the backing of a powerful external supporter, Pakistan will find it impossible to maintain the artificially erected balance of power in the region and may be persuaded to be more accommodating. India, with the benefit of hindsight, may recognize that it cannot repeat its mistakes of the 1950s.[5]

It might be argued that it was perhaps India's failure to accommodate Pakistan's legitimate security concerns that was instrumental in pushing Pakistan into an alliance with the United States in 1954.[6] The consequent U.S. intervention helped Pakistan to maintain a lopsided balance despite India's enormous superiority. The experience since World War II has clearly shown that the involvement of extraregional powers in the subcontinent has been detrimental to India's interest and has prevented that country from exercising its "natural" leadership in the region. Both India and Pakistan appear to have lost their superpower backers. The Soviet Union has collapsed and is in no position to continue its assistance to India. At the same time the end of U.S. and Russian intervention in Afghanistan and the demise of communism in the former Soviet Union has virtually ended U.S. interest in Pakistan. At one level both India and Pakistan, deprived of their traditional security moorings, are genuinely worried. On the other hand, past experience should militate against seeking external redress. As noted, neither country (as opposed to sections of the ruling elites) can claim to have benefited from external intervention. The arguments against repeating the mistakes of the past are self-evident. Pakistan has genuine security anxieties that India will have to allay if it wants to prevent Pakistan from being pushed into seeking external alliances, especially amongst the Muslim countries. Nor can India afford to miss an opportunity for building confidence amongst its neighbors by being more sensitive to their security perceptions. It is in Indian interest to keep external powers out of the region.

It is as yet too early to assess the full impact of the end of the Cold War on South Asia, but the prospect of external powers extricating themselves from South Asia has opened up new opportunities for improved relations between India and Pakistan, and in the region generally. There is already enough evidence to suggest that changes of far-reaching significance are imminent in the latter 1990s.[7] The combination of dramatic changes both globally and within the region is, probably for the first time, making the old policies of confrontation untenable and in fact appears to have created a suitable environment in which a lasting solution to the Indo-Pakistan conflict might be found. Both the principal regional protagonists appear to recognize the inefficacy and limitations of their external backers. There is a discernible change of attitude among the new generation of the ruling elites in the subcontinent.[8] Both the Indians and the Pakistanis are belatedly recognizing the incontrovertible fact that the relationship between the two countries is a central determining factor in the domestic and foreign policies of both countries. More important, it is obvious that continuing hostility between the two countries has had an adverse impact on the development and aspirations of the peoples of both countries. It is precisely because both sides recognize that another round of Indo-Pakistan war will be economically and politically unsustainable that they have been careful to not allow the tensions resulting from the uprising in Kashmir to escalate into a war between the two states. The severity with which Pakistani security forces held back the Kashmiris from crossing over the cease-fire line was indicative of the regime's determination to avoid another clash with India. At the same time both India and Pakistan are, albeit reluctantly, coming round to understand that the problem in Kashmir is no longer merely a bilateral issue between the two countries. The failure of the Indian forces to suppress the uprising in Indian-occupied Kashmir and the rejection by the youth in Pakistani-occupied Kashmir of being integrated into Pakistan are clear indications that Kashmiris have plans for their future that are at variance with those of India and Pakistan. In my private conversations with the leaders on both sides, they acknowledged that the solution lies in a united and autonomous Kashmir (with certain territorial modifications), but neither are willing to broach it publicly because the people in both countries are supposedly not ready for it. Old habits die slowly, but each side is anxious to get rid of the millstone around its neck.

There is another obvious fact that is not often fully appreciated. Neither Pakistan nor India has been successful in achieving its own national objectives. The two persistent themes in Pakistan's foreign policy are the demands for self-determination in Kashmir and the understandable concern about its territorial integrity. Ironically Pakistan has not only failed to wrest Kashmir from India but was itself truncated in 1971. India, too, cannot claim to have been successful in its objective of playing a preeminent role in the region, which it is entitled to by virtue of its size, population, and resources. The intervention of the extraregional powers in the subcontinent came about largely because of India's failure to accommodate Pakistan's perceptions of its legitimate security concerns. Besides, reliance on external powers for military and economic assistance has infringed on the national sovereignty and limited the autonomy of both countries in international affairs. No less important, the massive arms race has been economically ruinous and has done little for large numbers of people in both countries living below the poverty line.[9] In the case of Pakistan, the persistent conflict with India has legitimized the army's domination of politics for much of its history.

There are admittedly widespread fears among the states of South Asia that with the disengagement of the external actors from the region, India will attempt to establish its hegemony. These fears, although genuinely held by the smaller states, can easily be dispelled. India is easily the most powerful state in the region, but its ability to use force is seriously circumscribed. The experiences of the two superpowers in Vietnam, Afghanistan, and Iran have already exposed the limits of military power against ideologically inspired nationalist movements. India's belated pursuit of military power understandably alarms its neighbors. But the ability to use coercion is questionable in a world where military force is becoming rapidly less effective politically. Iraq could not subdue Kuwait; and despite the cynical abandonment of Bosnia by the big powers, the brutal Serbian genocide has not been sufficient to wipe out the Bosnian Muslims. Recent events in South Asia have to some extent confirmed the limits of India's ability to impose its will on its neighbors. There can be no doubt that India's intervention in Sri Lanka has gone a long way toward ending the repression of the Tamils and also helped to provide the mechanism for the resolution of Sri Lanka's ethnic conflicts within the framework of a united country. Similarly, in Nepal, India's stance on the Indo-Nepalese trade and transit treaty was impeccable from the point of view of international law. But in both cases India burned its fingers.[10] The inability of 100,000 crack Indian troops, highly experienced in counterinsurgency, to subdue a small force of Tamil guerrillas in Sri Lanka and the near universal disapproval of its allegedly bullying tactics in Nepal were not only embarrassing but a cogent reminder to New Delhi of the pitfalls of meddling in the affairs of smaller neighbors. Moreover, Rajiv Gandhi's inability to reverse his declining political fortunes at home confirmed the limited electoral gains that can be obtained from foreign adventures. The examples of Japan and the newly industrialized countries of East Asia are a constant reminder to many Indians that status and power come from economic strength. The economic imperatives of the Indian government will make it politically impossible to sustain military expansion. It is obvious to many that India cannot maintain its current defense expenditure and at the same time expect to alleviate the grueling poverty of its people.

The arguments for moving away from confrontation to cooperation not only have become compelling but also are beginning to be appreciated at last.[11] It is significant that despite the escalation of tensions in Kashmir, both India and Pakistan have shown remarkable constraint. At the same time the persistent paranoia amongst the smaller states about the need to resist India's supposed expansionism has been tempered with a dose of realism.[12] The recent experiences of Sri Lanka and Nepal have left the smaller states under no illusion that extraregional powers are not only unwilling to be dragged into subcontinental conflicts but also, and perhaps more important, are unwilling to antagonize a powerful India for the doubtful benefit of acquiring a small client state.

Much of the optimism in the foregoing analysis is premised on the assumption that with the end of the Cold War the external powers will disengage themselves from the region and that lessons from the past will militate against attempts by the states of South Asia to involve the extraregional powers in the affairs of the subcontinent. There is no certainty that either of these two assumptions will be fully borne out by actual developments. In the first place, the promise of short-term gains or expedience may once again encourage or entice the South Asian leaders to enter into an alliance with an external power. Second, the West cannot altogether ignore South Asia. There is a growing concern about the proliferation of nuclear weapons in South Asia and the supposed rise of Islamic fundamentalism in Pakistan. Suppressing Islamic fundamentalism and preventing the spread of nuclear weapons are high on the list of priorities of the Western governments. In other words, new compulsions or "logic" for external intervention seems to be manifesting that may inhibit the disengagement of the external powers from the region.

The end of the Cold War and the collapse of the Soviet Union have left both Pakistan and India without an ally, and there is considerable anxiety in all South Asian countries about their security. With the United States now no longer interested in the conflict in Afghanistan, with the end of the Cold War and the virtual demise of communism in the former Soviet Union, the Americans have little interest in Afghanistan and still less any desire to see the installation of a fundamentalist Islamic regime in Kabul—and consequently the importance of Pakistan as a front-line state containing Soviet expansion has become irrelevant. Not only has Pakistan lost its status as the "most allied" ally of the United States, but in the changed circumstances the United States is showing concerns about Pakistan's nuclear program and what it mistakenly perceives to be the growth of Islamic fundamentalism. Despite

Pakistan's valuable support during the Gulf crisis, the United States has been exerting both economic and diplomatic pressures to force Pakistan to abandon its nuclear program. Fears that the United States might use force to destroy Pakistan's nuclear capability are frequently expressed in Pakistan.

In contrast, the U.S. attitude toward India appears to have become markedly conciliatory. In part this stems from the fact that following détente with the Soviet Union, the United States no longer views India as its enemy's friend; and the ostensible show of warmth may also be intended to bring pressure on Pakistan. But it may also be conjectured that the overture to India is a part of new U.S. strategic planning, which envisages the possibilities of being engaged in two regional conflicts simultaneously. With the demise of communism and the breakup of the Soviet Union, the only remaining threat to Western interests is perceived as coming from the Third World. The United States is the only remaining superpower, but the end of the bipolar international system has not led to a unipolar system dominated by the United States, as many had imagined. Although the shape of the new international system is far from clear, it is more likely to be multipolar, with several centers of power.[13] The United States, albeit a military superpower, lacks the financial resources (as was evidenced during the Gulf War) to be able to play the role of a hegemon on its own. Its ability to control the international system will depend largely upon its ability to work harmoniously with the other "great" powers or "pillars" in the new multipolar structure— the European Community, Japan, the Commonwealth of Independent States (or at least the Russian Republic), China, and India. To that end it is quite conceivable that the United States may envisage India as one of the supporting pillars of the U.S.-dominated international system. The co-option of India and China as allies would not only greatly facilitate U.S. influence over the system but would also eliminate any credible challenge to the international society.[14] With Iran emaciated and Iraq both economically squeezed and isolated, there would appear to be no other obvious challenger to the West from the Third World. The prospect of a U.S.-Pakistan alliance being replaced by U.S.-India collaboration cannot be altogether ruled out.

Indeed, India may well be tempted to ally with the United States. The virtual breakup of the Soviet Union has deprived it of a major ally and seriously dislocated its defense, since nearly 70 percent of India's imported weapons came from the Soviet Union. Moreover, India has embarked on a program of economic liberalization whose success depends upon access to credit and structural adjustment loans from the World Bank and the IMF—both of which could be jeopardized by hostility to the United States. And if U.S.-Pakistani relations deteriorate as a result of the tensions over Pakistan's nuclear program, it will not be difficult to understand why many in India might well find it hard to resist the temptation of reciprocating U.S. overtures to get at the old enemy.

But there are clear limits to the possible extent of the U.S.-Indian accommodation. Not only do the two countries have a widely different perception of each other but also there is scarcely any consensus between the two on any major international issue.[15] India and the United States have disagreed over a whole host of issues. In the past the United States found India's nonalignment morally reprehensible and was greatly chafed by India's vigorous advocacy of the rapid decolonization of the European empires in Asia, Africa, the Caribbean, and Oceania. They have differed on the questions of Palestine, South Africa, Cambodia, Vietnam, Afghanistan, Iran, and Cuba; they have also held antagonistic positions in the debate on the New International Economic Order, in the GATT negotiations, on the nuclear nonproliferation treaty (NPT), and in the UN. The end of the Cold War has certainly eased some of the differences between the two countries, but the world's two largest democracies remain divided by their fundamentally divergent views about the international order. India has not yet altogether acquiesced in an international system that is tilted in favor of the advanced economies. There is plenty of room for improved relations between the two countries by the removal of minor irritants, but it is extremely implausible that India will agree to become a part of the U.S.-led new world order and thereby help legitimize the existing iniquitous system. Not only would this mean a repudiation of India's past commitments and ideals but also there is no guarantee that the U.S. commitment to India will be any less fickle than it has been to Pakistan or its other Cold War allies. President Clinton's pressure on the Russian president to stop supplying missile engines to India is just one evidence of the distrust between the two countries.

To argue that the end of the Cold War will lead to the disengagement of the external powers from South Asia and a deescalation in intensity of rivalry between the states of the region is not to suggest that all conflicts will disappear or that peace is about to break out in the region. Regional conflicts have their own dynamics. Suspicions and hatred built up over decades will not disappear instantaneously. Although there can be no doubt that the superpowers have played an important role in escalating low-intensity regional conflicts into major wars, it would be inaccurate to suggest that interstate and intrastate conflicts in the Third World are entirely the product of superpower rivalries or external intervention.[16]

To a large extent, tension and conflicts are inherent in developing societies as they seek to evolve into nation-states and assert their national identities. Most of the postcolonial states in the Third World are artificially constructed and consequently extremely vulnerable. The ethnic, religious, linguistic, and tribal diversities, coupled with uneven economic development and regional diversities, have made difficult the evolution of national identities and the building of political institutions. This is not entirely surprising. It took Western Europe several centuries to establish a comparatively stable state system based on the principle of national self-determination.[17] In South Asia, as elsewhere, interstate and intrastate turbulence is deep-rooted.

There are numerous sources of dissonance between the states of the region.[18] India is a secular state; almost all its neighbors give primacy to religion in governmental politics. The Indian federation is organized along linguistic lines and to a large extent recognizes the autonomy of the states; its neighbors have centralized regimes dominated by the majority ethnic group. Most important, India and Sri Lanka have fairly well established democratic systems; authoritarian regimes have tended to dominate the other states. The organizing principles of one state are viewed as a threat by another. Moreover, because authoritarian regimes lacking in legitimacy have no popular support base, they become more dependent on external supporters and are thus more amenable to pressures and manipulation from outside the region.[19]

Although South Asia with its well-defined external boundaries constitutes a coherent region, its internal political geography follows no clear lines of demarcation. This is to be largely expected in such an ancient crucible of civilization—where peoples, cultures, and religions are inextricably interwoven. Boundary demarcations invariably cut across communities and tribes. The three major river systems—the Indus, the Ganges, and the Brahmaputra—by cutting across the boundaries of India, Pakistan, Bangladesh, and Nepal, have further exacerbated the tensions between them resulting from disputes over the share of water.[20] Moreover, five of the six states in South Asia have borders with India, and this has resulted in inevitable complications, since all these states are in their infancy and in several cases the boundaries are not yet firmly settled.[21] India, which looms large as the centerpiece, shares ethnic, religious, and cultural affinities with all its neighbors. In times of conflict in neighboring countries, this becomes a source of acute tension. Spillover of domestic crises across frontiers is not uncommon. Millions of Bengalis in then East Pakistan fled across the borders to India in 1971 to escape the atrocities of an invading Pakistani army, leading to India's direct intervention in Bangladesh's war of liberation. The Tamils of Sri Lanka sought refuge in India and launched their insurgency from Tamil Nadu across the Palk Straits, thereby heightening tension between India and Sri Lanka. Nearly 3 million Afghans crossed over to Pakistan following the Soviet intervention in their country in 1979, exacerbating the Pakistan-Afghanistan relationship. Since the mid-1970s, Chakmas from the Chittagong Hill Tracts have sought asylum across the border to avoid genocide by the Bangladesh security forces. Similarly, some would-be secessionists such as Sikhs from the Indian Punjab and Muslims from Indian-held Kashmir have found sanctuary in Pakistan in their struggle for autonomy. It is very likely that such low-intensity conflicts will continue in South Asia until these states have evolved a national consensus and found a way to politically accommodate minority groups.[22]

UNEVEN GLOBALIZATION AND SOUTH ASIA

The end of the Cold War, the incorporation of the former Soviet Union and Eastern Europe in the capitalist world economy, and the creation of an integrated market in Europe have altered the pattern of international economic linkages and trading relations, which will inevitably have their resonances in South Asia. There is a distinct possibility that the Third World countries will become increasingly marginalized as their strategic significance diminishes and the developed world becomes more preoccupied with its own immediate problems.[23]

The "opening" of Eastern Europe might also have further implications for South Asia. South Asia will now have to compete with Eastern Europe in a whole array of economic matters. Until now the region's attraction to foreign investors has been due not only to attractive incentive packages the governments of these countries offer to investors—tax holidays, cheap credit, subsidies, and foreign exchange concessions for exports—but also because South Asia is one of the few regions outside the developed world that offers access to a potentially vast market, cheap and skilled labor, a large pool of managerial and scientific personnel, attractive real estate costs, and a sound legal and banking system. However, the region's comparative advantage is likely to be challenged as the Eastern European economy is opened to the West. Eastern Europe has a natural and cultural affinity with the West, enjoys geographical proximity, and is comparable, if not superior, in infrastructure to South Asia; and like South Asia, it too has a large trained workforce and potentially a sizable market. It should therefore be hardly surprising if Western capital and technology flows to Eastern Europe in preference to South Asia.

In the short term the region is also likely to suffer from the "fortress" policy of the EC: Imports into the EC are being discouraged by nontariff barriers, the so-called voluntary restraints by the exporters, the multifiber agreement, the imposition of quotas through bilateral agreements, and now, more ominously, the requirements of "standardization." South Asia not only features at the bottom of the list of the EC's trading partners[24] but now, in its concern with Eastern Europe, the EC is likely to draw its attention further away from South Asia. The EC is coordinating the efforts of the European Bank for Reconstruction and Development, whose members include, in addition to the EC countries, the United States, Japan, and ten non-EC states, in raising funds—estimated to be larger than those for the Marshall Plan for the reconstruction of Western Europe after World War II—for reviving the collapsed economies of Eastern Europe. In the competition for resources and markets, the claims of South Asia will invariably be accorded a lower priority.

The comfortable assumptions on which the ruling elites of the Third World have come to base their economic policies are rapidly becoming obsolete. Economic policies can no longer be predicated on the annual pilgrimage to Paris, where the so-called aid consortium doles out the checks. The consequences of concessional economic assistance ceasing to flow or even slowing down are bound to have a serious impact on the economies of the region, as different countries are in varying degrees dependent upon foreign aid. But even though the transition is bound to be painful, these changes offer fresh opportunities for South Asia. In the long run, the countries of the region will learn to mobilize their own resources for development. This will reduce external dependence and may help to foster greater popular accountability and democratization of governments. And as the region is left more to its own devices, it might be argued, the countries of South Asia will be compelled to develop closer links with each other.

And yet the responses of all the South Asian governments show a remarkable reluctance to face up to the new reality. Instead of rethinking their economic strategies, necessitated by a qualitative change in the international system, the leaders, including, surprisingly, those of India, have allowed themselves to be cajoled by the donors and the International Monetary Fund into accepting the free-market philosophy as the panacea for all their economic problems. The free-market doctrine now appears to have become the new orthodoxy in all the South Asian countries. Each country is vying with the other both in terms of the speed with which the economy is being "liberalized" and also in their effort to attract foreign investors by offering an attractive package of incentives. In some of the countries, notably in Bangladesh, economic liberalization is also seen, albeit mistakenly, as a necessary condition for ensuring the flow of aid.

The attractions of a market economy are understandable. With the collapse of communism in Eastern Europe and the former Soviet Union and their conversion to free-market ideology, it is argued that only the free market can ensure both economic growth and democracy. In February 1990 Barber Connable echoed the triumphal return of market forces and the primacy of economic growth: "If I have to characterize the past decade, the most remarkable thing was the generation of a global consensus that market forces and economic efficiency were the best way to achieve the kind of growth which is the best antidote to poverty."[25] The central message of those who advocate the market economy is simple: an imperfect market is better than an imperfect state. The simplicity of the market logic, its internal coherence, and its instinctive appeal to the strong in society have made economic liberalization the accepted orthodoxy. All state intervention in economic life in the form of constitutional, legal, or administrative regulations must be eliminated so as to free entrepreneurs from stifling bureaucratic control. The emphasis is on the primacy of economic growth—only by enlarging the size of the gross national product, it is argued, can the governments address the problem of poverty. The free marketeers argue that a major constraint on Third World development has been the ineffective allocation of scarce resources: If we let the market determine the allocation of resources in the short term, economic development in the long term is also ensured. The triumph of free-market ideology and the return to the emphasis on growth as the central tenet of development strategy have virtually stymied the debate on development.[26] They have intensified pressures on the governments of the developing countries to move away from planned development to a market economy. With ever-increasing globalization of the economy, the compulsions toward economic liberalization are inescapable, but nonetheless it is important to debate the appropriateness of the doctrine for South Asia.[27]

Some of the features of economic liberalization have considerable merit. Even before socialism was buried in Eastern Europe, it had become increasingly apparent that state-controlled and centrally planned economies had their limits.[28] There could be no denying that centralized planning was stifled by bureaucratic control and that it was inflexible, often unimaginative, and insensitive to the actual needs of the people or to the diversities and particularities of different regions. But most important, in many of these states the governments were not sufficiently accountable to the people and the economic policies were mainly designed to reflect the interests of the decision-makers; consequently the main beneficiaries of state-controlled development were those who had access to the government or were members of the ruling elite. The state machinery became an instrument in the hands of a small ruling oligarchy and its client-supporters for monopolizing the benefits accruing from the state. State intervention in the economy therefore came to be discredited not because it had failed to stimulate growth (which was only partially true) but because of the inability of the state to distribute equitably the benefits of development, which was one of the primary rationales for state-controlled socialist policies. The situation can be remedied not by whittling down the government but by empowering the people through the strengthening of the civil society so that government becomes more sensitive to the electorate.[29] Since 1950 donors have poured vast sums of money into economic development projects without adequately considering the effectiveness of the political institutions on which the successful implementation of such projects depends. Not surprisingly, even the best-conceived poverty alleviation schemes have mainly benefited the better-off groups and those individuals with access to the government. Bangladesh alone has been the recipient of over US$20 billion in that many years with little to show for it except that the rich have become more affluent and the poor more emaciated.[30] It can be argued that if only a quarter of that aid had been earmarked for the development of human resources and institution-building, there might have been a very different picture.

Liberal economic policies might have served the needs of the advanced economies quite well, but applying them mechanically and indiscriminately to the developing societies presents different problems.[31] The advocates of economic liberalization, although decrying the inefficiency of the state, fail to take into account that markets in the developing societies are also imperfect—and extremely limited. In countries of South Asia, where a sizable part of the population lives below the poverty line and for all practical purposes subsists outside the domain of the market, the relevance of the free market is at best limited. Such a market cannot allocate goods and services with the same efficiency as it does in the developed countries. In other words, in societies where markets are socially ineffective and dominated by the economically and politically powerful, the weakening of the governments will leave the vulnerable at the mercy of the strong. There is a distinct danger that in opting for the "inefficient market" in place of the "inefficient state," the developing countries may end up throwing out the baby with the bathwater. As Michael Lipton pointed out, there is a market-government dilemma in which each tries to undermine the other—one encroaches at the cost of the other.[32] The solution to the economic problems of the Third World is not to unleash the market by emaciating the government but to ensure good governance and strengthen the capability of the people so that they can realize their entitlement.[33]

Development in Asia and Africa has clearly shown that unless governments make a special endeavor, the benefits of development—access to health, education, sanitation, recreation, jobs, or even to crude patronage of the state—are usually monopolized by the elites and seldom reach the poor. Even programs ostensibly designed for the poor are usurped by the politically and economically more powerful. This is scarcely surprising, since the poorest section of the population is not only economically insecure but also illiterate, lacking in skills, often in debt, and politically not well mobilized. The history of developed countries has shown that only when governments are popularly elected and dependent upon the vote for remaining in power do they begin to show a concern for the voters. The poor also discover strength in their numbers and use their newfound political muscle to extract from the elected leaders a commitment to popular welfare. The welfare states of industrial societies—capitalist or communist—emerged only when workers and peasants were able to exert their influence on the governments either through the ballot or a revolution.

LIBERAL DEMOCRACY AND GOOD GOVERNANCE

The democratic transformation of South Asia in the aftermath of the Cold War has been breathtaking. Bangladesh, Nepal, and Pakistan have installed popularly elected governments; and India and Sri Lanka have shown that despite assassinations, political turbulence, and the rise of sectarian militancy, democratic institutions have remarkable resilience. The international environment in the post–Cold War world is very conducive to democracy. Democracy has emerged as the triumphant ideology and seems to have de facto emerged as one of the criteria by which the standing of a state will be reckoned in the new world order. It seems that Western aid and trade will in future be increasingly linked to a country's democratic and human rights credentials.

Even though democracy is seen to be triumphant, ironically the Western commitment to it in the Third World is quite ambivalent. Western support for democracy movements and human rights did much for the overthrow of the authoritarian regimes in Eastern Europe and the former Soviet Union; and yet it was those same Western states that supported authoritarian rulers in the Third World. Some of the most tyrannical rulers—the shah in Iran, Ferdinand Marcos in the Philippines, Zia ul Haq in Pakistan, and Saddam Hussein in Iraq—were allied to the Western democracies and received the lion's share of their military and economic largesse. In an almost perverse way, some of the Western powers did a great deal to sustain authoritarian regimes and give them a cloak of legitimacy. It has been argued that in the changed international environment the ability of authoritarian regimes to secure Western support is greatly diminished. This requires some elaboration.

Since authoritarian regimes lack popular legitimacy, they seek to compensate for their vulnerability and insecurity (domestic and external) through external alliances and assistance. The external "props"—economic assistance and military support—become integral to the survival of these regimes. Rapid and prestigious development (for which domestic resources are just not available) is crucial to their acquiring popular acquiescence, to creating a network of collaborators and clients through the dispensation of patronage, to buying off the potential opposition, and to bolstering and securing the loyalty of the armed forces. In short, the survival of an unpopular regime often hinges on its ability to ensure the flow of foreign economic and military assistance. Authoritarian rulers in the past were particularly successful in obtaining aid. A cursory glance reveals that many of the donors had a marked preference for authoritarian regimes—at least in so far as this is revealed by the volume of aid that was offered to repressive regimes.[34] It is not difficult to explain this odd behavior of the donors. Both the United States of America and the USSR, who were by far the largest donors, viewed aid as an instrument for furthering global strategic interests and could not be too scrupulous about the democratic credentials of their allies. With the end of the Cold War, the strategic significance of South Asia has diminished; and even though Western support for democracy in the Third World is as yet inconsistent and opportunistic, there is nevertheless a popular perception in the region that authoritarian regimes are no longer in favor with the West.

However, a word of caution is in order: The election of a popular government is merely the first step in the restoration of democracy and not an end in itself. The evidence from all the countries of South Asia suggests that the democratic process is still far from secure. Movements by the people have been instrumental in toppling authoritarian regimes and forcing popular elections, but thereafter the masses appear to have been marginalized. Despite the transition to democracy, the class composition of the leadership has remained very much the same; and indeed, the elites associated with previous regimes are also prominent in the new order. This can be partly explained by the fact that in the ultimate analysis the transition to democracy was not the result of a complete defeat of the elites who stood behind the previous authoritarian rule. The actual transfer of power was, in fact, the result of negotiations between the old and the new elites, in which, although a few heads rolled, the status quo essentially prevailed. Although the new leaders have come to power through popular mobilization and the electoral process, the leadership is essentially drawn from a narrow group of "ruling" elites, and their interests and outlook are not substantially different from those of the people they have replaced. Both groups have a stake in preserving the social and economic status quo. And the outgoing elites have not altogether lost their ability to interfere in the democratic process in order to protect their interests. In fact, there is evidence to suggest that democratic regimes have entered into agreements or implicit understandings that define and protect the interests of that group.

Much more important, the democratic regimes have done little to give the people a stake in the survival of the democratic order. The gap between the ruled and the rulers remains as before: The people's access to the government is reduced by the bureaucracy and the security cordon, and popular feedback, the main source of information for the elected government, is filtered through the intelligence apparatus. For democracy to survive there has to be a continuing partnership between the elected leaders and the electorate so that the electors develop a stake in the preservation of their elected government. That still remains a distant goal.

REGIONAL INTEGRATION

With the end of the Cold War and the European schism, South Asia, like the rest of the Third World, is faced with the ever-increasing prospect of being marginalized in the international economy. In the circumstances regional cooperation is no longer just an option but a necessity thrust upon the countries of South Asia as a result of global changes. It is obvious, after nearly half a century of independence, that none of these countries pursuing development strategies based on aid and trade with the developed world have been significantly successful in alleviating poverty; and their export performance has been uniformly sluggish in the face of the protectionist policies of their main trading partners in the developed world. The stalemate in the North-South dialogue, the worsening terms of trade in international markets, growing dependence on external assistance, and the mounting debt have turned the vision of the New International Economic Order into an illusion.

The potential for regional cooperation in the changed international and regional environment is considerable. It is perhaps the only viable alternative to South Asia's dependence on the developed world as both a market for its agricultural products and the source of its manufactured goods and technology. But breaking away from old habits of mutual antagonism and hostility will not be easy. Translating the hope of regional cooperation into a meaningful reality will require a fundamental restructuring of the economy based on mutual advantages for all the countries.[35] And the move toward economic integration will invariably provoke a backlash from each nation's bourgeoisie. Because of the excessively narrow support bases of most former regimes in the region, it is surprising that governments have failed to muster the political will to challenge the elite. In other words, regional cooperation, like economic development, is dependent upon a democratic revolution that will strengthen the entitlement of the people. Here the indications are hopeful. The ability of the elites to continue resisting regional economic and political cooperation will be greatly weakened as the countries of the South become even more marginalized in the new global order. Moreover, with the establishment of democratic institutions and the consequent empowerment of the people, the stranglehold of the elites is likely to be reduced. Contrary to the widespread gloom, the drying up of foreign assistance may have some beneficial impact: It will call for greater self-reliance, increased husbandry of domestic resources, and South-South cooperation; it will compel self-reliance and encourage popular participation; and, most important, determined efforts will have to be made toward regional cooperation to compensate for the loss of markets in the developed world.

CONCLUSION: A NEW ERA OF REGIONAL COOPERATION

The prospect of external powers extricating themselves from South Asia following their détente has opened up new opportunities for improved relations between India and Pakistan and in the region generally. However, because regional conflicts have their own dynamics, the suspicions and hatred built up over the years will not disappear instantaneously. Nevertheless, the prospects for peace in the subcontinent appear to be better than at any time before. Not only have both the principal regional protagonists recognized the inefficacy and limitations of their external backers but also important changes are taking place both domestically and in the region that appear conducive to a political rapprochement.

The developments in Europe will also have important repercussions for South Asia. The collapse of authoritarian regimes in Eastern Europe and their gradual incorporation into the capitalist economy and the creation of an integrated market in Europe have altered the pattern of international economic linkages and trading patterns, which will inevitably have their resonances in South Asia. These changes have brought both fresh challenges and opportunities for the region. In the short term the different countries of the region will have to cope with declining amounts of foreign assistance and the prospect of a slowdown in economic growth. India will have the additional problem of finding a substitute for its privileged trading links with Eastern Europe in the face of competition from Western manufacturers. In the long term, however, the countries of the region will have to learn to mobilize their own resources for development. The transition is bound to be painful but will reduce external dependence and may help foster greater popular accountability and democratization of the regimes. But most important, as the region is left to its own devices, the countries will be compelled to develop closer links within the region.

The compulsions toward South Asian regional cooperation cannot be ignored. However, meaningful regional cooperation will require a fundamental restructuring of the economy based on mutual advantage for all the countries. Enormous possibilities exist for economic cooperation through structural adjustments, but such a policy will not be easy to adopt because it is bound to be resisted by the national elites of all countries. Overcoming such resistance will require enormous political will, but given the narrow support base of most regimes in the region, none of the governments are likely to muster the will until the governments become more responsive to popular opinion. The transition to democracy in Pakistan, Bangladesh, and Nepal is a promising start.

❧ 5 ❧

China in the Post–Cold War Era

ZHANG YUNLING

Dramatic changes have taken place with the collapse of the communist system in Eastern Europe and the disintegration of the Soviet Union. And change continues; the "world order" is still on the road toward restructuring.

The old world was characterized by a pattern of integration-division-exclusion. Integration, or globalization, has been reflected mainly in rapid increases of international trade and investment, which have made the national economies more and more interrelated and interdependent. In other fields, such as security and the environment, globalization was also increasingly significant. Nevertheless, the world was a highly divided one. The inequality between North and South made the world economy and world market highly asymmetric, and the confrontation between West and East provided for the structure of "cold war." The feature of exclusion is striking. For example, during 1980–1990, the shares of the 102 poorest countries in the world's exports declined from 7.9 percent to 1.4 percent while the shares of the core regions, North America, Western Europe, and Japan, increased from 54.8 percent to 64 percent. The former Soviet Union and Eastern Europe were also almost excluded from the major part of the world economy and the world market. Their share of exports and imports in world trade never exceeded 10 percent.[1]

With the end of the Cold War the confrontational division between East and West is no longer there, and in that sense the world is more united. The transformation of the Eastern bloc toward a market economy has marked the end of the history of two "parallel economies." Obviously, the economic and political consequences of change are significant. However, this does not mean that a new order, substantially different from the old one, will be swiftly established. We are in the midst of a transition. Many of the basic features of the old order may continue to exist for a long time. It is too early and also too difficult to draw a clear picture of a new order.

China

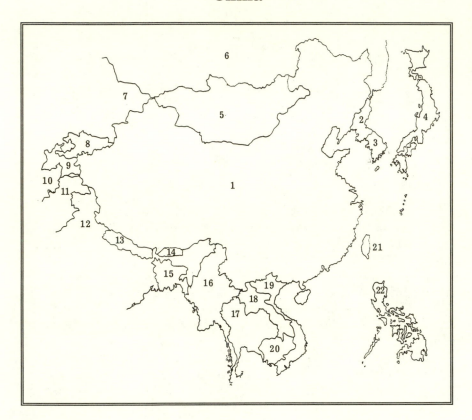

1. China	9. Tadzjikistan	17. Thailand
2. North Korea	10. Afghanistan	18. Laos
3. South Korea	11. Pakistan	19. Vietnam
4. Japan	12. India	20. Cambodia
5. Mongolia	13. Nepal	21. Taiwan
6. Russian Federation	14. Bhutan	22. Philippines
7. Kazakhstan	15. Bangladesh	
8. Kyrgyzstan	16. Burma	

The reform and open-door policies of China are not the result of the end of the Cold War per se, since they began in the late 1970s. Significant changes have taken place not only in China's economic, political, and social structures but also in its position and role in the region and in the world. China is in a process of transition toward a market economy, modernization, and internationalization. Great challenges have to be dealt with both in its domestic development and its international relations.

"The end of geography" (see Chapter 7) due to the end of the Cold War has placed China in a unique position in world politics as a modernizing socialist power. With increasing participation in the world market, China has become more and more dependent on the world economy. As a large country with rapid growth, China finds it vitally important to pursue a pragmatic policy in both the region and the world. Furthermore, in a wave of drastic changes, pressures of disorder and even chaos may increase. China has to walk a tightrope, carefully balancing stability, transformation, and development.

CHANGES IN THE WORLD

The world has witnessed dramatic changes since the late 1980s. Many, if not all, are the results of the ending of the Cold War. The consequences of these changes are not uniform. Some see them leading to the "end of history," that is, the collapse of communist systems and the total triumph of capitalism.[2] Others argue that the world is in a state of disorder with increasing instability and polarity between the rich and the poor. But the fundamental question is, What are the consequences of the changes, and how can we deal with the new problems?

The End of Confrontation

With the collapse of the communist system in Eastern Europe and the disintegration of the Soviet Union, the confrontation of two power blocs ended, and the security of the world is no longer tied to the relationship between them. However, the new situation and the new relationships of the post–Cold War era are far from clear. The dramatic restructuring of the international system is still under way. The redistribution of power is one of the most striking phenomena. World politics and relations still continue to be shaped by one superpower heading a small group of leading powers. The United States wants to play the leading role of superpower and hopes the world will accept an American hegemony.[3] But the United States is no longer a superpower. It lacks the economic strength to run the post–Cold War world. The European Community, as a highly integrated body, wishes to play a more independent and stronger role in international affairs and a major role in European affairs. Yet it is currently much constrained by its own difficulties and the regional unrest in Europe. Japan, with its significantly increased economic power, does not want to be a political dwarf and demands a share of power in a tripolar world. But it is still constrained by its constitution, internal opposition, and mistrust of the international community. Against this background, is it realistic to envisage a tripolar structure with a high capacity for world leadership and, if yes, will the world accept this new "super leadership" (new order)?

It must be remembered that with the overlay of confrontation between two superpowers lifted, "the regional powers have far greater latitude to pursue their own policy."[4] The increase in conflict caused by competition for regional supremacy, the division of the new nation-states, and the reshaping of the major powers against a background of ethnic and religious strife are the most serious threats to the stability and order of the post–Cold War world. It is a world neither controlled by the United States nor by the tripolar powers. Of the many kinds of new conflicts in the post–Cold War era, the most dangerous are those between the new minipowers, often involving ethnic, religious, and nationalist antagonism as well as the proliferation of nuclear technology. The major concern is the danger in conflicts expanding from the internal to the regional or international level. Existing regional or international organizations are at a loss about what to do. It is true that the role of the United Nations has been strengthened in intervening and handling domestic as well as regional conflicts. One may find UN involvement in almost every corner of the world nowadays. However, its role in solving internal wars or regional conflicts is rather restricted and limited because of its lack of military and financial resources. In the case of large action, direct participation and organization of the big powers remain necessary. This is made difficult by the existence of different or even antagonistic interests among the leading core countries. In other words, the end of the Cold War has changed the formation of the power structure but not the essence of continued dominance of the big powers in international affairs.

The Transition to Democracy and a Market Economy

The collapse of the communist systems in Eastern Europe and the Soviet Union, and their subsequent transformation toward capitalist market systems, appears to have made democracy and the market system the winner of the great contest between East and West. Yet this has not brought about stability and prosperity for the countries concerned. In the former Eastern bloc, the transition has caused all kinds of crisis and instability:

1. Economic crisis has created a serious threat to stability. The economies have experienced sharp decline, which has resulted in continuous worsening of the living standard of the people. The problem is that there seems to be no sign of quick improvement of the situation. The economic, social, and welfare costs of the transformation are thus extraordinarily high.

2. Political conflicts among different interest groups struggling for power have created disorder and the risk of chaos. For example, the confrontation between the Russian parliament and president is obviously a negative factor increasing the difficulties of the transition. In other states, the political struggles sometimes even lead to internal wars.

3. The most serious threats are regional conflicts and wars. The war in the area of former Yugoslavia and military clashes in the former Soviet Union

have ended the "tranquility" of Europe, lasting for more than 40 years after World War II. It seems that Europe has had a peaceful revolution, but hardly a peaceful transition. The danger is that existing European organizations are not effective enough to handle the problems. People now worry about "the return of history" (to a situation comparable to nineteenth-century Europe) following the "end of history." In other areas, such as the Middle East and Africa, the conflicts or wars not only continue but also escalate.

Moreover, it is not clear that this transformation will necessarily lead to a stable democracy or a prosperous market economy. In Russia, present instability continues to be a threat, and future prospects give cause for alarm. As Andrei Kozyrev, minister of foreign affairs, warned, "History has witnessed many times how the domestic problems of Russia made that state a dangerous and unpredictable participant in international affairs."[5] It seems too early to say whether Russia will emerge a partner or an adversary to the Western world. The transition of the other countries in the former Soviet Union are even more complex and unpredictable.

The Integration of the World Economy: Uneven Globalization

The world economy witnessed a fast progress of integration after World War II. The major elements of the integration are trade, direct investment, and other capital flows. The integration of the world economy is characterized by two striking features: First, it has mainly taken place among the developed countries, typically among the triad (United States of America–EC–Japan); second, it has mainly been undertaken by transnational corporations (TNCs). For example, in 1990, the triad countries share around a total of 65 percent of world export and import, out of which 70 percent is conducted among themselves, mainly by TNCs. The developing countries and the former Eastern bloc countries are largely excluded.

Yet from a global point of view, the world economy has become more integrated in the sense that the East European countries and Russia as well as the other countries of the former Soviet Union have discarded the planning system, rejected their inward-looking economic strategies, and become members of the international economic and financial community (IMF, World Bank, GATT). Against this background, it should be easier for the international community to take effective steps to coordinate and adjust global development. Therefore, the trend of economic integration is likely to be further strengthened. Nevertheless, the nature and structure of international organizations have not changed very much with the participation of new groups of countries. It is still the "rich club" headed by the major powers that plays the major role in intervening and coordinating economic and financial policies.

Seen from the logic of power and economic wealth, the economic field has not changed much. The old structure continues to dominate. The division of the world between rich and poor remains a striking feature of the world economic system (see Chapter 2).[6] Trade, financial, economic, social, and technological indicators confirm the deepening of integration among the developed countries on the one hand and an increasingly impoverished and slowly growing Third World on the other. Here the parts are less and less integrated, moving to isolation and exclusion from the other parts of the world, as well as from each other.

The developing countries have not received any peace dividend from the end of the Cold War. Internal conflicts and wars have even worsened in some countries following the release of previously repressed contradictions, which in turn have made the economic situation deteriorate even more. It seems the gap between rich and poor will continue to grow, since more and more resources and wealth flow to the North; the North itself is increasingly shifting its attention away from the developing countries toward Russia and Eastern Europe. Moreover, the end of the Cold War does not touch the uneven structure of the international division of labor, in which the poor countries have a very unfavorable position.

The developing countries themselves are increasingly differentiated in economic terms. A few of the successful exporters among the NICs are close to the income level of the developed countries. But at the same time, quite a few have fallen behind and continue to plunge deeper into poverty. The restructuring of political forces within a country or a region has often contributed to the deterioration.

There are other problems than those relating to economic equity. A general global maldevelopment associated with misuse of natural and human-made resources and the corresponding increase in ecological and environmental problems are also of utmost importance. The end of the Cold War itself does not appear to have improved the prospects for successfully dealing with these issues.

The Process of Regionalization

Together with integration, regionalization is an outstanding feature of the world economy. The regional economic integration pioneered by the European Community (EC) has been followed with increasing interest worldwide. By setting up a regional economic community, or zone, the EC is not only aiming at increasing regional cooperation but also at confronting competition with outside rivals. For a growing number of countries, regional integration and cooperation appears to be an increasingly necessary strategic choice in order to survive and develop. In addition to the EC, several regional economic organizations have been set up. However, most of them are still in an initial stage. The lower level of integration concerns establishing a customs union or an internal free-trade zone; the higher level involves building an internal market with free flows of capital, personnel, goods, and services. The North American Free Trade Agreement (NAFTA) is an example of low-level integration with the participation of the United States, Canada, and Mexico. The EC's European Single Market is high-level integration.

Regional economic organizations have to give priority to the interests of their members; in that sense regional blocs are by definition protectionist and exclusivist. Nevertheless, the integration of the world economy at large may be intensified on the basis of regional integration to the extent that regional groups are organized as open systems.[7]

Yet regionalization is no panacea. First, regional cooperation or integration is often built on a very weak base due to internal contradictions in economic interests, other disagreements, or worsening economic conditions or crises (sometimes also political disputes). One can see how the economic crises of the EC are now damaging the process of its integration. As a result of the economic crisis, not only the Maastricht Treaty but also the European Single Market have been negatively affected. Second, in a world of integration or exclusion, resources will continue to flow to the "rich clubs" and thus the conditions of the "poor clubs" may not improve very much. Further marginalization may even be in the cards.

A call to build a New International Economic Order was heard as early as the 1970s. But almost nothing has happened in this respect. The world system, especially a post–Cold War world system, ought to reflect not only the interests and requirements of the big powers but also the interests of the majority of developing countries, especially the least-developed ones. Moreover, without further economic development of the majority of developing countries, the growth of the world economy will be restricted or even disrupted.

CHINA IN TRANSITION

China's reform and open-door policy started long before the end of the Cold War. The reform is a radical break with earlier policies. Great achievements have been made since 1978, when the reform started. From 1978 to 1990, the average economic growth rate was in double digits, and GNP quadrupled.[8] In 1991, 1992, and 1993 the economy continued to grow even faster than in the 1980s. Yet it is not the mere figures that are most important but the changes in the structure and institutions of the entire system.

Transition to a Market Economy

The reform started with the family contract system in the rural areas, from where it expanded to other regions. The core of the reform is to move the basic economic mechanism away from central planning toward a market economy. Dramatic changes can be seen in three dimensions. The first is the structure of the economy. State-owned enterprises now coexist with collectively and privately owned companies, with a majority of nonstate-owned units. For example, 55 percent of industries are now owned by collectives or private entities (both are known as township industries). The remaining state-owned industries will have to change according to the requirements of market competition. At the same time, the private shareholding system is going to expand further.

The second dimension is the role of the state, which has moved away from direct control toward indirect management. Most state central planning of production has been given up. Now more than 90 percent of production and retail are not under state command and the prices have been liberalized. Government intervention has shifted toward conventional monetary and financial macroeconomic measures, that is, long-term monetary policy, financial policy, and so on.

Third, rural society is moving toward industrialization through the fast development of township industries. More than one-third of the national income now comes from township industries, and around 120 million workers are employed by them, more workers than employed by state-owned industries.[9]

The greatest achievement of China is that drastic reform has been accompanied by extremely rapid economic growth, and the average living standard of 1.2 billion people has significantly improved. The reforms must be considered irreversible now; they have gained their own internal momentum and can no longer be stopped politically.

From Closed-Door to Open-Door

One of the most significant changes in China is its fast opening up to the outside world. The open-door policy has closely interlinked the Chinese economy with the world market. Between 1978 and 1990, the total value of exports and imports increased from $20.6 billion to $115.4 billion, an average growth rate per year of more than 15 percent. In southern China, a large number of manufacturing industries are highly export led.[10] Foreign direct investment (FDI) in the Chinese economy has increased quickly. By the end of 1992, the total value of effectuated or agreed upon FDI was $108.9 billion. FDI plays an important role in export-led industries, in particular in the special economic zones and the coastal areas.[11] In 1991, China became the largest recipient of capital inflows in Asia, and the second largest (after Mexico) among all developing countries.[12] Following this opening toward the outside, the structure and working of the Chinese economy has changed dramatically. The institutions, mechanisms, and policies of the Chinese economy increasingly conform to world market economic standards. Chinese growth is now highly dependent on the world market, since foreign trade amounts to more than one-third of GNP. The process of integration has created interdependencies between the Chinese economy and the outside world through the linkages of international trade and financial markets. With China's huge population, fast economic development, and increasing income level, the significance and influence of its economy in the world market can hardly be overestimated.

China is a latecomer in the world market, but it has become a successful player very quickly. Some argue that China will become a superpower by the early 2000s, second only to the United States.[13] Although this is probably an exaggeration, it is true that economic interests are a major factor in shaping China's relations with other countries and its policies in international affairs.

A New Position and Role in the World?

The collapse of the Soviet Union meant a serious challenge to China, since it left very few countries, actually only one big country, insisting on the leadership of the Communist Party. It was argued that China's position in world politics would decline because the "China card" could no longer be played. Nevertheless, the changes imply opportunities. No longer having to maneuver inside the narrow space of superpower confrontation, China may have more options in handling international relations. As a big country with increasing influence through its reform and open-door policy, China can play a more important role not only in the region but also in the world.

For a long time after World War II, China focused its foreign policy on its own security through targeting both of the superpowers. However, this strategy did not work well. China started to change its theory and strategy of foreign policy from the early 1980s. A more positive, pragmatic, and flexible policy was adopted following the end of the Cold War.

China argues that the major concern after the Cold War should be peace and development. This is because China needs a peaceful international environment to support its open-door and modernization policies. China does not endorse the existing structure of the world economy and politics, but it does not want to isolate itself. Therefore, China has operated pragmatically due to its priority interest in upholding a stable world order. In the UN Security Council, China has taken a flexible and cooperative approach. China understands that it can play an active role only through participation and cooperation in international affairs. For its immediate and long-term interests, China will have to manage to improve relations with the developed countries, especially with the big powers, because its modernization program relies heavily on their capital, technology, and markets. China might be more and more willing to participate in a central coalition of big powers in keeping international order. However, it will surely not share all views of the other powers. China does not belong to the West. It has its own culture and civilization. Clashes may be expected on issues such as democracy and human rights.[14]

From an ideological point of view, China has become isolated. Yet its open-door policy, causing increasing integration, has brought it closer to the outside world. Obviously, the existing world economic structure, or order, set up after World War II is outdated and unjust. Uneven globalization has adverse effects mostly in the developing countries. But China does not want to launch a movement to disrupt these trends even though in principle it supports the idea of a new economic world order: Above all China supports stability and peace. China's top priority appears to be active participation in and use of the existing market and division of labor for the benefit of its own development and modernization. Of course, China belongs to the developing world and shares many interests with the developing countries; but it can no longer represent the interests of the developing countries, since they are rather diversified. At the same time, China has become a strong competitor facing the other developing countries in an increasing number of areas of the world market. Many of the developing countries will have to painfully confront China's economic challenge in the near future.

Emphasizing the Regional Focus

China is an Asian country. Pacific Asia, where China is situated, has gone through a number of positive changes since the ending of the Cold War. First, wars and conflicts have been substantially reduced or put to an end. The normalization of Sino-Soviet (now mainly Sino-Russian) relations, the settlement of the internal war in Cambodia, the mitigation of the situation in the Korean Peninsula, and the improvement of Sino-Vietnamese relations all mean that the region is transforming toward more peace and stability. Second, economic development has accelerated, making Pacific Asia one of the most dynamic regions in the world. The optimistic view argues that the next century will be a Pacific Asian era due to the region's extraordinary economic dynamics. Third, regional cooperation and coordination have developed new strength in both economic and political fields through interregional organizations, such as APEC (Asia Pacific Economic Cooperation).

At the same time, Pacific Asia contains a variety of political systems and economic models, as well as a diverse pattern of alliances. It is by no means a peaceful oasis. Historically, there have been a number of territorial as well as ethnic conflicts. In a sense, the stability of the region is largely dependent on its relations to the big powers. Fortunately, these relations are no longer shaped by the confrontation between two superpowers. On the top level, there is a quadrilateral structure, that is, China–United States of America–Japan–Russia, among which the triangle of the former three is considered to be vitally important.[15] At the sublevel, relations between the United States and Japan, between the United States and Russia, between China and the United States, as well as between China and Japan, are of a different nature. The United States and Japan are political allies, the Sino-Japanese relationship has changed from hostility toward friendship, and relations between the United States and China are troublesome but not antagonistic any more.

Thus, a higher degree of coordination or even cooperative relations appears to be possible. China is neither a close partner nor an enemy of the other three. It will carefully manage its relations with them, for example, by strengthening cooperation with Japan without compromising its relationship with the United States.

From China's perspective, relations with the neighboring countries are extremely important. For a long time, relations between China and its neighboring countries were troubled, but they have greatly improved in recent years. Since the late 1980s they have benefited from China's new "good neighbor policy." From North to South, and from East to West, for the first time in a long period it seems that China may feel released from the threat and encirclement by its neighbors.

In a process of redistributing the balance of power in the region following the end of the Cold War, China is one of the most important actors. China has the geographical advantage of being the largest country in the region in terms of territory and population. Economically, although China is still a developing country, its potentials and fast development are increasingly recognized. Politically, as a permanent member of the Security Council of the United Nations, China has a special influence. Furthermore, China also enjoys a cultural advantage, since Chinese culture, known as Confucianism, has a strong impact on not only ideology and politics but also the economies of the other countries. In sum, without China's participation almost no important action can be taken now concerning regional affairs; China's position is often decisive. Yet although China is a strong regional power, it is not yet a world power and should not attempt to play the role of a superpower in regional affairs.

The following principles ought to be central for China in dealing with relations with the countries in the region:

1. China should continue to improve economic relations with the neighboring countries. It is a healthy strategy to develop "open-border zones" with the neighboring countries or regions. China has shown strong interest in opening its border areas, in setting up "special border development zones" with its neighboring countries or regions. In the Northeast, a zone (known as the Tu Men River Development Zone) is starting to develop with Russia, North and South Korea, and Japan. In the Southeast, there is a vast zone with Taiwan–Hong Kong–Macao as the nucleus, but there is also close economic cooperation with the ASEAN countries. In the South and Southwest, a zone including Vietnam, Thailand, Pakistan, and India is now being established. In the Northwest, a development zone including the Central Asian countries of the former Soviet Union can now be found in its embryonic form. It is of course not just China's aspiration to develop these border

zones. The neighboring countries and regions have shown increasing interest and have participated actively. However, this kind of open economic strategy will integrate China (like a real "middle kingdom") into a vast region, linking it not only to directly neighboring countries but also to a number of others. In economic terms, this is a huge market with vast resources, and politically, integration will help create a peaceful and stable area. However, uneven development in and between the zones is a source of instability, and there is the danger that in the absence of central control, China will be divided into regions dominated by local interests.

It remains difficult to foresee Pacific Asia as a highly integrated body, but some institutional cooperation can be developed further. China may use its advantage in the ethno-Chinese economic network in the region to develop its economic relations and cooperation with the other countries, but certainly it does not want to create a separate Chinese bloc or a "great Chinese community." China now is an active member of APEC. As a first step, some interregional trade arrangements may be agreed upon, and then, as a second step, a general trade agreement would be possible. If it is too difficult to make an agreement through APEC, then it would be necessary to promote an agreement in a smaller area, for example, in East Asia. These prospects depend in particular on the attitudes and policies of China and Japan. China's attitude is, however, changing from inactive toward constructive engagement.

2. China should promote political as well as military coordination and cooperation. Political and military relations are more complex than economic ones. It is important to set up an interregional coordination mechanism for solving disputes, reducing tensions, and controlling the buildup of armaments. So far, China has given special attention to improving bilateral relations with countries in the region. But it begins to pay more and more attention to multilateral arrangements. The principle of laying aside the issue of sovereignty, cooperating in development, and making use of resources proposed by the Chinese government is meant to ease tensions and to set up bilateral and multilateral mechanisms for coordination and cooperation in the region. The South China Sea is considered to be an area of potential conflicts, since there are territorial disputes concerning the Nansha Islands (also known as the Spratley Islands). Some worry that violent conflict might break out if China adopts a power-oriented policy. However, it is highly unlikely that China will risk disturbing the balance of power to the brink of going to war with other countries, possibly with the involvement of other big powers, because this would put the ambitious modernization program in jeopardy.

A number of observers have taken a skeptical attitude toward China's future behavior and role, since it is still undergoing a process of transformation that might be long and unstable. Given the thrust of modernization in China, however, China will most likely play a positive rather than a negative role in regional development.

CONCLUSION: CHINA IN A CHANGING WORLD ORDER

There is great vigor and dynamism in current development in China. But there are also a number of challenges. Even if evolutionary reforms have proceeded smoothly so far, a number of structural problems stand in the way of further development. The old planning system has been discarded, but a new system of economic macromanagement for a market economy is not yet fully in place. For example, there is no strong and independent central banking system, and the commercial banking system is far from perfect. Reform of the state-owned industries is still rather slow and difficult even though more than one-third of them continue to lose money; the problem is not one merely of efficiency but also of employment and social stability. The impetus that has come from removing features of the old system will not continue. An institutional macrostructure compatible with the market economy is urgently required. Economic development will not maintain steam for long in a half-baked system. In addition, fast growth itself has caused additional imbalances. There are built-in impediments such as bottlenecks of infrastructure and resources.

At the same time, the economic problems are related to the political system. It is increasingly recognized that without a corresponding political reform, many problems cannot be solved quickly and thoroughly. The economic reform itself, with the structural changes and emergence of new forces and interests, has created internal pressure for political changes. However, any drastic move toward deep-going political reform will probably cause a chain reaction of disorder and chaos. China has to strike a balance between dynamic development and stability. In the near future, an evolutionary path involving a state that is strong in terms of both economic intervention and political control may be a realistic and pragmatic choice. Such a path would lead, in effect, to a socialist market economy—an East Asian model with Chinese features!

The emergence of Chinese power together with the end of the Cold War has caused apprehension among other countries in Pacific Asia, especially in East Asia. China is increasingly looked upon as a superpower that will naturally expand and strengthen its regional influence and power. In economic terms, China is now a strong competitor, expanding its market shares and hosting large amounts of foreign investment. The fact that millions of Chinese live in other countries in the region increases anxieties concerning the creation of an "invisible Chinese kingdom." China must take such fears seriously and avoid power-oriented policies, which will only create tensions in the region and eventually hurt China's interests in development and modernization. Therefore, China will have to resist the temptation to fill the regional vacuum left by the end of the Cold War.[16]

❧ 6 ❧

Russia: Between Peace and Conflict

VLADISLAV M. ZUBOK

Years after the destruction of the Soviet Union, its effective heir, Russia, is still trying to find its place in the world economy and international relations. All quantitative parameters considered, Russia is a highly industrialized country with enormous potential for development in terms of both resources and existing infrastructure and has an educated urban population. However, Russia has been cut off from the global economy and the international financial system. It has to build its democratic institutions from scratch while at the same time dismantling and transforming the institutions it inherited from the authoritarian past.

Most of the other regions of the world began to grapple with the various challenges of global interdependence before the end of the Cold War: In Western Europe and in the United States, the state, civil society, and groups from the intellectual elites have been experimenting and searching for new solutions for a long time. Russia is unique. The country owes its existence to the yearning of some of the Soviets to join the political and economic mainstream of the "civilized world." This yearning more than anything else brought about an end of the Soviet Empire and the Cold War. Yet Russia, the eager convert to the "new world," was completely unprepared for the new realities. Its political and intellectual resources had been much too concentrated on reforming (or dismantling) the communist regime. The people who were catapulted to power in August 1991 were as overwhelmed as the Bolshevik leaders were in October 1917. In Russia, therefore, the building of state structures, emergence of societal institutions, proliferation of market relations, and exposure to all the effects of global interdependence are happening simultaneously and in extremely intense ways. The country is like the "sleeper" of the oxygen bubble who suddenly, after several decades, woke up and broke out into the street. Russia might survive, but at what cost to itself and to others?

Former Soviet Republics

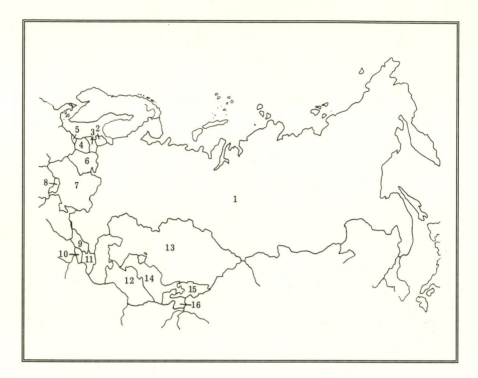

1. Russian Federation
2. Estonia
3. Latvia
4. Lithuania
5. R.F. (Kaliningrad)
6. Belarus
7. Ukraine
8. Moldova
9. Georgia
10. Armenia
11. Azerbaijan
12. Turkmenistan
13. Kazakhstan
14. Uzbekistan
15. Kyrgyzstan
16. Tajikistan

The following issues are discussed in this chapter: (1) Russia's responses to security challenges and multiplying conflicts at its boundaries; (2) the impact of the exposure to the world market economy and trade on Russia's economy and welfare; (3) the dynamics of domestic politics and perspectives for society and the state.

From the viewpoint of international relations, Russia ceased to be the focus with the collapse of the bipolar structures of the Cold War. But the Russian perspective raises new interesting issues for international relations theorists. Russia, and some other successor states of the Soviet Union (Ukraine in particular), are tottering on the verge of the so-called zone of conflict, as full-fledged civil wars in Tajikistan and Georgia and the October 1993 violence in Moscow demonstrate.[1] In world economic terms, Russia may join the countries in the semiperiphery. By virtue of its size and geopolitical importance, Russia is bound to influence the future configuration and the character of international relations: If Russia preserves its unity, it will be an important pillar of peace; if Russia slips, many other parts of Eurasia will be affected.

DOMESTIC AND INTERNATIONAL ORDER: WHICH PLACE FOR RUSSIA?

The Soviet Union played the role of the scarecrow, the bête noir, in the old global order during the Cold War. The unseemly manifestations of the Soviet utopia contributed to political tolerance, multiculturalism, and economic integration in the West. As Samuel Huntington once noted, in many ways there was only one superpower, the United States, at the hub of that order. But in one sense the Soviet presence was a big bonus to world peace. From the nuclear deadlock between the Soviet Union and the United States emerged the tradition of cautious, more or less rational behavior of adversaries in international conflicts.

The Soviet elites, dealing with the problems of security and international affairs, were the product of these circumstances. They felt humiliated by the illegitimacy of the Soviet regime and, at the same time, grew accustomed to informal, tacit cooperation with the West. That converted some of them, in Gorbachev times, into ardent Westernizers. At the time of their conversion they absorbed much of the modern jargon of interdependence and the "global village." Soviet "new thinkers" under Gorbachev tried to adapt the ossified communist ideology to these visions of the twenty-first century and almost inadvertently tripped over the threshold to radical changes that made disintegration of the old Soviet system inevitable.

Many in Boris Yeltsin's administration actively attempt to distance themselves from the new thinkers of the Gorbachev administration. But in reality the Yeltsin foreign policy elite and the former policymakers of the Gorbachev team are two sides of the same coin; even some of the players remain the same.[2] But their thinking has changed perceptibly. In place of Gorbachevian grandstanding and globalist pretensions based on the "new political thinking" came a more pragmatic and modest mentality, more "realist" in the traditional sense of the word.

To a large extent this change is a reflection of new geopolitical realities. Moscow is no longer the capital of the Soviet Union but the clearinghouse of weak and struggling Russia. On the map, the country resembles more the "appanage Rus" of the fifteenth century than the tsarist empire of the nineteenth. Russia is without a strong center and well-established natural boundaries and has almost no outlets to the sea. The state structure is in crisis: Russia is a quilt of 88 "subjects of federation," of which 22 in early 1993 proclaimed their sovereignty. Therefore, the country may, as Bogdan Szajkowski put it, "disintegrate into Bantustans."[3] Russia's traditional security problems with its borderlands are formidable: It faces a huge power vacuum on its southern borders. And for the first time since the first half of the eighteenth century there are signs of Islamic and Turkish ascendancy to the south and the east. Ethnically, it is still far from homogeneous, with 19 million non-Russians out of a 149 million population. At the same time 26 million ethnic Russians live on the territories of other successor states—the biggest diaspora in the world after the Chinese.

It is significant that Russia as a country has become less European and more Asian. A brief look at a world map shows that European Russia is a truncated appendix to the huge Asiatic chunk of land, spanning across many time zones to the Pacific. Most of the old "warm" ports connecting Russia with Europe now belong to the Baltic states and Ukraine, states not necessarily friendly to Russia or sympathetic to her commercial and geostrategic needs.

Siberia and the area between the Volga and the Urals dominate the country's economy, and (due to Yeltsin's origins) Russian government. It would not be an exaggeration to say that Russia's political center of gravity has shifted to somewhere between Kazan and Novosibirsk. The potential implications of this shift look even greater if one recalls that since Peter the Great this center of gravity has resided, some argued artificially, in St. Petersburg, the "window to Europe."

These shifts increase the problems for Russia's self-definition and legitimacy as a state. The Russian elites cast off the old Soviet legitimacy as a spent force. Unlike the leaders in other successor states, they could not build a new kind of legitimacy based on the ideas of "antiempire" and nation-state, or even (as the Balts did) on the sense of belonging to European civilization. What is left is the century-old debate between the Westernizers (Atlanticists), who argue that Russia's future and security lies in its integration with the West, and the Eurasians, who point to Russia's special location, history, and interests as excluding a one-sided Western orientation. This discrepancy reveals itself in the comparison of two official documents: the foreign policy doctrine, announced by the Russian foreign ministry, and the outlines of a new military doctrine, drawn up by the Russian General Staff. The first puts a premium on a diplomatic alliance with Western countries on the basis of "common values." The second stresses the primacy of geostrategic "spheres of influence" for Russia, covering the Baltics, Eastern Europe, "all Commonwealth states (CIS)," and the Near, Middle, and Far East.[4] The Eurasians seem to be gaining ground, as the Russian military is increasingly seen as the only guarantor of Russia's territorial integrity and the security of 26 million Russians living in other successor states. Russian troops became engaged in fighting Muslim forces in Ossetia and Tajikistan and, as mercenaries, in Armenia. The borders of Tajikistan with Afghanistan are considered by some as "the forward bastion of Russia."[5] The most Westernized representatives of the Russian elites were propagating a sort of Monroe Doctrine for Russia, that is, the right to intervene in the name of "human and minority rights throughout the entire territory of the former USSR."[6]

Some observers worry that Russia might become a revanchist state. Indeed, Russia in 1994, from the viewpoint of history and realist theory, falls into the same category of a loser nation as Germany did in 1919–1933, with the same disastrous consequences. This Weimar scenario is supplemented by one where Russia might become "a sick person of Eurasia": a disintegrating country supported by other great powers for the sake of world stability but eventually bound to collapse in the sea of ethnic and religious strife, like Turkey and Yugoslavia did in the past.

Is Russia doomed to take the irredentist road and to repeat its historic swing from "the time of troubles" (a state of virtual disintegration in the early seventeenth century) back to the land empire? Or will it disintegrate into one of the largest zones of conflict by the end of this century? In what way do long-term global trends affect the chances of these dismal scenarios?

It is far from clear how the current structure of international relations, based on the unipolar domination of the United States and economic integration among all capitalist power centers, might affect Russia's future. The democratic, liberal nature of the "core" exercises a positive influence on the orientation of the country's elites and their experiments in political and economic fields. The United States, preoccupied with nuclear proliferation, is interested in Russia's territorial integrity and even can go along with the use of Russian "peacekeeping" troops in troubled areas such as Georgia.[7] But this influence might one day be challenged by a backlash against the West when Russian dinosaur industries fail to adapt to the world market and massive unemployment results. What will the core then do to stop the Turkish or even the Weimar scenario from becoming a reality in Russia?

The disappointing performance of the international organizations makes such outcomes even more probable. As Russian nationalists look at the failures of the UN and NATO in Bosnia and Somalia, they can hardly be deterred from reckless irredentism in the Caucasus and the Crimea. And the activities of the IMF and the World Bank in Russia, whatever they do, will be always controversial, making these organizations easy targets for communist and neo-Nazi demagogues.

However, there is a limit to what the West, at the peak of its power, can do for Russia. Russia still remains, by the consent of other great powers, the mainstay of geostrategic constructions spanning from the Atlantic to the Pacific and is the only legal heir of the superpower's paraphernalia, including embassies abroad and the permanent seat on the UN Security Council. The story of nuclear proliferation in Ukraine and Khazakhstan has demonstrated that the United States failed to guarantee Russia's nuclear monopoly in the Commonwealth of Independent States. Some Russian officials strongly suspect that the United States of America played a double game on this issue.[8] The Washington establishment is divided between Russophiles, standing on the platform of geostrategic realism, and Russophobes, who for a variety of other reasons prefer to deter Russia and to build up checks and balances to the West of Russia, from the Baltics to Ukraine.

Finally, whatever the West's intentions, it can do little to alleviate Russia's worst security dilemmas, which stem from regional conflicts and problems. And increasingly the majority of Russian elites come to realize it. If Russia stays away from Tajikistan, the vacuum there will be filled by militant Islamic fundamentalism or, in some combination, by "enlightened" Turkey, Pakistan, and Iran. If Russia does not check the tribal violence in the Caucasus, it will spread further (Russian leaders often express the sentiment that either Russia will control the Caucasus or the Caucasus will control it). Not only Western powers are important for Russian diplomacy as it faces these conflicts; so are relations with the People's Republic of China, Iran, Pakistan, and Turkey. Since May 1992 (the Treaty of Tashkent) Russia has been cobbling together regional structures to preserve stability in Central Asia.

Security concerns, however, are not likely to become the prime ones in the immediate future. The nuclear arsenal, in addition to smaller mobile conventional forces, might somewhat allay Russia's fears. Though the Russian General Staff does not consider nuclear weapons sufficient for deterrence of the new type of threats (regional conflicts, terrorism, and fanaticism to the south of Russia), society at large seems to hold that no war or serious external danger can threaten a country protected by nuclear arms. The Russian public's lack of concern about the external threat is striking if one takes into account the centuries of turbulent Russian history and the "hostile encirclement" propaganda of the communist regime. Quite a few Russians like to groan about the collapse of the country, but precious few believe that foreign occupation is a real threat.

Summing up, from the Russian perspective the new world order increasingly looks not like salvation and a security dream but like a club of the rich to which Russia will not belong for a long time to come. International organizations and alliances with great powers cannot solve Russia's security problems. When Russian elites look at the outside world, what they see more and more is their "near abroad": small states of Eastern Europe and the Baltic who fear Russia's resurgence and want to join NATO, the rise of Islamic militancy in the South, and the regional conflicts that only Russian troops can contain. In the short term Russia's focus on the "near abroad" gives impulse to a regional security system with Russia as a leader and other members of the Commonwealth of Independent States (CIS) as followers.

THE RUSSIAN ECONOMY AND UNEVEN GLOBALIZATION

The global dichotomy between haves and have-nots leaves Russia in a precarious position. Russia's emerging market has few regulations and norms. Most entrepreneurs still complain that state structures, legislation, even the constitution itself, are constructed in a way totally inimical to and incompatible with private property and business. As one perceptive Western cartoon observed, one has to wait until business groups in Russia become big and powerful enough to rewrite the constitution and legislation to their liking. It seems that decades will pass before liberal economic philosophy will become a societal force powerful enough to glue Russia together. Economic disintegration finds different expressions: quasi-feudal-type regimes in Central Asia and a return to self-sufficient "natural complexes" in agricultural areas of European Russia. Old industrial complexes, formerly linked among themselves by the logic of the division of labor, are now breaking into an anarchy of primeval capitalism. There is no central pool for investments, no program of priorities for conversion. Instead, each one tries to survive independently. It remains to be seen whether the emerging forces of the market economy will install in Russia some of the liberalism and peacefulness that flow from economic interests or will aggravate its security dilemmas.[9]

The short-term prospects for the Russian economy look disastrous, but medium- and long-term results of the current transformation are more ambiguous. Russia's foreign policy—and its emerging market economy—are increasingly influenced by the rich capitalist economies of the North. If Russia could follow the tactics that some European countries adopted inside the U.S. "empire by invitation" in the 1950s, (Geir Lundestad called it "tyranny of the weak"), it might get critical Western aid and, more important, be admitted into the economic and financial club of world powers.[10] Though this will not trigger a Russian miracle immediately, one could argue that it might produce a new vision and new hope for Russian elites and the population that in the next century Russia could become a full-fledged member of the world economic core.

Much of this scenario has indeed been coming to life. Russia under Boris Yeltsin has acquired, with the help of the U.S. administration, a status as observer in GATT, in the World Bank, and, most prestigious of all, at the regular summits of the seven great industrial and financial powers of the world (G-7). Apprehensions that the austerity measures of the IMF might arouse anti-Western feelings in Russia forced the IMF to modify its rules for Moscow. In brief, on the organized level of the global economic system, Russia is not treated as Peru, Nigeria, or Mexico. As far as symbolism goes, Russia got far better treatment than did the Third World.

But all this should not mislead. In the international division of labor and capital Russia is far behind a country such as Mexico, which is now part of the North American Free Trade Agreement (NAFTA). And again, there is little the West can do about this. The Russian economy has to go through a long and painful process of complete restructuring before massive foreign investments (as distinct from foreign aid) will come and before Russian-made goods will enter the world market. Until then Russia remains part of the world economy only by virtue of three factors: import of a broad variety of consumer goods into Russia, export of raw materials, and sales of arms. There are singular successes in the integration of Russian and Western firms, for example, in aerospace and computer software. There is also the less cheerful prospect of increased drug trafficking from Russia.[11] But they are not going to match "the big three," just mentioned any time soon, particularly in their impact on Russia's goals and its conduct in international affairs.

The economic problems are compounded by the failure of the Russian presidency and the parliament to generate a coherent industrial and trade policy. So far the state has not been able to establish a proper framework for international business in Russia (financial infrastructure, norms, and regulations) conducive to business activities and investments. Corruption has increased to the point that Western donors have refused to channel their aid through central authorities. In this partial political and legal vacuum the major trade and economic forces have to organize into a loose semblance of lobbies, or as Russians prefer to say, mafias, that include industrialists, businesspeople, state officials, and various mediating players.

The most important of these is undoubtedly the oil and gas lobby. Head of the oil industry Viktor Chernomyrdin became Russia's prime minister. This lobby's power can flow in different directions. As a primary source of hard currency, oil and gas exports may encourage trends toward interdependence and cooperation in Russian politics. The oil industry is also likely to get immediate foreign investments, which it badly needs. Other successor states, Kazakhstan and Turkmenistan, have already gone down this road. Khazakh president Nursultan Nazarbayev in a $20 billion 40-year deal agreed to lease the Tengiz oil field to the multinational Chevron. A Khazakh analyst praised this deal as Alma-Ata's stepping-stone to "successful economic growth."[12]

The response in Russia was mixed. Some in Moscow realized that the export of oil and gas provides Russia with powerful leverage over her neighbors, the countries of Eastern Europe, and most of the former Soviet republics, including, most importantly, Ukraine and the Baltic countries. Oil exports to "the near abroad" might, therefore, remain hostage to strategies of regional security, or even to irredentist policies.

As the history of OPEC (Organization of Petroleum Exporting Countries) demonstrates, the old diplomacy might work both ways: So far the balance is in favor of cooperation and reasonable commercial profits. The Russian oil and gas lobby pioneered the creation of a northern version of OPEC. An accord was signed between Russia and 11 CIS states to set up the Intergovernmental Oil and Gas Council.[13] After some arm-twisting, Russia resumed oil supplies to Ukraine and Estonia. The oil industries obtained a decree from Yeltsin that would allow them to use a considerable part of the earned hard currency for capital investments.[14] Russian ties with Arab OPEC are of positive significance. They are based on the assumption about a mutuality of security interests, that is, the containment of troublemakers that are located between Turkmenistan and Kuwait, primarily Iraq.

The influence of the arms sales lobby on Russia's international behavior has been evidenced by the U.S.-Russian conflict over the transfer of Russian ballistic missiles and satellite technology to India. This episode made many Russian elites relapse into a typical Third World criticism of the United States for its double standard and defense of U.S. trade privileges. Russia's arms sales were reduced by five times, according to official (not very reliable, though) statistics, down to the level of $1.9 billion (1992 figures). This was a hard blow to Russian military industries that already were in dramatic decline. It has been the perception in Moscow that the U.S.-based producers of armaments picked up most of the former Soviet arms market, especially in the Arab world.[15] Russian arms salespeople have been making frantic efforts to regain their old clients and to make inroads into other crucial markets. They are likely to take advantage of the old and emerging regional security structures that produce regional arms races: among the People's Republic of China (PRC), both Koreas, and Taiwan; between India and Pakistan; among Iran, Iraq, and the Persian Gulf monarchies; and so on. Arms exports are likely to rebound dramatically. In 1993 Russia agreed to sell $1.9 billion worth of arms to China alone. These sales are viewed by many in the Ministry of Defense and the Ministry of Foreign Affairs as a road to Russo-Chinese strategic cooperation, a goal that, if achieved, might solve the Russian security dilemma in the East. But this basis for cooperation between the Russian military and diplomats evokes controversy and rivalries with other lobbies. Some lobbyists from desperate arms companies suggest that Russia should ignore the Western sanctions and sell arms to Serbia, Libya, and Iraq (Russian losses from the embargoes on those countries and the frozen Libyan and Iraqi debts to the USSR are currently estimated to be US$16–$18 billion in total). These radical voices are reminders of the real dangers (including illegal leaks of nuclear technology) stemming from the Russian economic collapse.

Another, less obvious, danger comes from the domestic significance of arms sales: They will be the staple of self-support for the Russian army in the age of hyperinflation and budgetary deficit. The arms lobby, encouraged by the military authorities and some diplomats, is determined to catch up with Western arms producers in both quality and quantity of marketable and exportable goods.[16] This might not only generate the cycle of sales-rearmament-sales but also help transform the military into a class unto itself, ambitious enough to play a crucial role in future Russian politics.

The third, vague but numerically gigantic, lobby consists of private entrepreneurs, organized profiteers, and moguls of the so-called black market and individual peddlers who travel to neighboring countries to bring back a gamut of consumer goods. This trade has already transformed the life of consumers in European Russia and, even more so, in Russia's Far East. The bulk of imported goods comes from the new rim of producers that have replaced the West: Turkey, Pakistan, and the vibrant economies of Southeast Asia.

The economic impact of these imports on Russia is negative (in the absence of trade tariffs they stifle domestic industries). But in terms of exposing Russian society to the realities of the world market, this trade has no parallels in Russian history. For the millions of unknown "heroes" of marketization who shuttle as business tourists year-round, the world has become a global village. Those of them who are socially conscious look to China, South Korea, Thailand, and Taiwan as beacons for Russia. The Sino-Russian trade is rapidly relinking the Russian Far East and Manchuria, since the economic profiles of the two are "wonderfully complementary."[17]

The emergence of the "import lobby" improves Russia's chances to emulate the group of Pacific Asian countries that have constructed healthy networks between the core and the periphery, preventing possible antagonism between the two. The import lobby will almost certainly contribute to the emergence of Russia's own goods-producing industries, with or without protectionist policies. But even if Russia's security dilemmas finally catch up with it, the presence of this lobby, unlike all the others, could undeniably check the backlash and the sliding toward the periphery and toward conflict.

All these factors taken together have potential significance for Russia's future orientations. Trade relations with Turkey are important because of the geographical proximity of Istanbul and Ankara. Russo-Turkish official relations, however, can be greatly complicated by the dispute over Central Asia and, perhaps, Transcaucasia. Pan-Turkeyism is viewed in Moscow not as a preferable alternative to Islamic fundamentalism but as a historical threat to Russia's geostrategic interests. Confidential memos of think tanks as well as newspaper articles are filled with concern about a potential Muslim superstate to the south of Russia, populated by 160 million Turks and spanning from the Adriatic to Mongolia.[18]

At the same time, grassroots uncontrolled trade with China and "dragons" of the Far East coincide with the long-term priorities of the arms lobby, as well as the strategic schemes advocated by Eurasians (and former Westernizers). Western investors' frustrated expectations and the slow interpenetration of Western and Russian markets stand in sharp contrast to growing hopes about the potential of trade and economic relations with the Pacific Rim countries.

Russia's place in the world economy remains the factor of biggest uncertainty and will be decided by the course and results of domestic reforms. Yet it is already clear that liberalization measures and the uncontrolled entrance of thousands of atomized economic "subjects" into the world market have a limited and mostly destructive impact on Russia's future. The increasing pressure of world competition from outside and powerful oligopolic lobbies from within might force the Russian state to return to heavy regulations on economic activities in the country.

DOMESTIC POLITICS:
JEFFERSON VERSUS PINOCHET

Russia remains, in Samuel Huntington's definition, a "torn country" whose elites try to join "the Western Civilization" while the rest of society is cut off from it by "the Velvet Curtain" of history and culture.[19] Right now the iron grip of history on Russia's future is less firm than many would think. The years of Soviet power transformed Russia from what was predominantly a peasant country into a country of urban educated people with many orientations and demands that are more middle-class than Russian. The vast majority of Russian elites share a middle-class mentality: They want property and stability, not revolution and expropriation. If Russia's fate is to be decided in the voting booth and by political means, the key factor in the immediate future will not be industrial workers or collectivized peasants but the urban middle class.

The biggest impediment to the evolutionary transformation of Russia's politics toward modern democracy is a woeful absence of institutions that could take up the role of civil society. Professional associations today are mostly minireplicas of the old socialist welfare state, demanding a bigger slice from the state budget pie. For most professions outside of the working class, there are no associations at all. Newspapers and electronic media are losing their grip on the educated audience they enjoyed in the times of glasnost. The Orthodox Church is in profound crisis and is unlikely to play the role of a substitute for civic bodies. All the political parties in Russia, except for the Communist Party, are just tiny clienteles of a few ambitious politicians.

This situation is ideal for a fascist type of movement that could emerge from nowhere and provide immediate links between the middle class (as well as other groups) and the state. This danger has not escaped the attention of Russian analysts. Some believe that a Russian Pinochet could save Russia for a democratic future by guiding it around the dangers of the transitional period with an iron hand. Others think that any compromise of liberal principles will only play into the hands of the lurking reactionaries, primarily the communists, who have merged with xenophobic, aggressive nationalists. Again, the urban population resurfaces as the key factor: Will all the economic dislocations and a growing sense of insecurity push these people into the embrace of a new extremist ideology?

This possibility, unfortunately, cannot be totally excluded, as Russian elections in 1993 demonstrated. But several important factors make this outcome different from that in Germany in 1933. The attractiveness of ideologies of any kind is decreasing in Russia. Some Russian observers, such as Dmitry Furman, categorically state that "ideological thought is weak and dying."[20] The long experience of imitating the ideological life (when nobody believed in official communist doctrine but paid lip service to it) produced whole generations of cynical relativists. So far no single idea, including, unfortunately, Christianity and Western liberalism, has made considerable inroads into Russian mass consciousness.

From the age of state-controlled media and Orwellian mechanisms of indoctrination, Russia seems to have taken a leap into the age of diversified informational networks. The biggest audiences can still be claimed by state television, but there are many others, for example, Radio Liberty and the videocassette recorder (VCR) industry (pirating Western movies from Singapore and Hong Kong). The proliferation of fax machines and, in some instances, even e-mail indicates the direction this process is taking—toward more pluralist communication networks.

Another phenomenon, so typical of the core, is sinking its roots in Russia. This is the shrinking role of the state and, even broader, of the whole idea of national sovereignty. It is not simply that many Russians are sick and tired of the state after the years of communist rule. One could foresee a critic arguing that the dilemma between imminent anarchy and a despotic state will be resolved in favor of the latter if anarchy reaches intolerable proportions. But what would be seen as intolerable anarchy in Russia? The current situation, from the viewpoint of many Western observers, already deserves this definition. Not so for most Russians. The years since the breakup of the Soviet Union, despite all hardships and chaos, were not anything like anarchy for the majority in Russia. Many of them, for the first time, realized that they could not wait for the state to provide for their needs. The cutting off of the umbilical cord linking most Russian citizens to the state, painful and dangerous as it was, became a necessary part of the birth of individualism and social creativeness. The change in mentality emerges as the most astounding of all changes since the breakup.

The revolution of expectations is, to a large extent, imported from the West through modern mass media and travels abroad (the number of travelers exploded from 2 million in 1987 to 12 million in 1992). It brings about further decline of the role of the state. Many young Russians are no longer satisfied with the mediocre, median living standards that state employment could guarantee. Their skyrocketing demands can be met only by nonstate activities (bureaucratic corruption is a separate issue), mostly by private profiteering. Needless to say, this is a trend with highly ambiguous consequences. But as long as the Russian potential for such profiteering is enormous, this boom mentality deflects the sense of growing anarchy among the young, who would be likely recruits into fascist-type movements. Thus, the inevitability of a dilemma between anarchy and a despotic state is postponed.

There are other factors of tactical significance. The arrival of new groups of elites to the pinnacle of power in 1991–1992, their rivalry, and the clashes between the presidency and the parliament provided many Russians with an opportunity to learn the relative merits of the idea of checks and balances, as opposed to the old Russian tradition of the good tsar. At least several times the Russian Constitutional Court played a role of umpire between the legislative and executive branches. The new people at the top also learned that there are no permanent allies but only diverse interests.

The problem of territorial sovereignty is the most poignant in Russia. Until recently the Russian central government has been ready to make considerable concessions to regionalism, primarily by reducing the meaning of "sovereignty" to the bottom line of territorial integrity while putting aside the huge area of interregional and international economic activities that used to be the privilege of the Soviet state in the past. Ironically, it is the lack of legitimacy of the ruling groups in Moscow, be they former parliamentarians in the White House or the "Sverdlovsk mafia" in the president's administration, that prevents them from rising above other elite groups in other cities and areas of the Russian Federation. The executive power has been taking extraordinary measures to restore its legitimacy by means of new elections and plebiscites, but so far the president has been more successful when using emergency measures and frightening local authorities with the use of force. The continuing constitutional crisis of the central power more than eco-

nomic decentralization (and certainly more than local anti-Russian nationalist and regionalist sentiments) is the biggest contributor to the prospect of
the "Bantustanization" of Russia. Those who make up the popular majority
and who initially supported the parade of sovereignties among the subjects
of the Russian Federation no longer harbor illusions that regional independence might make them better off economically, and they certainly do not
believe that local efforts can replace a national program of protection
against unemployment and other hazards. The temptation will grow, therefore, to resort to the methods of progressive authoritarianism to restore the
center rather than waiting for the creation of a complicated, and to many in-
comprehensible, system of checks and balances.

CONCLUSION: QUO VADIS RUSSIA?

Russia demonstrates many features that pull it in the direction of the periphery of the world system. Its basic motives as an economic and political entity
are survival and territorial integrity. Security dilemmas set Russia apart from
the core and push it toward creation of regional structures not necessarily
compatible with the new world order of the West. In the economic sphere,
Russia is cut off from the core by the Soviet history of self-inflicted isolation
and by the failure to create established norms and regulations similar to
what became accepted by liberal societies in the West as the basis for the "enlightened" realization of economic interests.

These woeful facts, however, coexist with many important achievements
indicating that a new Russia might eventually follow the path of the Pacific
"dragons" rather than suffer the fate of prerevolutionary Turkey. Quite a
few observers of Russia agree that available statistics seriously underrate the
rapid expansion of the private sector of the economy. Yet since the prophe-
cies of doom prevail, I have tried in this chapter to present some of the reasons for a more optimistic view. My main conclusion is that current world
developments do have a positive influence on the transformation of Russia's
society and domestic politics, but this influence does not come *directly* from
the West. Rather, it is most pronounced when it coincides with experiences
and processes indigenous to Russia. Most of the direct effects of the outside
world on Russia are either ambiguous or downright ruinously counterpro-
ductive.

Many Russians run twice as fast now in order to survive. But the spurt of
entrepreneurial energy is not primarily the result of a primitive urge but an
alternative to the feeling of emptiness and anarchy in political, social, and
national life. An important distinction between Russia and Yugoslavia is
that instead of fighting for the preservation of territory and state, most Russians prefer to haggle for profits and property. The disintegration of the Soviet Union has been met either with indifference or with enthusiasm by most

Russians because it was widely perceived that, in economic terms, the Soviet Union wasted Russia's resources, natural as well as human.[21]

Now, when the euphoria of liberation is giving way to the hardships of life, most Russians still do not support the idea of restoration of the Union, propagated by some demagogues on the right. The reluctance of people (even the famed Cossacks) to be empire-builders at Moscow's service might be Russia's blessing in disguise. Perhaps Russia will eschew a bloody road of realization of the ideas of the nation-state or another land empire. Perhaps it will manage its security dilemmas and develop as a trading state, with far better chances for peace and economic integration with the core countries of the world. Unless a strong fascist-type movement emerges, Russia will probably combine security regionalism with bandwagoning with the West.

7

Dialectics of World Order:
A View from Pacific Asia

TAKASHI INOGUCHI

Pacific Asia is one of the most dynamic regions in the world. Of all the world regions, it has been enjoying the highest annual economic growth rate in the fourth quarter of this century. At the same time, a vague angst about the future of the region has been present under the surface of its thriving business and increasing self-confidence. Pacific Asia, ranging from Korea, Japan, Mongolia, and China to the ASEAN and Indochinese countries and Myanmar (sometimes including Australia and New Zealand and Russia's Far East), has been changing fast, which has made it somewhat apprehensive of the consequences of rapid change, not only economically and technologically but also in social, political, and military terms. I shall attempt to identify the emerging features of the global transformation by looking closely at Pacific Asia.[1]

In my view three kinds of change can be identified on a global scale. For the sake of convenience I call them the end of the Cold War, the end of geography, and the end of history, respectively. The three phrases have been used to denote certain events in the past. George Bush certainly had his way of defining the end of the Cold War—as the victory of the United States. Richard O'Brien, who has authored a book so subtitled, defined the end of geography as the disappearance of the tyranny of distance in economic activities. And Francis Fukuyama, who authored a book that gave birth to the phrase "the end of history," has his own way of defining the term.[2] I use the terms somewhat freely to mean what I believe is the primary feature of change unfolding on a global scale in the three areas of international security, the world economy, and domestic societies. As the editors of this volume argue, one can maintain that technological change is a *long durée* variable, in a Braudelesque sense, accelerating uneven globalization in the world, and that the end of the Cold War is *évenementielle*, again in a Braudelesque sense in

Pacific Asia

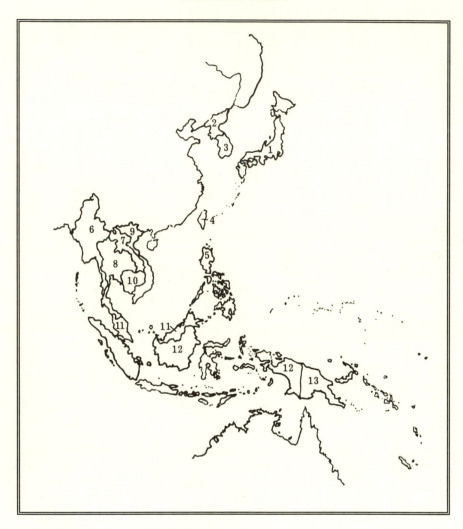

1. Japan
2. North Korea
3. South Korea
4. Taiwan
5. Philippines
6. Myanmar
7. Laos
8. Thailand
9. Vietnam
10. Kampuchea
11. Malaysia
12. Indonesia
13. Papua New Guinea

Pacific Island States:

Solomon Islands
Nauru
Vanuatu
Kiribati
Tuvalu
Fiji
Western Samoa
Tonga
Federated States of Micronesia
Marshall Islands

that it precipitates certain sets of events in the three areas of security, development, and democracy.

At any rate, by "the end of the Cold War" I mean the uneasy coexistence of U.S. absolute military supremacy on a global scale, both in strategic and conventional terms, and the U.S. perception of its longer-term deterioration of the technological and economic competitiveness sustaining its military supremacy. By "the end of geography" I mean the uneasy coexistence of removing barriers and impediments and codifying common sets of rules and standards to the extent of realizing a borderless global economy and a single world market on the one hand, and encapsulating certain sectors of the national and regional economies from global capitalist market forces on the other. And by "the end of history" I mean the uneasy coexistence of loosening the regulated economy and the authoritarian polity on the one hand and coping with destabilizing consequences of this loosening on the other.

In other words, what we have been witnessing in the world is characterized not simply by the victory of the United States, the victory of international liberalism, and the victory of market capitalism and liberal democracy but more importantly by the contradictions intrinsic to all these three supposed victories. That is why I say that I use the three "end of" phrases somewhat freely.

More concretely, the United States has demonstrated its military supremacy in strategic nuclear forces by cornering the Soviet Union into a series of agreements concerning stable reductions of strategic nuclear weapons, and in conventional forces by successfully waging the war against Iraq. U.S. military supremacy and the collapse of the Soviet Union have made it very clear that in the area of international security the United States is the sole military superpower to be reckoned with when it comes to deploying massive destructive forces far beyond national borders. But U.S. military supremacy has its weaknesses.

First, the sudden disappearance of the enemy, the Soviet Union, has led the U.S. public to believe that drastic reductions of U.S. military forces must be a legitimate peace dividend. U.S. military supremacy is discredited when faced with all the disintegrative and disaggregative conflicts taking place in the world along ethnic, religious, linguistic, and other lines. Second, the technological and economic foundations of U.S. military supremacy are perceived as so steadily weakening as to undermine severely whatever military supremacy the United States might have for the moment—thus the political imperatives of focusing its efforts on enhancing and solidifying its technological and economic competitiveness.[3] Furthermore, the U.S. government's efforts in pursuing competitiveness-enhancing goals do not seem to be well orchestrated. They lack correct instruments and well-thought-out implementation schemes deployed with a longer-term commitment solidly ensured by public opinion, political parties, the bureaucracy, and the business community.

Third, U.S. military supremacy itself does not seem to ensure automatically the consent of U.S. friends and allies. They perceive the somewhat close-to-desperate need for the United States to obtain their acquiescence if it is to achieve its international goals. Once the Soviet threat is gone, the solidarity of the Group of Seven countries seems to wane.[4] The Group of Seven declarations concerning economic policy coordination have been watered down considerably since the Munich summit of 1992, and its agreement to assist Russia financially has revealed more divergence among member countries in their declared commitments.

In the world economic area too, technological progress has promoted an irreversible trend to open the economy, to liberalize the economy and to compete globally. Just like the two great depressions, the one in the fourth quarter of the nineteenth century and the other in the 1930s, the stagflations related to the two oil crises of the 1970s were followed by more liberal trends in the world economy. Not only former communist countries have been moving in the direction of a market economy; a large number of developing countries have also been deregulating their tight bureaucratic protectionist mantles. Yet the internal contradictions of global economic liberalization are becoming no less pronounced.[5]

First, globalizing economic activities means that economic actors must adapt to the changing economic environments adroitly. It means that comparative advantage tends to change constantly when national barriers are lowered. It also means that technological innovation becomes more costly and must be made with more agility. Cognizance of their probable inability to adapt to changes is bound to lead economic actors to act defensively. This takes various forms. Barriers and hindrances are kept high or new ones are created to prevent global market forces from permeating the national economy; regional economic blocs are built to maximize the benefits accrued from liberalization and to minimize the costs of building walls against nonregional actors; bilateral trade deals are made to ensure sufficiently limited transactions in the form of cartelized arrangements; and modes of economic activities are subjected to bilateral or regional standardization or commonization, typically discriminating against those economic actors who may not subscribe to such a "universal package" of economic activities. Multilayerization is created in the liberalization scheme so as to give a uniformly liberal semblance to international economic agreements at the community or federal or national level and yet give autonomous power to local units such as provinces and prefectures to declare exceptions to such agreements. In other words, the globalization of economic activities prompts the opposite forces to prosper. They are called protectionism, regionalism, new regulations, subsidiarity, and cartelization.[6]

In the area of domestic societies too, technological progress has created a trend of a deregulated economy and a less authoritarian polity. This trend coincides with the three liberalizing periods of the twentieth century, the first quarter, the third quarter, and the post–Plaza Agreement (1985) fourth quarter.[7] Yet loosening economic and political forces from tight regulation and oppressive arrangements has encouraged the opposite forces to burgeon and blossom everywhere. And some of them have become intensely destabilizing forces. For instance, India has been loosening its bureaucratic economy since Rajiv Gandhi was prime minister. But economic and social deregulation often means an intensification of brutish and nasty market forces assaulting less-privileged strata and thus inviting them to strike back politically. Algeria has been trying to make a transition to democracy. Yet the increasing exposure to global market forces and the concomitant domestic economic deregulation have accentuated income inequality, thus enhancing the attractiveness of Islam, which preaches the absolute equality of everyone before Allah. The prospect of a political party based on Islamic fundamentalism taking power once a free and secret election was conducted led the military to put democratization off for the time being. These destabilizing forces have been so desegregating that the power bases of the nation-states are quite visibly eroding.

Two phenomena associated with the end of history are regional economic bloc formation and humanitarian military intervention. Geographical closeness, economic deregulation, and economic expansion have prompted the creation of de facto economic blocs. Not only formal groupings like the Asia Pacific Economic Cooperation conference but also de facto groupings such as Singapore-Batham-Johor, Hong Kong–Guangdong–ASEAN, Taiwan–Fujian–Hong Kong, Slovenia-Croatia-Austria-Germany, California-Texas-Mexico, and Kazakhstan–Turkey–Asian Development Bank have been receiving increasing attention. In tandem with the birth of these de facto economic groupings, the fledgling economic regimes of common norms and rules emerge. Some may become fully fledged economic regimes and others may not. The important thing is that they tend to defy the conventional national and regional geographical demarcations.

In a similar vein, humanitarian military intervention is getting increasing attention as it looks more feasible with the increasing acceptance of the notion of international security. But it is also more difficult because of the actors' different attitudes to the rationale and scheme of intervention. As desegregating forces are getting stronger and stronger, national sovereignty has become a thing of the past in cases such as Somalia, Yugoslavia, and Cambodia. The U.S.-UN military intervention in Somalia has evoked the notion of humanitarian military intervention because there was no request from the Somalian government for the intervention and because there was no Somalian government worthy of the name. The Yugoslavian Federation collapsed and yet no effective military intervention has been attempted so far, either by the United States, the United Nations, the West European

Union, the North Atlantic Treaty Organization, or the European Community. Cambodia has been trying to move in the direction of national unity on the basis of the Paris agreement of 1991. Accordingly, the United Nations Transitional Authority in Cambodia (UNTAC) was set up to carry out free and secret elections in Cambodia. Yet one of the three parties, the Khmer Rouge, has been taking issue with the Paris agreement and openly defied it. It did so allegedly because of UNTAC's tacit acceptance of the other parties' violation of the Paris agreement on the withdrawal of Vietnamese soldiers, arguing that some Vietnamese soldiers have remained in Cambodia disguised as Cambodians.

All these observations are made in order to give more concrete flavor to my view of the global transformation. From my explication of three types of global change, I will move on to study Pacific Asia, starting from the same set of changes.

VIGOROUS AND UNCERTAIN PACIFIC ASIA

It is my task to look into what has been taking place in Pacific Asia from the same three perspectives: the end of the Cold War, the end of geography, and the end of history. Pacific Asia, the most dynamic economic region of the world, is by definition vigorous and uncertain. Rapid economic change in Pacific Asia fosters structural transformation in noneconomic areas as well. I will examine the three areas of international security, the world economy, and domestic societies one by one.

International Security

Pacific Asia is said to be one of the regions not much affected by the end of the Cold War. The United States has been downsizing its military presence in Pacific Asia, but not as drastically as it has done in Western Europe. Russia has not reduced its military power in Pacific Asia to the same extent as in Europe. Ironically, this is largely because of the noncentral importance of Pacific Asia during the Cold War period. Pacific Asia was not the primary area for the starting and ending of the Cold War.[8] Europe played the primary role. Pacific Asia may have reinforced Cold War hostilities in the past, but not anymore. Rather, Pacific Asia, like most other non-European regions, was given a cause célèbre named the Cold War to promote locally whatever grand schemes political actors might have had. Even if this cause célèbre is gone, in other words, even if the mantle of justification is gone, local politics has remained. After all, all politics is local. Thus it is natural that Pacific Asian politics has become even more intensely local after the Cold War. Even the continuous presence of U.S. military forces in Pacific Asia and also Russia's presence may be explained nicely by this. Local politics has not given the United States or Russia any strong excuses to drastically reduce their military forces in Pacific Asia or to withdraw those forces from Pacific Asia.

Three major local factors explain why Pacific Asia has not manifested drastic changes in its international security configuration. First, aside from the bilateral agreements between the United States and its allies and between the Soviet Union and its allies, there have not been any effective, sufficiently all-encompassing, multilateral security arrangements in Pacific Asia. Without them it would be too much of an irresponsibility on the part of the United States and Russia to abandon their self-appointed roles as the guardians of the national, regional, or global interests with or without bilateral agreements. Russia has none of its erstwhile bilateral agreements with Mongolia, North Korea, China, or Vietnam. The United States abandoned its military forces in the Philippines recently but has kept such agreements with Japan and South Korea and retained cordial relations with such countries as Thailand, Taiwan, and Singapore in terms of military-related cooperative arrangements.

Second, Pacific Asia has been the most vigorous world region in terms of economic development. This vigor creates a vast range of uncertainty. Military expenditure tends to go up in tandem with economic growth, and Pacific Asia is no exception to that. Pacific Asia gives an ominous picture of vigorous military expansion. The region is now surpassing the traditionally number-one area in this regard, the Middle East.[9] Furthermore, if recent annual economic growth rates are a good indicator of military expansionary propensity, then China, Indonesia, and India may become military powers to be reckoned with in Pacific Asia—along with the United States, Russia, and Japan, all of which tend to register much lower economic growth rates of late. In addition to the steady advance of military buildup, more specific worries exist as to the possibilities of a nuclear arms race. North Korea announced in March 1993 its withdrawal from the Nonproliferation Treaty to reject the International Atomic Energy Agency's (IAEA) inspection of possible nuclear facilities in Yongbyong.[10] North and South Korea had concluded an agreement declaring their nonnuclear status in 1991, when they also agreed to facilitate peaceful exchanges between the two Koreas. North Korea's economy had been stagnating for some time already, but after the Cold War, it went downhill dramatically. Russia has ceased to supply it with petroleum. China wants business and in North Korea there is not much business. Japan has not gone in the direction of giving aid to North Korea, as the latter would like. Reacting to the U.S.–South Korea naval exercise, North Korea resorted to its rejection of the IAEA's inspection. If North Korea goes nuclear, Japan and South Korea will have a hard time not doing the same.

Third, traditional rivalries are strong in Pacific Asia. Traditional rivalries are strong almost anywhere, but the history of supranational community-building efforts is less pronounced in Pacific Asia than in Western Europe.

Certainly empire-building efforts are not lacking in the region. But there has never been an instance of one united empire covering the whole region of Pacific Asia for a considerable period of time. In Western Europe one can point to the Roman Empire and a series of efforts to revive and rebuild some sort of community, religious or political. But in Pacific Asia such conscious community-building efforts are a far more recent phenomenon. Often, people in neighboring countries are ignorant of each other's language or history; more often than not they are more aware of the language and history of colonizing patrons. The end of the Cold War has thus helped to revive some elements of traditional rivalries in Pacific Asia. So far, they have not surfaced to any considerable extent for two major reasons: the U.S. military presence has been a positive factor in mitigating such rivalries, and the prosperity of Pacific Asian economies has been long dependent on Japanese-driven dynamism and U.S. market access. Pacific Asians have not been bothered too much by traditional rivalries as long as their prosperity continued. But more recently other factors have come into the picture. U.S. market access looks increasingly questionable over the longer term. And in addition to Japanese-driven dynamism, Chinese-driven dynamism seems to be emerging on the horizon. This perception can be glimpsed in the editorial of a Singapore newspaper arguing that the nongovernmental Beijing-Taipei agreement of May 1993 has signified the emergence of the China-Taiwan-ASEAN Chinese bloc as a fourth economic superpower in addition to the three existing ones, that is, the United States, the EC, and Japan.[11] One might say that the agreement merely represents a competitive spirit among Pacific Asians. In any case, one has to be cautious not to make a premature judgement given the intensity of traditional rivalries and the durability of historical memories.

The World Economy

The end of geography seems to affect Pacific Asia more than other regions. The fact is that the Pacific Asian region is less closed and institutionalized than other regions. After all, it is in Western Europe that we find the architects of first the Rome and then the Maastricht Treaty, leading toward deeper integration of the 12 member countries. It is in North America that market liberalization in the unilateral and bilateral contexts among the three giants, that is, Canada, the United States, and Mexico, is being vigorously carried out. It is only in Pacific Asia that regional integration has not been institutionalized by formal agreements. The Asian Pacific Economic Cooperation (APEC) conference represents the most institutionalized form of economic coordination and cooperation within an area encompassing Australia, New Zealand, ASEAN, Vietnam, China–Taiwan–Hong Kong, Northeast Asia including Russia, Canada, the United States, and Mexico. But its degree of institutionalization is much lower than the European Community and the North American Free Trade Agreement (NAFTA). Of all the international institutions in Pacific Asia, the Asian Development Bank (ADB) may be one of the most powerful. Its budget is very likely to surpass that of the World Bank if Japan's initiative to increase its own and other major countries' contributions is successful. But the Asian Development Bank is not an institution designed specifically for regional integration. Both the APEC and the ADB are institutions primarily designed for facilitating economic development and cooperation in the region. Pacific Asia places utmost emphasis on market mechanisms to facilitate regional transactions.

Three major factors explain why Pacific Asia has been basically reluctant to go ahead with regional integrative institutionalization. First, it is not likely to benefit from regionalist self-enclosure. It benefits from an open trading system. It desperately needs open access to the big markets of North America and Western Europe. Given the relatively poor endowment of food and energy resources in relation to the large demographic size and rapid speed of industrialization, it needs to manufacture and export to the rest of the world. This picture applies not only to such obvious countries as Japan and South Korea but also to such countries as China and Indonesia. Even if the other two economic regions resort to regionalist and protectionist solutions, Pacific Asia cannot afford to resort to any institutionalized form of regionalism and protectionism. That is widely perceived in the region to be suicidal.

Second, Pacific Asia is a world of corporate networks that often involve governments. In many cases these networks effectively prevent foreign or extraregional actors from entering into markets. Pacific Asia is not alone in having corporate networks and government-corporate alliances. Continental Western Europe is another region known for these associations. Names and forms may differ, but the basic fact is that networking matters both in Pacific Asia and in Western Europe. You may call it keiretsu, guanxi, cartel, corporatism, or whatever. Especially noteworthy here are Japanese government-business relations beyond borders and Chinese business networks across borders. Japanese government-business relations, nurtured since the times of the industrialization drives of the 1930s through the 1960s, are important in linking business firms, banks, and government agencies in an organic fashion through financial market and other kinds of bureaucratic regulations and keiretsu and other kinds of business practices.[12] Although much of the keiretsu relationship melted away in the wake of the collapse of the "bubbled" economy in the early 1990s and a bulk of bureaucratic regulations were liberalized in the 1980s, close government-business relations in such areas as official development assistance, foreign direct investment, and foreign trade (in a descending order of importance), do remain solid. That is why Japanese-driven dynamism in Pacific Asia is called keiretsu practiced abroad. The causal relationship is roughly as follows: Japanese official development assistance to other countries relies very much on Japanese business firms' (especially trading corporations') assistance to the Japanese government in terms of identifying potential projects and executing feasibility studies with partners in those countries. Then Japanese business firms are given some preferential treatment by the recipient country's government in the form of procurements of construction contracts and exports of products and parts. Since Japanese official development assistance traditionally places emphasis on developing and enhancing industrial infrastructure in recipient countries and on the manufacturing capacities of recipients, Japanese construction, telecommunications, transportation, and manufacturing firms benefit enormously. Japanese exports of products and parts increase accordingly. In tandem with the gradual improvement of the business climate in Japan, helped in part by official development assistance, Japanese direct investment increases. That normally further increases Japanese export of capital goods to the recipients because local factories tend to import capital goods from Japan. The bulk of the products manufactured by Japanese–recipient country firms in Pacific Asia goes to the U.S. market.

The other, increasingly important network is that of the Chinese throughout Pacific Asia.[13] The higher-than-average economic growth-rate pattern of China–Taiwan–Hong Kong has given extraordinary impetus to the power of Chinese business networks across borders. The strength of Chinese business networks is found in the transnational nature of Chinese family and geographical networks. Thus they work across borders effectively. When Japanese business firms trade and invest in Southeast Asia or China or Vietnam, the key, or liaison, local firms are headed by Chinese. Most foreign investors in China are Chinese from Taiwan, Hong Kong, Singapore, Thailand, Malaysia, the Philippines or the United States. Another possibly important attribute of Chinese business networks is their relatively small size. Because they tend to be based on family and ancestorial and linguistic lines, this is somewhat inevitable. Comparing Taiwanese and South Korean firms, one notices immediately that Taiwanese business firms are much smaller. South Korean business firms are organized in gigantic "chaebol" groupings. Many Taiwanese firms are smaller because they grew from the Kuomintang government's piecemeal privatization program of selling companies cheaply to Kuomintang loyalists. Many South Korean chaebol groupings grew from the ashes of the Korean War and became fat through the close relationship with the government in the form of preferential allocation of foreign reserves.[14] The reason Chinese-style smaller business firms may be increasingly stronger is that in an era of intermittently strenuous structural adjustments, and of increasingly high costs of technological innovation, small can be beautiful. Small firms can be more adroit and agile in adapting to changing market conditions. That is why many business conglomerates of the United States, Germany, Japan, and South Korea, for instance, have been suffering more severely from maladjustments.[15]

Another important factor to be reckoned with is the growing manifestation of the U.S. government corporate-alliance strategy applied to Pacific Asia, as well as to the rest of the world. The strategy is to solidify the relationship between government and business in relation to achieving market liberalization and trade agreements with Pacific Asian countries.[16] Especially in Pacific Asia, but also in Western Europe, local governments and local private firms cooperate closely. The proponents of this strategy ask, Why should the Americans not do similarly? The prescription has three components. One is the close teamwork between the government and private firms. The second is the bottom-up strategy. In other words, instead of working from the top down, as is the case with the GATT-type trading negotiations, the strategy is to work from below and bilaterally (taking advantage of U.S. hegemony in most bilateral contexts). The third component of this strategy is to effect a deeper version of the GATT-type, shallow-integration strategy, which conceives of shaping economic rules as a universal package, that is, as formulating not just trading rules but also domestic economic rules and structures.[17] Since the United States has been experiencing trade deficits vis-à-vis many Pacific Asian countries, this strategy has increasing appeal to the U.S. government. The aggressive U.S. trade and liberalization negotiations vis-à-vis Pacific Asian countries has created somewhat negative feelings toward the United States in the Pacific Asian region.

It is clear that the Pacific Asian economies are not moving toward forming an exclusive economic club and that only a few efforts to form some regionally specific economic institutionalization are under way. The first is the universalist, shallow-integration strategy of the GATT and the APEC, encompassing not only Pacific Asia but also North America and Oceania and beyond. Japan and Australia, among others, are the most ardent supporters of this line of free-trade regime. The second is the East Asian Economic Council strategy, whereby Pacific Asian countries exert influence vis-à-vis the United States in their trade and economic negotiations as a bloc. Malaysia is the initiator of this strategy. Although more weighty Pacific Asian countries such as Japan and Indonesia played down this strategy somewhat in the early 1990s, they share Malaysian sentiments about the United States and seem to be paying renewed attention to this strategy. The third is the NAFTA strategy applied to Pacific Asia and Oceania as well. This means bilateral negotiations whereby the United States and some smaller Pacific Asian countries such as Singapore, Taiwan, Australia, and South Korea—as well as the colony of Hong Kong—conclude agreements like the U.S.-Mexico and U.S.-Canada free-trade agreements. The focus of this strategy is to push market liberalization and accelerate deeper integration. One cannot identify the Japanese, Chinese, or U.S. strategies with any single one of these initiatives. Japanese, Chinese, and Americans all give priority to market forces. But although the Japanese may like the GATT and APEC styles more than the NAFTA style, the Chinese may move to form a fourth pillar of a greater Chinese economy in harmony with the APEC and GATT frameworks. Americans may like the NAFTA style more than the APEC style, not to mention the GATT style.

Despite what has been said about regionalism and different strategies in Pacific Asia, the key fact about the region remains that it is and will be the most dynamic area of economic development in the world for some time to come, especially when China, Vietnam, Indonesia, Russia, the Central Asian republics, and even India come to prosper together. "The end of geography" is most appropriate when applied to Pacific Asia.[18]

Domestic Societies

Domestic societies are relatively stable in Pacific Asia. Despite the disappearance of communism in Europe, it lives on in Pacific Asia: in China, Vietnam, and North Korea. Despite rapid economic change, politics has been relatively stable in the region. Tiananmen Square, Bangkok, and East Timor, for instance, have not triggered great transformations, although they have raised local consciousness about the importance of human rights and democratic participation.

Two major factors are noteworthy in explaining this relative stability. Most important, most people in the region perceive steady economic growth as having had ameliorating effects on whatever negative consequences economic and social dislocations may have had. When the economy grows, employment possibilities grow and so does the overall income level. This simple fact enables many to adapt to structural adjustments relatively calmly. Yet if we look more closely, many are exposed to hardships during the initial phases of industrialization. Furthermore, the often widening income gap during such phases creates discontent among those with a relatively stagnant income level. In some cases the egalitarian appeal of certain religious beliefs such as Islam can create political turmoil. But in most parts of Pacific Asia such potentially destabilizing elements tend to be played down by the lure of growth and opportunities. Second, the transition from authoritarian to democratic politics seems to be conducted step by step, not drastically, in most parts of Pacific Asia. In many cases the system whereby regulated economics and authoritarian politics were conducted retains some of its old essential elements. By "essential elements" I mean the continued solid power position of internal security apparatuses and macroeconomic management institutions. Needless to say, internal security apparatuses have to become more conscious of the need to adapt to liberal politics and democratic rules of conduct. In many cases the apparatuses adopt more low-key roles while continuing to perform effective monitoring functions. Macroeconomic management institutions are important in Pacific Asia for a number of reasons. First, governments are devoted to running the economies properly. They are keenly aware of the simple fact that steady economic growth tends to ensure political stability even if authoritarian politics is practiced. Second, Pacific Asia desperately needs an international (i.e., global) free-trade regime for continued prosperity. Governments are constantly monitoring economic changes throughout the world in order to spot economic sectors in need of structural adjustments. Third, Pacific Asia being a mosaic of networks, governments are intensely involved in economic activities through a substantial range of discretionary power and a large number of bureaucratic regulations.

The human rights and market liberalization issues are central to these important policies. Pacific Asia is peculiarly vulnerable to human rights issues because of its tenacious belief in putting the collective interest first and the individual interest second and putting economic development first and social redistribution second.[19] The United States is a society where the human rights issue is also important domestically. It is only natural that many Americans stress human rights internationally also. They disclose severe violations of human rights in Pacific Asia. Yet many Pacific Asians are weary of U.S. preachings on human rights, recalling what Pacific Asians see as the U.S. government's gross infringements on human rights in such cases as Rodney King in Los Angeles and David Koresh in Waco, Texas. Possibly more important, the enormity of the poverty and crime problems in the United States does not encourage Pacific Asians to place too much trust in U.S. preachings. Here is an irony: While Americans preach human rights both at home and abroad, Pacific Asians tend to take American criticisms of their violations of human rights as politically motivated and possibly even racist statements that aim to undermine their political and social stability.[20]

Market liberalization issues also touch the nerves of many Pacific Asians. The reason is that Pacific Asia loves free trade externally but hates interference into internal affairs. It regards money, finance, tax, and tariffs as matters of sovereignty. That is why the doctrines of neoclassical economics are well represented at academic and policy levels in most of Pacific Asia, and why what John Maynard Keynes would call the outdated doctrines of relatively obscure economists prevail in practicing economic management. Thus when the U.S. government attempts to liberalize markets in Pacific Asia, uproar and despair are expressed. The opposition to financial market liberalization has been especially strong. In Japan, for instance, the exceptionally powerful Ministry of Finance resists any suggestions. The U.S. government and many Japanese securities houses and nonbanks have been unable to persuade it to liberalize the financial market. The Japanese Liberal Democratic Party, the governing party between 1955 and 1993, tried in vain to strip the Ministry of Finance of all its monetary functions, leaving only the fiscal policy functions intact. The Ministry of Home Affairs wants to take away more government revenues from the Ministry of Finance's jurisdiction by federal-

izing the political system and giving far more taxing power to the
prefectorial governments (these are under the jurisdiction of the Ministry of
Home Affairs). So far the prospects for its success are not very bright, despite
the new coalition government's stress on decentralization.

LESSONS FOR INTERNATIONAL RELATIONS

With the metaphors of the end of the Cold War, of geography, and of history
used fairly freely to characterize how the world has changed and how Pacific
Asia has been evolving during the time of a great transition of the late twentieth century, I have now come to the point of reflecting on these changes. A
number of theoretical traditions exist to describe and explain them. They include a long list: structural realism, liberal institutionalism, functionalism,
world systems analysis; there is a natural law theory, a realist theory, a fide-
ist (a defender of the faith) theory, a rationalist theory, a historicist theory,
and so on. Some of them have been scrutinized elsewhere already, so severely
as to give many of them a death sentence.[21] Since all these and other theories
have not been employed in Pacific Asia as often and intensely as in North
America or Western Europe, the purpose here is to suggest which issues and
approaches might be fruitfully emphasized and elaborated. The following
three key questions should be asked.

   1. How can a security regime be constructed in a region where there has
      been no strong tradition of multilateral security arrangements and
      where there have been intense traditional rivalries?
   2. How can a free-trade regime receive a revitalizing initiative from an
      area where there has been a strong developmental state mind-set and
      institutions and where deeper global economic integration is looked
      upon with suspicion?
   3. How can liberal and democratic institutions be solidified in a region
      where collective welfare is placed before individual welfare and where
      economic development is put before political freedom?

   These key questions are posed as if they were policy questions. But asking
them helps us to think more deeply about what kinds of approaches should
be further developed in international relations theory. The trio of complexity, rapidity, and uncertainty in the evolution of Pacific Asia has defied the
application of much of international relations theory in the recent past. Ironically, this might help international relations theory to emerge from Pacific
Asia even if it might not reach the level of generality and abstraction of some
of the North American international relations theories.
   To answer the first question, one must look into how some recent security
arrangements have been developed in Pacific Asia. One might look into the

United Nations Transitional Authority in Cambodia and how it came into being on the basis of the Paris peace accord. One might also look into the International Atomic Energy Agency's nuclear inspection in North Korea on the basis of the Nonproliferation Treaty. Another relevant item is that police coordination to reduce crimes and drugs across borders and other cooperation networks are developing from a very low level. And one cannot overemphasize that the United States Armed Forces in Asia and the Pacific has been playing the role of a linchpin, even without a multilaterally organized, unified command and force structure. More recently, the U.S. armed forces tried to get regular consultation and active cooperative arrangements with China and India started, in addition to those they already have with traditional friends (Japan, South Korea, Thailand, and Singapore). Given the pragmatic and adaptive nature of Pacific Asian arrangements in the past, the approach suggested here stresses a rich and deep description of how multilateral cooperative institutions developed based on the vague notion of generalized reciprocity.[22]

To answer the second question, one must look into how developmental state mind-sets and institutions have coexisted with a free-trade regime and realize that market liberalization is seen in Pacific Asia both as the positive reflection of growing interdependence and as a negative force that undermines the basis of a developmental state. One must also examine Pacific Asian policymakers' attitudes toward deeper interaction, seen both as the positive force of dismantling developmental states and their firms, possibly enabling them to adapt to the end of geography much more smoothly, and as a negative force eroding the distinctively national features of many economic and political practices.[23] Data on Japan, the front-runner in Pacific Asia both in terms of the dismantling of the developmental state and in terms of deeper integration with the world economy, might provide the answers to these questions.

To answer the third question, one must look into how Pacific Asia's emphasis on developmentalism and industrialism has promoted the view that the collective interest is above individual interest and that economic development should be given the highest priority, and how Pacific Asia might be able to reverse these priorities in favor of postdevelopmental, postindustrial, and postmodern values. Again, data on Japan, the front-runner in Pacific Asia in terms of economic development and democratization, might provide the answers. The optimist would say that the generally bright prospect for steady economic development in the region means that those mind-sets and institutions associated with certain stages of economic development stand to be weakened considerably. The pessimist would say that the prospect for Pacific Asia's economic success will prolong the life of those mind-sets and institutions, which will be further reinforced by collectivist cultural traditions.[24]

In addition to considering this set of three new research areas, we might ask another three research questions specifically addressed to Japan's role in security, development, and democracy vis-à-vis other countries in Pacific Asia and vis-à-vis the rest of the world, given the major present and future importance of Japan in regional and global development.

Japan's regional security role is expected to grow steadily to cope with the uncertain vigor of Pacific Asia and the rest of the world. The sophistication of technology in many civilian areas enables Japan to acquire and apply many high-tech items for military purpose. Despite 1993's lowest level of defense spending in relation to total government expenditure since 1960, two areas are given priority: First, the conventional area-defense capability has been armed with Air Warning and Air Command System–equipped aircraft and various missile defense systems. These weapons have been purchased from the United States in response to the growing force-projection capability of North Korea in recent years. Second, the capability to undertake transportation of forces has been enhanced in light of the need to send personnel and extend logistic support to UN peacekeeping and other kinds of operations abroad, most recently in Cambodia and Mozambique. They include medium-sized transport ships and transport aircraft. None of them can be characterized as "normal" aircraft carriers or "normal" transport aircraft. They do enable the Japanese Self-Defense Forces to operate independently abroad, albeit on a relatively small scale.

Japan's growth prospect for the twenty-first century is not greater than that of other Pacific Asian countries such as China, Vietnam, and Indonesia. Yet it will probably register a somewhat higher growth rate than most Northern Hemisphere countries in North America and Western Europe, pulling up the region and the rest of the world (especially North America) to a more vigorous level of economic activities. As a major dynamo in the region and the world, Japan has the prospect of a continued respectable growth for the twenty-first century; Japan will not turn into a minor actor in the region. In other words, the late-comer economic boomers—China, Vietnam, and Indonesia, along with India, Russia, and the Central Asian republics—are likely to occupy a remarkably strong regional position. But they will not play a predominant economic position in Pacific Asia, or in the rest of the world. Conversely, the prospect of Japan or the United States dominating the region or the rest of the world seems less likely. At the same time, the technology level and all the associated resources of the United States and Japan seem to enable them to play an important role both in Pacific Asia and in other regions toward the next century.

Japan's peculiar role of being the first non-Western country to achieve an advanced industrialized and democratic status seems to place the country in a unique position to advance democracy in Pacific Asia and the rest of the world, in particular the non-Western world. Many Japanese leaders seem to be content with the role of go-between, bridging the gap between the United States and the rest of Pacific Asia in quietly encouraging the latter toward becoming more democratic.

But there are diverging attitudes in Japan. One extreme is to react very critically against the U.S. call for human rights in Asia. Some Japanese representatives at the 1993 Bangkok conference on human rights did exactly that. The other extreme is to ally completely with human rights activists in the United States, accusing most Pacific Asian governments of shortcomings in respecting human rights. The picture is complex, as the former reaction is not necessarily tied in with the political right-wingers (Asianists), and the latter is not necessarily expressed by the political left-wingers (Westernizers).

In addition to this complex ambivalence, the idea of using official development assistance as an instrument to guide often blatantly authoritarian developing countries to more democracy and prosperity on the basis of the Japanese economic development model has been popular for some years in Japan. Whether and how Japan might be able to do so in concrete situations remains to be spelled out.

CONCLUSION: UNEVEN GLOBALIZATION AND THE END OF COLD WAR IN PACIFIC ASIA

Rather than proceeding from the nature of global change through its distinctively regional features and flavors to the development of new theories, this chapter has come to an end at the second stage. Instead of formulating new theory, I have proposed new sets of research questions that could be profitably pursued. That is perhaps inevitable because where there is no merciless destruction, there can be no earthshaking creation. In Pacific Asia there has been no merciless destruction of pre–Cold War structures and actors.

Of the two major independent variables, uneven globalization and the end of the Cold War—and their effects on the three areas of security, development, and society—globalization, which has been unfolding at a steady pace in Pacific Asia, seems to be far more important than the end of the Cold War. After all, the former is a *long durée* variable and the latter is *événementielle*. More important, communism is alive in China, North Korea, and Vietnam, and the U.S. armed forces are not planning as drastic a reduction of forces in Pacific Asia as we have seen in Europe. Even if one can argue that peaceful evolution is taking place in all three communist countries due to globalization and liberalization of economic activities, the end of communist dictatorship has yet to come. Furthermore, even if one may argue that the U.S. armed forces are bound to leave in the longer term, their regional security role has been enhanced in the short term due to the prospect of increasing competition and growing uncertainty.

It appears that a model of Pacific Asia circa 2000 looks as follows in the three areas of security, development, and politics: In security, there are concerns such as China's new emergence as a military power on solid economic feet, North Korea's nuclear possibility, and Japan's emergence as a high-tech military power active in UN peacekeeping and other kinds of operations. Such concerns are pulling the United States in the direction of staying in the region. The reasoning is, if you cannot beat the Pacific Asians in terms of economic competitiveness, then join them, anchoring them to the United States. In development, the globalization of Pacific Asia is proceeding based on the vigorous economic growth prospect and the aggressive thirst for global market access. The institutionalization of regionalism remains a soft formula, based on competing versions of loosely knit networks. In politics, liberalization and democratization proceed underneath the facade of continuing authoritarian legacies in such countries as Indonesia, Malaysia, Singapore, and, possibly, China. Given the robust nature of regional economic development and self-confident governing, evolutionary change seems more likely in politics, even though Pacific Asia might appear as less liberal than some other regions in the transitionary period.

Needless to say, if the vigorous prospect for regional economic development is jeopardized by global protectionism and regional self-enclosure as well as by domestic political destabilization and acute international insecurity, a different model might emerge: In security, a warring period starts with the United States unable to play a balancing role effectively. In development, global protectionism and regional self-enclosure lead Pacific Asia to adopt a more institutionalized regional economy based on various types of networks. And in democracy, Western protectionism and regional self-enclosure breed the legitimization of various Pacific Asian paths of development and democracy, with less liberal elements remaining strong.

In conclusion, more continuity and more stability amidst breathtaking change dominate the scene. It is not *plus ca change, plus c'est la meme chose.* Rather, "change takes place under the facade of continuity," seems to better capture the dialectics of Pacific Asia.

The Challenge of Globalization and Individualization: A View from Europe

MICHAEL ZÜRN

Europe is arguably the one region in the world that has changed the most since the mid-1980s. But what has changed and why? Most of the change in Europe that has occurred since 1989 can be understood as a fundamental turbulence regarding the level and scope of political regulation. In Eastern Europe, centralized units of political decisionmaking are seriously challenged, and many newly established smaller units strive for participation in international institutions. In Western Europe, a powerful movement toward more political integration faces a similarly powerful nationalism even in those countries that are strongly integrated into the European Community. States such as Spain, Italy, and Great Britain are challenged by secessionist movements. I will argue that this turbulence is due to the dynamics of globalization and individualization. Both processes generate social change that continuously challenges the same competitive international system that compelled states to unleash these forces in the first place. Although this by no means is a historically new process, in Europe a new phase in this development began in the late 1980s. A development resembling the "great transformation" that disturbed Western Europe 100 years ago seems to be under way.[1] Whereas during the second half of the nineteenth century, the great transformation consisted of a removal of political regulations on the local level and their reconstitution on the national level, currently, uneven denationalization undermines national political arrangements.

WHAT IS CHANGING?

To begin with, there are different notions of what Europe is. Some refer to Europe as the European Community or even only to its core area, that is, the

138

Europe

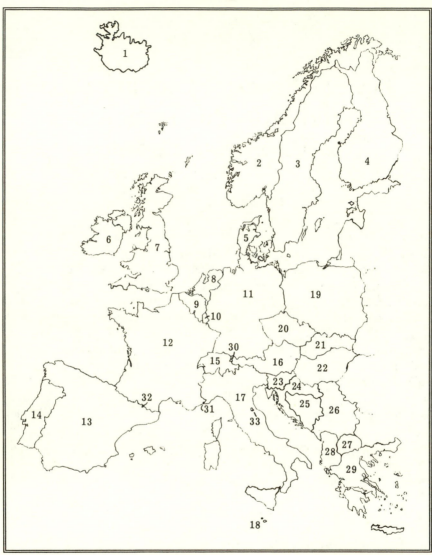

1. Iceland	12. France	23. Slovenia
2. Norway	13. Spain	24. Croatia
3. Sweden	14. Portugal	25. Bosnia and Herzegovina
4. Finland	15. Switzerland	26. Fed. Rep. of Yugoslavia
5. Denmark	16. Austria	27. F.Y.R. of Macedonia
6. Ireland	17. Italy	28. Albania
7. The United Kingdom	18. Malta	29. Greece
8. The Netherlands	19. Poland	30. Liechtenstein
9. Belgium	20. Czech Republic	31. Monaco
10. Luxembourg	21. Slovak Republic	32. Andorra
11. Germany	22. Hungary	33. San Marino

six countries that signed the Rome Treaties in 1957. Others have a more encompassing understanding and point to the so-called CSCE (Conference on Security and Cooperation in Europe) area, which includes not only all the former Soviet republics but also the United States and Canada. In this chapter, "Europe" refers to a region comprising the European Economic Area (the EC countries plus the former EFTA [European Free Trade Association] countries) and those countries of Eastern Europe that have the best chances of integrating into this region, that is, Poland, Hungary, the former Czechoslovakia, and parts of former Yugoslavia.

This Europe has witnessed dramatic and perplexing events and developments since 1989. The fall of the Berlin Wall brought down the other physical barriers between the East and the West. At the same time, democratization made dramatic progress in most East European countries. Yet racism, secessionism, and nationalism appear to have grown since then; thus the political systems of EC core countries such as Italy, Germany, France, and Belgium face considerable instability. The Single European Act and the Maastricht Treaty temporarily set aside any doubts about the future of the EC. Yet the integration project for Western Europe was soon weakened due to a crisis in the European Monetary System and domestic resistance, especially in Great Britain and Denmark. The CSCE Charter of Paris and the democratization of Eastern Europe even fed hopes for "eternal peace" in Europe in its most encompassing definition, hopes that were, however, quickly belied by the balkanization of Eastern Europe.

Obviously, these events and developments do not allow for any straightforward interpretation about the direction of change and thus are not easily grasped as one inseparable set of changes. Yet any casuistic account of the different changes neglects interrelationships among them. Therefore, I suggest conceptualizing the current change in Europe as consisting of two simultaneous *movements*—one toward political integration and one toward political fragmentation. *Political integration* refers to the extension of political regulations governing societal transactions and the interaction of political units (governance). It describes a process of coordination or integration of previously uncoordinated or even competing policies, most often accompanied by a sense of community defined as "agreement on at least one point: that common social problems must and can be resolved by processes of 'peaceful change.'"[2] Political integration takes place when the density of international and transnational institutions increases in a given issue area. By contrast, *political fragmentation* refers to the reduction of the scope of political regulations. It describes a process of dissolution of previously harmonized or integrated policies, sometimes but not always accompanied by the willingness to employ force as a means to prevail in conflicts. Political fragmentation is indicated by a reduced density of international and transnational institutions in a given issue area.

WHAT HAS CAUSED THE CHANGES?

Most explanations of change in Europe refer at some point to the concept "the end of the Cold War." For some, the end of the Cold War is the dependent variable in the study of change in European politics, for others, the major explanatory variable.[3] However, both predominant conceptualizations fail to see the end of the Cold War as part of a broader turbulence that not only has affected the former socialist countries but continues to affect European and world politics as a whole.[4] Hence both conceptualizations, the one considering all changes as part and parcel of the end of Cold War and the one seeing the changes as part of the Cold War's consequences, are not capable of taking into account the progress in European integration between 1986 and 1991. Moreover, both are bound to regard the balkanization of Eastern Europe as almost a necessary consequence of the end of authoritarian rule. To the contrary, the end of the Cold War is considered here as one instance of change (among others) that can be categorized as a case of movement toward political integration in Europe. To be sure, the end of the Cold War was followed by many instances of political fragmentation, thus pointing to the possibility of specific Cold War consequences that are at least partially independent of the forces that produced the end of the Cold War in the first place. In this sense, the end of the Cold War represents an "intervening variable" rather than merely a dependent or an independent variable in the study of turbulence in European politics.

The simultaneous movements of political integration and political fragmentation raise two questions. First, when did the double movement originate? Current developments can be seen as an acceleration of long-term trends. By the end of the nineteenth century only 34 independent political units existed worldwide. Since then, empires have fallen apart and decolonization has rapidly increased the number of independent political units. Furthermore, due to secession movements in all areas of the world, the number of independent states has increased: In 1994, the United Nations had 184 member states. Simultaneously, however, international institutions have, except for the interwar period, grown in number. For example, in 1850, there were exactly 4 international governmental organizations, the number of which had grown to 26 by the end of the century. In 1994, there were about 300. In other words, the double movement of political integration and fragmentation had begun already in the second half of the nineteenth century and has been accelerating ever since the mid-1970s.

Second, what kind of underlying forces prevailed in the latter half of the nineteenth century and through which causal mechanisms are the underlying forces linked with political integration and fragmentation? I argue that the simultaneous occurrence of integration and fragmentation *in governance* can best be understood as the consequence of two accelerating developments that represent *social change*. These developments generate forces favoring both political integration and political fragmentation. The first one can be called *globalization* and refers to the extension of societal transactions from the local to the national and from the regional to the global level. Any broadening of the borders of these transactions—"the place where there is some critical reduction in the frequency of a certain type of transaction"[5]—signifies globalization. The flow of trade and foreign investment, global ecological interdependence, and the distribution of weapons of mass destruction can be seen as indicators for globalization. Globalization currently increases interdependence among societies, thus providing the necessary condition for international institution-building (political integration); it also creates enormous political complexity and many "modernization losers," both of which are the seeds of political fragmentation. The second social development can be called *individualization*. It refers to the widening and deepening of the principle of individual self-determination accompanied by a dissolution of traditional alignments and the tendency to evaluate things on the basis of individual cost-benefit calculations.[6] Change in the structure of the average family may well be a good indicator for this social process.[7] Although individualization contributes to the democratization of societies, thus increasing the number of constitutional democracies and stabilizing existing democracies, it also often leads to the creation of new social cleavages and thus destabilization. Both, the process of globalization and the process of individualization, accelerated during the second half of the nineteenth century as well as from the mid-1970s on and thus may well account for the double movement of political fragmentation and integration.

WHAT ARE THE THEORETICAL CONSEQUENCES OF THE CHANGES?

Explaining integration and fragmentation in governance with the social processes of globalization and individualization implies a distinction between society and governance on the international level that parallels the society-state distinction on the national level. According to the logic of the society-state distinction, the state does not represent a "territorial association of people" but a "specific set of administrative and coercive institutions" that is influenced by and in turn influences societal demands.[8] Similarly, change in international governance need not necessarily be the result of interactions between states. It can also be caused by change in transnational social constellations, and in turn, transnational social constellations may be shaped by international governance. If globalization and individualization indeed need to be taken into account when explaining the current change in world politics, then the most fundamental consequence of theorizing about world poli-

TABLE 8.1   Principles of Governance and Waves of Social Change

Century	Principles of Governance	Waves of Social Change	Outcome
17th–19th	Territorial state—mercantilism		Stability: coinciding capability of and demand for governance
Second Half 19th		Globalization and individualization	
Late 19th/Early 20th	Nation-state—popular nationalism		Turbulence: demand for governance outstrips supply
Second Half 20th	Nation-state + international institutions—embedded liberalism		Stability: coinciding capability of and demand for governance
Late 20th		Globalization and individualization	
Late 20th/Early 21st	Ineffective nation-state + international institutions—uneven denationalization		Turbulence: demand for governance outstrips supply
?	?		?

tics runs as follows: The study of social change must supplement the study of international politics to understand change in world politics.

Table 8.1 is a periodization sketch of modern history based on this postulate. It shows the relationships between principles of governance, waves of social change (globalization and individualization), and the degree to which governance of societal transactions is provided. It suggests that currently, as in the late nineteenth century, waves of social change undermine existing governing arrangements and provide the dynamics for turbulence. The model summarizes the correlational argument and provides the organizing scheme of this chapter.[9]

Globalization and individualization were originally put into place by a competitive state system in which external power considerations dominated political choices. Although this system already carried its seeds for transformation, it proved stable for more than two centuries (see the section on the rise of the territorial state and mercantilism). The section on the great transformation and popular nationalism shows that the first wave of globalization and individualization brought with it the rise of popular nationalism in the nineteenth century. As a result, domestic considerations increasingly influenced international politics and caused turbulence that led to the great transformation. The section on the rise of international institutions and embedded liberalism argues that postwar international institutions that are based on the principle of "embedded liberalism" grew out of the ensuing interplay between domestic and international interests and allowed for a short period of stability. These international institutions shaped states' practices so that short-term interests had less influence on the choice of policies than before. In the section on the loss of national effectiveness, I argue that embedded liberalism, despite leaving room for national policies and peculiarities, nourished a further acceleration of globalization and individualization, leading to what I call uneven denationalization. Uneven denationalization carries the potential for another great transformation, challenging the most fundamental principle of governance in the modern state system: the sovereign nation-state as the predominant unit of decisionmaking. Against the background of the historical sketch, I outline, in the section on causes and consequences of uneven denationalization, a model of the causal mechanisms through which social changes shape the turbulence in world politics; hereby we may speculate about the consequences of uneven denationalization. Finally, I offer some reflections about the consequences for theorizing in international politics.

THE RISE OF THE TERRITORIAL STATE AND MERCANTILISM

During the twelfth and thirteenth centuries, the process of fragmentation that emerged from the fall of the Roman Empire came to an end. At this time, a fatal competition between differently organized political units set in and military battles intensified. While these wars further increased the suffering of the rural population, military occupation paid off for the successful lords.[10] Some of them prevailed in certain areas and built the foundations of the territorial state by disarming competing princes and magnates.[11] There has thus been an intimate relationship between wars, the necessity for extracting the means of war, and the establishment of an administrative apparatus for extraction.[12] The warriors and lords of the thirteenth century were spontaneous racketeers, and the territorial state that emerged between the sixteenth and the eighteenth centuries had a somewhat different character. In a system characterized by competition, war, and conquest, a growing administrative apparatus gathered resources for the provision of security against military threats from similar but external units.

The Westphalian Peace formalized a state system that comes close to Hobbes's view of anarchy, defined by the absence of a central authority *and* the absence of governing institutions. Freedom of action characterized the policies of the European powers, since no remaining concept of public law effectively circumscribed the behavior of states after the medieval idea of *res publica Christiana* had dissolved. This anarchy often culminated in diplomatic treachery. War coalitions were formed with little regard to tradition, religion, or dynastic marriage. Except for the united provinces, every European state fought both with and against the French during the reign of Louis XIV.[13]

Facing this predicament, the rulers realized that they needed a strong and autonomous economy to defend and expand their position. The fierce competition created incentives for the development of technologies and for political institutions that increased economic power. It was the age of Colbert's mercantilism. Louis XIV's minister employed policies to stimulate the French economy, yet in doing so, his primary goal was not to improve the standard of living of the French population. He aimed at accumulating resources to finance wars and maintain a large standing army. The modern state was consolidated and organized internally to increase its power externally.[14] Whereas the competition between states was almost unrestrained, mercantilism proved to be stable from the early seventeenth century until well into the nineteenth century, with the great revolutions in France and America as forerunners of coming turbulence.

THE GREAT TRANSFORMATION AND
POPULAR NATIONALISM

Until the consolidation of the modern state system, the activities of monarchs and princes were more or less restricted to matters of warfare. They waged wars to eliminate external rivals, protected the population against tribute-takers from outside, and extracted the means for warfare from the population of the territory they controlled. In addition, the monarchs and princes extended the monopoly of force by eliminating internal rivals. The size of these newly emerging states was often much larger than required for the effective political regulation of societal transactions. The borders of the territorial state were more or less shaped by military calculation and thus sometimes encompassed large areas. The borders of societal and economic transactions (the lines beyond which one can observe a critical reduction in the frequency of those transactions) defined much smaller areas, mostly on the local level.[15]

To be sure, because of competition, states developed additional activities over time: They distributed and guaranteed property rights, they adjudicated social conflicts, and finally they shouldered functions in the sphere of production. The territorial state thus fostered the "nationalization" of markets. Yet the economic change met growing resistance. Using all the means at their disposal, local authorities defended the principle of a noncompetitive local trade and an equally noncompetitive long-distance trade carried on from town to town. Hence, for some time to come, many political regulations remained on the local level: "The relations of master, journeyman, and apprentice; the terms of the craft; the number of apprentices; the wages of the worker were all regulated by the customary rule of the guild of the town. What the mercantile system did was merely to unify these conditions either through statute as in England or through the 'nationalization' of the guilds as in France."[16] However, the circumstances changed dramatically with the industrial revolution. It was at this point that the mercantilist equilibrium was undermined by social change and moved into a turbulent phase.

Globalization

The expansion of societal exchanges and transactions first led to deregulation, that is, a reduction of local regulations. The rise of competitive capitalism did not happen spontaneously; it required a state determined to create an integrated, formally free labor and commodity market on the national level. "Laissez-faire was planned."[17] This process is best illustrated by what took place in England. In 1795, a pauper law was introduced (in Speenhamland) that granted subsidies in aid of wages in accordance with the price of bread so that a minimum income was guaranteed to the poor independent of their earnings. To be sure, most of the poor in Europe still were subject to the whims of their landlords and had hardly any rights. Yet unemployment was much less consequential than in a free labor market. People who lost their employment did not necessarily have to move to a place where it was available. Only in 1834 did the capitalist employers in England get their way with the introduction of a Poor Law Amendment that created a national labor market and left the remaining small subsidy payments to the hopelessly overburdened parishes.

Not until the 1870s were the workers capable of organizing themselves to demand protection either by a strong workers union (as in England) or by the reintroduction of welfare payments from the state (as in continental Europe). By 1914, social insurance and legal protection for trade unions were introduced in Great Britain, France, and Germany. During the 1920s, even unemployment insurance and the eight-hour day (to be abandoned during war preparations thereafter) were established in these countries. Active state policies to ease economic downswings or to protect the environment were not established until the 1930s. In sum, the state-induced extension of the scope of economic exchanges and transactions first led to a deregulation of societal transactions and only subsequently to political regulations that restored protection of the poor (redistribution) and the provision of public goods on the national level.

What were the consequences of the extension of societal transactions? The development of a national market economy and the industrial revolution produced unknown wealth. However, blatant social inequalities and the pauperization of considerable segments emerged to the extent that national political regulation lagged behind social nationalization. Although the growth of the intervention state in Europe alleviated the worst of these inequalities in a later period, it also established bureaucracies governing the local habits and creating the perception of an aloof power center. For the people, especially for the lower-middle classes, these complexities and uncertainties gave rise to feelings of being overwhelmed when faced with modernity. Therefore, the extension of societal and economic transactions not only laid the ground for the nationalization of regulations but provoked strong and disturbing resistance pointing toward fragmentation.

Individualization

The eventual establishment of national markets resulted in a shift from mercantilism to popular economic nationalism, which was paralleled by a political shift from absolutism to democracy—a form of political organization that emphasizes individual self-determination as a source of political legitimacy. The rise of the national market economy required enough people with a basic education, so that communication could take place across regions and so that individual workers could be replaced. Therefore, a demand for a centralized national education complementing the local acculturation arose. The provision of national cultures was facilitated by new forms of communication (journals and later newspapers). As a result, national languages and identities developed.[18]

Of course, the content of the communication was not neutral. In the spirit of the enlightenment, traditional certainties and orientations were questioned and finally put aside. In their place, principles such as rationality and self-determination shaped the new communication and education. The complementariness of nationalism and democracy, as practiced by the American Revolution, thus determined largely the political ideas of the nineteenth century. Individual self-determination and the foundation of an independent national political community governed by the people appeared to be two sides of the same coin.[19] The extension of the principle of individual self-determination went along with the democratization of the nation-state as well as with the nationalization of democratic movements. The first long wave of democratization took place.[20] During this democratic phase of nationalism, the definition of the nation was still determined by bourgeois rationality.

The rationale for the need of centralization was now largely economic. The notion of a minimal territorial size as a criterion for a legitimate and democratic nationalism was predominant; it was seen as a requirement for successful development.[21]

What were the consequences of individualization? Two consequences of individualization and democratization stand out. First, the process of democratization strengthened the social forces preferring liberalization, so feudal resistance to modernization could be defeated even faster than before. Indirectly, this development further increased inequalities in terms of material distribution. Second, the process of democratization increased the number of people involved in political decisionmaking, at first primarily in the form of elections. Increased participation, however, changed the meaning of nationalism during the world economic crisis (1873–1896) dramatically. Whereas the impoverished masses displayed discontent and threatened the established political order, many manufacturers pushed governments to support their search for new markets and to protect home markets. Nationalism, freed from its democratic component, was in this situation the ideology of the political establishment. The fanatic, nondemocratic version of nationalism that began to fashion the map of European politics during the fin de siècle became an instrument for generating domestic legitimacy as the internal pressure for changing the distribution of political power and economic distribution mounted. Governments had a considerable domestic interest in mobilizing nationalism among their citizens to maintain their power.

Nationalism finally transformed into an ethnic-racist amalgam as migration patterns grew throughout the world economic crisis. The petty bourgeoisie, who felt their status threatened, became the principal agent of fanatic nationalism, whereas the dominant classes, who originally utilized it, became its prisoners. As to foreign policy, nationalist rhetoric reduced the zone of international agreements considerably and so caused the fall of old and prevented the rise of new international institutions. Domestically, nationalist rhetoric fostered "isms" that created additional cleavages within the national societies, especially along ethnic-racist lines. In sum, individualization not only strengthened centralizing but also freed fragmentizing social forces.

THE RISE OF INTERNATIONAL INSTITUTIONS AND EMBEDDED LIBERALISM

If dependence is described as a situation in which the effects of one actor's specific actions are contingent upon another actor's actions, European states were dependent upon each other from the very beginning of the modern competitive state system.[22] The success of a state's attempt to achieve economic and military superiority over another was to some extent dependent upon actions of the other state. Throughout the seventeenth and eighteenth centuries, there was only weak regulation of this state interdependence. It rested mainly upon kinship bonds among the rulers and their ad hoc negotiations. This changed with the treaty agreed upon at the Congress of Vienna. The powers now agreed to hold meetings in the future to enforce the treaty and take up new issues as they arose. Several congresses resulted, which are of significance as an "experimental step toward international regulation" of European affairs.[23] Although the Congress of Vienna indeed represented a forerunner of modern international institutions, it soon was outmoded, for it exclusively addressed state interdependence, that is, issues emerging from a system in which national borders were relatively impermeable to external activities. With the emergence of national economies, however, transnational exchanges grew considerably and events occurring within one European society affected events taking place in another without any state action being taken. Societal transactions across borders as well as states' interactions needed now to be regulated. This led to the rise of modern international institutions: international governmental organizations and international regimes.[24]

With respect to the regulation of transnational activities, economic issues were for a long time the most important. Besides allowing for the standardization of industrial norms, international institutions aimed at limiting the tariff and nontariff barriers for international trade, at establishing a reliable international currency system, and at controlling financial markets. Those liberal international economic institutions operated more or less successfully under British leadership for most of the second half of the nineteenth century.

The effectiveness of these institutions decreased as the end of the century came closer. The decline of British supremacy was only one reason for this. Domestic upheavals and the rise of fanatic nationalism in most industrialized countries were others. European societies began to protect themselves from the repercussions of laissez-faire liberalism. Consequently, the nation-state became more interventionist and societies were no longer willing to adhere to rigid liberal economic regimes as created during the British hegemony. The rise of interventionist domestic politics led to policies seeking to externalize economic problems by erecting trade barriers and by unilaterally devaluating currencies. As a result, liberal international institutions broke down. Conversely, ineffective international institutions compounded national economic difficulties.

After World War II, the United States took the lead in building new international institutions. The GATT regime allowed for a liberalization of international trade, the Bretton Woods regime established a fixed exchange-rate system (which lasted until 1971), and the IMF-based regime controlled the flow of credits until the mid-1970s and then again from the early 1980s on. Furthermore, the EEC institutionalized a free-trade area in the core of Western Europe. It is important to understand the character of these institutions. Fundamental to them is the interventionist nation-state that funnels a large share of the GNP and that has developed a myriad of instruments to steer the national economy. The early industrial state of the nineteenth century mainly destroyed social regulation on the local level; the modern industrial nation-state has reconstructed an encompassing set of social regulations on the national level. Therefore, the postwar international economic institutions had "to devise a framework which would safeguard without, at the same time, triggering the mutually destructive external consequences that had plagued the interwar period. This was the essence of the embedded liberalism compromise: unlike the economic nationalism of the thirties, it would be multilateral in character; unlike the liberalism of the gold standard and free trade, its multilateralism would be predicated upon domestic interventionism."[25]

Although economic institutions based on the principle of embedded liberalism obliged states to keep their economic policies within certain margins, they left room for developing different national styles. Some European states used this freedom to develop a market system with a strong social component, interventionist policies, and a strong welfare component.

THE LOSS OF NATIONAL EFFECTIVENESS

The postwar order, built on institutions embodying the principle of embedded liberalism, was extremely successful. It allowed for stable growth of the Organization for Economic Cooperation and Development (OECD) and especially the European economies for almost 30 years; it promoted the integration of the world economy, thus strengthening those groups in European societies that prefer an open economy;[26] and it helped to avoid the closure of the national economies and the attempt to utilize devaluation for externalizing economic problems, when a new world economic crisis occurred in the 1970s. As a result, the consequences of the 1970s recession were much less disastrous than the ones in the 1930s. Moreover, in spite of the strong multilateral component of the postwar economic order, national protection from the worst consequences of unregulated market competition was possible. Postwar economic growth enabled some countries to develop their own economic policies with a focus on low unemployment and to extend their welfare system considerably.[27] In brief, during the height of embedded liberalism the capacity to govern coincided with the demand for governance determined by the scope of societal transactions. Embedded liberalism, like mercantilism, represented an equilibrium, whereas the period of popular nationalism embodied turbulence that led to transformation.

However, like the mercantilist policies in earlier centuries, embedded liberalism unleashed forces of globalization and individualization that undermined its very foundation. Especially in response to the recessions in the 1970s and 1980s and with the end of the Cold War, the effectiveness of national policies declined in an unknown way. As a result of accelerated globalization and individualization, the gap between the capacity to govern and the demand for governance was renewed. The ensuing turbulence may well cause a second "great transformation."

Uneven Globalization

The acceleration in uneven globalization since the mid-1970s has caused a loss of effectiveness of national policies in the spheres of welfare, culture and communication, and security.

Welfare. All the four principal forms of economic policies that emerged between the seventeenth and nineteenth centuries, that is, stabilization, allocation, distribution, and regulation, required a national market in order to be effective.[28] By the 1960s and 1970s, the growing importance of international trade as a component of a country's GNP restricted the effectiveness of national policies. The effects of any attempt to spur demand through increased government spending, for instance in France, will spread around the EC and, in fact, most of the OECD world. Since the mid-1980s, however, there have been additional major developments that suggest a leap in the process of economic globalization: (1) rapidly increasing foreign direct investments that grew four times as fast as world trade,[29] (2) a growing enmeshment of multinational corporations that for some now justifies the term "transnational" corporations,[30] (3) and an integration of financial markets caused by an increased capital mobility.[31]

Earlier forms of interdependence between national economies made a breakup of economic relations between two European nations a costly decision (giving up well-established comparative advantages); nowadays such a breakup is hardly conceivable without a fundamental change in the whole organization of production and finance. Because "almost every factor of production (money, technologies, factories, and equipment) moves effortlessly across borders," as Robert Reich contends, the very idea of national economies "is becoming meaningless," as are the notions of national corporation, national capital, national products, and national technology.[32] To be sure, there is still not one integrated world economy and not even one fully integrated European economy. Yet the mentioned developments do show a movement that goes beyond merely interdependent national economies. The new quality of interdependence in economic relations gives transnational businesses improved exit options: In case of an unfriendly tax policy, profits can be transferred to other branches of the corporation, and investments can be directed more easily than ever to regions that have low standards of social and environmental regulations. As a result, we have witnessed increased competition among "industrial locations" implying, of course, a restricted range of effective national policies. In the absence of international institutions this may lead to a lowering of social and environmental standards.[33]

Security. Although the means for national defense have often been abused in modern history, that the principal function of the state is to provide security against external forces can hardly be contested. However, with the development and deployment of nuclear weapons, even a powerful state is no longer able to provide security. Nuclear and other modern weapons of mass destruction tend to have irreversible effects, thus reducing the opportunity to wage war for the sake of national interest. In spite of this, during the Cold War the unilateral strategy of deterrence still prevailed. Since only few states had nuclear weapons at their disposal and since these states were considered as equipped with reliable control mechanisms and more or less reasonable leaders, nuclear deterrence provided the last resort of traditional notions of defense.

In 1994, the situation changed fundamentally. The dissolution of the Soviet Union and the increased proliferation of nuclear material suggest that the use of weapons of mass destruction is no longer restricted to a few well-known states. From a European perspective, there is a sharply increased likelihood that nonstate actors (for instance, terrorist organizations) as well as small states with insufficient political and technical control mechanisms will soon have those weapons at their disposal.[34] The whole notion of national security will then erode.

Thus, internal security is increasingly dependent upon the activities of nonstate actors who are outside the realm of the nation-state. Organized crime has built up a global network and is increasingly difficult to control through national measures. Global ecological dangers are even more important in this context. The basic conditions for a healthy life can no longer be supplied through national means alone. Growing awareness of both global ecological dangers, as well as the increasingly uncontrolled proliferation of nuclear weapons, has created something that can be labeled "world risk society." The dangers to survival and health tend nowadays to be irreversible and universal in impact, threatening everyone's lives to a similar degree and independent of national borders.

Culture and Communication. Although nationalism—especially in its new form of ethnonationalism, for instance, in the former Yugoslavia—is still shaking Europe, the role of the nation-state in providing the services that fed nationalism in the first place (a standardized language and education) has decreased remarkably. Besides the integration of markets, the spread of communication and information technologies is most important in this respect. Both of these developments allow for a further extension of an emerging (world) culture that is firmly based on Anglo-Saxon roots. American music dominates not only entertainment but increasingly classical music, too; American movies sell better and win more prizes than ever. Furthermore, English as the lingua franca seems today firmly established, and most computer programs are also of American origin. This success of Anglo-Saxon culture is, in my view, to a large extent caused by its integrative abilities and thus can be seen as an indication of a transnationalization of culture.

The transnationalization of culture takes away another fundamental task of the nation-state. The scope of necessary standardized communication and standardized fundamental education has broadened dramatically. The provision of educational services allowing people to communicate with each other has become more important than ever, but these services no longer need to be supplied by nationally defined units.

What are the consequences of globalization? Since the mid-1970s globalization has accelerated and the effectiveness of national policies to achieve desired ends has been drastically reduced. Therefore, interdependence among societies has increased. Societal interdependence, in turn, provides the most fundamental precondition for the rise of international institutions that foster the process of political integration. Seen from this perspective, the Single European Act and the Maastricht Treaty are not surprising at all. Hence, the current turbulence implies a profound challenge for the European nation-state: The legitimate authority of a state to make decisions within its jurisdiction may decline in favor of international institutions. Whereas secessionist movements in, for example, Scotland, the Basque provinces, Tyrol, and Lombardy are strongly resisting national obligations, they are apparently willing to comply with EC rules. However, as in the nineteenth century, when the transformation from local to national political regulation took place, any conceivable transformation process will hardly be smooth. It creates resistance and numerous uncontrolled dynamics. The resistance against the Maastricht Treaty, the crisis of the European Monetary System, and a renationalization in some Western European countries are only the most visible signs of this development.

One might object that nation-states respond to interdependence by establishing international institutions and thus maintain sovereignty as well as control over ultranationalist forces. Accordingly, "interdependence does indeed challenge the effectiveness of purely national policy, but not the formal sovereignty of states; and on the whole, international institutions *reinforce* rather than undermine formal sovereignty."[35] Along the same line, it has been argued that the EC integration increased rather than decreased the role of the nation-state.[36] Although it is correct that the absolute amount of state activity has grown with the rise of international institutions, the rise of international institutions is much too slow when compared to the speed of the process of globalization. As students of international institutions have shown in many case studies, the demand for international regimes is not directly translated into their provision. Other than a problematical social situation, which creates the demand in the first place, at least some supportive variables have to be in place.[37] For that reason effective international institutions are absent in many issue areas that actually display a demand for them. Although we have experienced unprecedented growth of international environmental institutions since the mid-1970s, from an ecological point of view they are far from sufficient.[38] Although the nonproliferation regime is an achievement as such, it is hardly prepared to control the proliferation of weapons of mass destruction after 1989.[39] Although the stability of international economic institutions "after hegemony" is striking, the new challenges caused by the globalization of financial markets and the rise in foreign direct investment are not managed appropriately through existing international institutions.[40] International governmental organizations (IGOs), indicating the internationalization of governance, have grown by a factor of approximately six since the beginning of the twentieth century. This is clearly much slower growth than that of transnational organizations—indicating the process of globalization—which have grown by a factor of approximately 27. Moreover, although in the 1980s there was a leap in globalization, the number of IGOs has not grown since the mid-1970s.[41] In sum, with respect to international governance, need outstrips supply; there is net deregulation (decline of the effectiveness of national regulations minus international regulations equals net deregulation), which creates political turbulence in much the same way as excessive national regulation did in the 1930s—though for different reasons.

In the long run, the failure to provide governance may bring people to question the nation-state as the focal point for decisionmaking. The repercussions of netderegulation are especially troublesome with respect to the distribution of socially valued goods. A polarization between rich and poor on a national as well as on a global scale has occurred since the mid-1970s and has resulted in a growth of poverty even in the industrialized countries. From the early twentieth century on, income distribution became somewhat more balanced in the industrialized countries, and the whole income level moved upward.[42] From the mid-1970s on, however, there was a remarkable shift: The shape of family income distribution shifted in almost all countries in favor of the richer quintiles, and the level of income did not grow any more.[43]

Whereas restoring political regulation on another level by developing international institutions has the potential to stop the widening of the income gap, it would aggravate another consequence of globalization—the general discontent with the complexities of modern politics. Citizens feel powerless when confronted with the political complexities created by the process of globalization and the restraints imposed by international institutions. Increasingly, there is resentment toward established politicians who govern "out of touch" in the capitals and in the cities where international organizations are located. The Eurocrats in Brussels are often seen as an unfortunate blend of bureaucrats and technocrats, as representing an insult to democratic thinking.

Together, increasing inequalities and decreasing opportunities for political control create discontent and feed those antiestablishment movements that offer simple national solutions. National right-wing parties in Western Europe ride on the ticket of simple anti-Europeanism. Therefore, it is not unlikely that we will witness a further rise of racism, national sentiments, and narrow-minded protest movements even in the most developed countries of the EC and the OECD. This will result in an increasing inability of democratically elected leaders to sell international agreements at home. The Uruguay Round of the GATT negotiations and the negotiations in the aftermath of the Maastricht Treaty are hardly understandable without reference to political leaders who desperately try to maintain support at home. Consequently, the gap between the process of societal globalization and the internationalization of governance may well widen and provide the basis for more fragmentation.[44] As a result, the legitimacy of the nation-state as the authority in political decisionmaking may decline, yet for completely different reasons than imagined by the internationalists.

Individualization

The spread of the principle of individual self-determination has also accelerated since the mid-1970s. The replacement of traditional orientations in favor of individual cost-benefit calculation is the essence of individualization. Sociologists point to the decline of the bourgeois family, consisting of parents and their offspring, and to the related pluralization of styles of privacy, which provides new opportunities to choose, as major indicators for this new wave of individualization in Western Europe.[45] Within these countries, individualization leads to the introduction of institutional and technological mechanisms that enlarge the sphere of individual self-determination.[46] In other places, the current wave of individualization embodies only the introduction of the bourgeois notion of privacy. One important consequence of this stage of individualization is the third wave of democratization in the late twentieth century. Since 1974, somewhere between 30 and 50 countries experienced for the first time free general elections.[47] Overall, it seems fair to conclude that democratic ideas have gained universal acceptance, even though we are far from their universal application.[48]

Although the third wave of democratization to some extent has origins similar to those of earlier waves, new factors are important. Probably the most important new factor is the supportive role of new communication technologies. They have led to a decline of states' effectiveness in determining the content of the culture and communication within their borders. The increased permeability of communicative borders has literally erased the possibility of a monopoly of information. As a result, democratic ideas were transplanted into societies governed by authoritarian regimes and strengthened by the success of democratic revolutions. The cascading breakdown of socialism in Eastern Europe in 1989 can be seen as a case in point.[49]

What are the consequences of individualization? The positive effects of democracies for political integration have been convincingly demonstrated. Democracies do not fight each other and they can coordinate and integrate competing policies based on a sense of community. Moreover, established democracies are much more resilient in the face of a performance crisis during an economic recession than are authoritarian regimes. It is thus argued that the stable democratic political systems of Western Europe will not give in to nationalist and other fragmentizing sentiments and that, in the long run, the social groups gaining from the process of globalization, which is arguably a majority, will prevail. Moreover, the enmeshment of international institutions in the pluralistic societies in Western Europe is already so advanced that only violent eruptions can destroy the networks of internationalized governance. In this perspective, it is furthermore expected that the new democracies in Eastern Europe will soon join the process of political integration in Europe.

However, there is an important difference between the state of democracy and the process of democratization. Once again, a look back to the nineteenth century, to the first wave of democratization, shows that this process has never been smooth. Currently in Eastern Europe, the two most immediate effects of the democratization of authoritarian regimes seem to be the liberalization of economic policies and the increased participation of the people, who are suddenly confronted with a lot of choices and uncertainties. The new wave of individualization in already consolidated democracies in Western Europe has similar side effects. Citizens reject any form of state tutelage, thus in effect paving the way for deregulation. The rejection of any rules of conduct based on tradition contributes to the lack of sources for identity formation, especially for younger people.[50] In addition, economic liberalization and deregulation further increase inequalities and aggravate social problems. Increased participation and the dissolution of traditional orientations may well inflame or even create cleavages and conflicts when desperate leaders use identity formation for rallying support. In times of turbulence, identities flow easily.[51] Whereas in the late nineteenth century fanatic nationalism seemed to be most effective for the purposes of conservatives, today references to ethnic groups, stirring up internal conflicts, or to notions of civilizations, creating external conflicts, are salient. In Western

Europe, especially in Germany and France, conservative politicians have used immigration and asylum issues in attempts to regain votes from right-wing extremist parties and to abash the more passive socialist parties. Elsewhere, over two-thirds of the states that have recently introduced electoral politics contain significant ethnic cleavages,[52] and polities in transition have a much higher incidence of interstate conflict involvement than polities without regime change.[53]

The general temptation to abuse processes of identity formation for electoral purposes is increased by other features of the current situation. First, the low effectiveness of national policies reduces the effective space for political choices regarding the really decisive yet complex issues in the areas of economy, ecology, and security. In order to rally support, politicians are especially tempted to reduce politics to matters of simple choices about values. Identity formation, the treatment of "foreigners," and the rightness or wrongness of certain sexual preferences or abortion are those value questions that create emotions and, at the same time, allow for simple national solutions—two properties of issues that are conducive to building political support. Those conflicts over values, however, have a high potential of creating rigid cleavages.[54]

CAUSES AND CONSEQUENCES OF UNEVEN DENATIONALIZATION

The fundamental challenge for European politics after the end of the Cold War consists in the following: Nation-states respond to a leap in globalization both too slowly and too quickly. Since the rise of international governance is slower than the process of globalization, the loss of effectiveness of national policies is not adequately replaced by effective international institutions. This causes a substantial deficit in the capacity to govern in all issue areas. As one domestic consequence, an increasingly unequal distribution of socially valued goods prevails within European societies. Since the rise of international governance is still remarkable but not accompanied by mechanisms for its democratic control, people become alienated from the remote political process. I call this process *uneven denationalization*. Because of uneven denationalization, the nationally oriented *citoyen* is increasingly powerless to curb the activities of the globally oriented *bourgeois*. The democratic state in Western Europe is confronted with a situation in which it is undermined by globalization and overarched by the rise of international institutions. This predicament resembles the one of uneven nationalization within most West European nations during the second half of the nineteenth century, when political regulations on the local level were pushed aside before new national regulations took place. Uneven nationalization led to the decline of mercantilism and the rise of popular nationalism. Today, embedded liberalism is challenged (see Table 8.1 for a scheme summarizing this correlational argument).

It is hard to predict the eventual outcome of uneven denationalization. One might distinguish an optimistic and a pessimistic scenario, both of them receiving support from the first great transformation as well as from developments since the mid-1970s. Whereas the pessimistic scenario points to instances of political fragmentation and emphasizes the disruption caused by turbulence, the optimistic scenario predicts, at least in the end, the triumph of political integration. The latter emphasizes, above all, the functional needs for international institutions that arise from increased interdependence among societies. In addition, it highlights the success of democracy and the rise of analytical skills among the citizenry that allow for the democratic control of very complex political arrangements. By pointing to the importance of increased interdependence, the rise of international institutions, the stability of democratic structures, and the civilization of the individual, optimists identify the major elements of political integration and of what might constitute a "process of civilization" of an evolving world society.[55] In the optimistic scenario, we would expect the growth of a complicated and intricate set of international, transnational, and subnational institutions, all built on nonhierarchical forms of political self-organization. "Complex international governance" might be an appropriate label for this scenario in which different kinds of partial orders, varying in regional scope and function, coexist.[56] Regarding such a vision, there is no question that (Western) Europe is one of the most promising regions in the world. Pessimists, however, emphasize first of all that durable governance requires a superior force as a necessary background condition. Since the nation-state hardly will give up its monopoly of force and the right to impose taxes on its citizens, international governance will necessarily remain underdeveloped. Moreover, the relationship between democracy and the nation-state is, according to the pessimists, so close that the democratization of international institutions is bound to fail. For these reasons, pessimists expect the unevenness of denationalization to increase, including all its negative repercussions such as inequality, lack of democratic control, and cleavages along ethnic and civilizational lines. All the mentioned problems are clearly visible in Western Europe; they are further aggravated by the huge economic and ecological problems in Eastern Europe. Taken together, the negative repercussions of globalization and democratization may cause a general breakdown in both domestic and international institutions, with no guarantee for the development of new instruments to maintain political and economic order.

FIGURE 8.1   The Sources of Uneven Denationalization

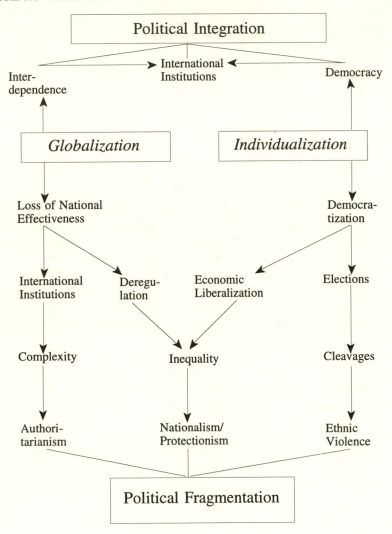

Figure 8.1 is a model of the causal mechanisms leading from globalization and individualization to the simultaneousness of political fragmentation and political integration. The model suggests that the mechanisms currently at work resemble the ones that brought about the transformation in the late nineteenth century. The model summarizes the *causal argument* of this chapter by pointing to the processes that undermined the equilibriums of mercantilism and embedded liberalism and, respectively, led or may lead to their transformation.

CONCLUSION: THE OBSOLESCENCE OF STRUCTURAL REALISM

What, then, are the consequences for theorizing about world politics? Figure 8.1 contains some categories that need to be considered in analyzing world politics; in this final section, I want to argue that the still-predominant theory of international politics, structural realism, does not offer a valuable alternative. Although the competitive self-help system that emerged in the sixteenth and seventeenth centuries is elegantly expressed in this structural realist theory of international politics, each change described in the preceding historical sketch undermined the adequacy of structural realist assumptions about world politics.

In an eloquent description, Joseph Grieco characterizes structural realism as based upon three such assumptions: "Realist theory assumes that states are the key actors in world politics, that they are rational, and that their preferences and choices are largely shaped by the absence of centralized international authority."[57] Without a central authority, states, due to their superior military capabilities, are the key actors in international politics. In this anarchic environment, it is in their best interest to maintain and to extend their power resources. In cases where states' leaders fail to further this interest or in cases where they act irrationally, they risk their state being eliminated. Therefore, only states acting in line with and thereby reproducing the rules of the competitive self-help system are able to survive.

Due to its static character, realist theory can neither explain social change nor, in turn, completely understand the consequences of social change for the interstate system.[58] Yet much social change has occurred since the seventeenth century, when the state system was first established in Europe. Ironically, it is the competitive character of the state system itself that compelled states to unleash the dynamics of globalization and individualization. As a result, the three aforementioned assumptions of structural realism do not fit the reality of world politics at the end of the twentieth century.

The Challenge of Domestic Politics

The rise of nationalist policies before and after World War I undermined the realist notion of a primacy of foreign policy, according to which states conduct their foreign policy for strategic reasons as a consequence of international circumstances and not to further domestic ends. Strong, unassimilated, preindustrial feudal and influential military elites, a cartelized political system, and misconceived utilizations of "myths of empire" against democratization movements were the conditions under which expansionist interests easily prevailed, even if it was definitely not in the best state interest to attempt expansion.[59] If the causes for aggressive policies are partially internal, then states and societies lacking the previously mentioned characteristics ought to behave more peacefully and cooperatively. Compatible with such reasoning, it has been shown that democracies do not fight each other[60] and that democratic countries characterized by the political dominance of economic sectors firmly integrated into the world market usually favor policies allowing for international institution building.[61]

One might place these findings about the relationship between domestic and international politics in a more general context. Since the mid-1970s, the central issue of academic debates about the modern democratic state has been the degree of its autonomy relative to the society it governs. Society-oriented positions reject the notion of state autonomy and explain state policies as mere outgrowths of the interplay between different interest groups in a given society. According to autonomy-oriented positions, however, states "pursue goals that are not simply reflective of the demands or interests of social groups, classes, or society."[62] The notion of relative state autonomy allowed for many interesting and important studies about the role of the state in the formulation of policies and the development of society. But note the carefully chosen formulation "not simply reflective" and compare it to the claim of structural realism: The state pursues foreign policy goals that (largely) derive from its position in the international system. By conceptualizing the state as a national-territorial totality, the structural realist theory of international politics has to assume something like *complete state autonomy.* However, the developments of globalization and individualization undermined complete state autonomy, if it ever existed. In 1994, to say the least, society may well be heterogeneous, consisting of different social classes and interest groups with different interests regarding world politics. The access of these groups to the state may be different depending upon the power and political skills of the groups as well as the strength and organization of the governing institutions—the state-society relation is a variable. Therefore, with the beginning of the twentieth century, structural realism's notion of state interests that are largely determined by the anarchic international system is at odds with what political science tells us.

The Challenge of Embedded Liberalism

The notion of embedded liberalism is yet another challenge to structural realists who do not expect that international institutions play a role in an anarchic self-help system. Although institutionalists often accept interstate power competition as a basic feature of the international system, they argue that states cooperated in many issue areas even "under anarchy" and that international institutions such as the EC or the international economic regimes influenced state behavior in favor of cooperation.[63] Institutions mattered, at least by changing incentives for cooperation, in that they provided information, reduced uncertainty, and reduced transaction costs. Already those functions of international institutions may well explain why international regimes created under the condition of U.S. hegemony persisted even after the relative decline of U.S. power.[64] In addition, international institutions influence domestic bureaucratic routines, create vested interests, and may foster a process of learning, thereby changing the domestic constellation of interests.

The mere persistence of international institutions and embedded liberalism after a change in power distribution poses a troublesome problem for structural realist theory. Therefore, structural realists argue that institutionalists failed to prove their claim, since they studied only economic issue areas in the OECD context. Accordingly, in those issue areas the emergence and persistence of international institutions can hardly be surprising. The institutionalist claim needs rather to be validated in "hard cases" such as security matters in a confrontational relationship, in which the relative-gains orientation of the states is predominant.[65] However, this structural realist defense disregards that in the 1970s international regimes came into existence even in the realm of the East-West relations and that those East-West regimes also proved resilient when the overall relationship between the superpowers worsened considerably in the early 1980s.[66]

The role of international institutions in world politics since 1945 thus casts doubt on the realist theoretical notion that states act permanently according to power considerations. In day-to-day interactions, states appear to follow institutional rules rather than constantly calculating the costs and benefits of their actions. This argument does not question the notion of rational pursuit of self-interest as such. It does, however, add the component of institutional rules and a sense of a priori obligation to follow legitimate rules.[67] In this sense, the age of embedded liberalism further weakened realist assumptions.

The Challenge of Uneven Denationalization

Both scenarios about the consequences of uneven denationalization, the optimistic one emphasizing political integration and the pessimistic one emphasizing political fragmentation, imply a vital challenge to the nation-state as the sole key actor of world politics—the most fundamental assumption of structural realism. The role of the nation-state will, according to the optimists, be drastically reduced in favor of other international and transnational institutions. In the pessimistic scenario, the nation-state, as the most visible political institution, could become the focus of protest and upheaval. Uneven denationalization, then, may well lead to increased questioning of the nation-state as the legitimate decisionmaking authority.

To be sure, the nation-state will not just be erased by the social responses to the challenge of uneven denationalization. The modern nation-state is more than just a political institution for regulating social transactions, it also

is a powerful corporate actor with enormous resources at its disposal. Therefore, nation-states will play a role of utmost importance in tackling the challenge. However, in a historical situation in which very different corporate
actors, the state being one of them, respond to uneven denationalization, the
future role of the nation-state cannot be taken as a given. Other powerful
corporate actors may prefer to utilize other, possibly more effective, institutions for the regulation of world politics, or they may aim at deregulation.
Correspondingly, people may increasingly look for other, subnational as
well as supranational, institutions as the foci of legitimate political authority. It may be that none of the European nation-states that existed in 1975
will exist in the same form in the year 2025. Some of them have already
changed their territorial foundation (the Federal Republic of Germany),
others were just dissolved (the German Democratic Republic, the Soviet
Union), and many new states have arisen (Russia, Ukraine etc.). Furthermore, the institutions of the EC seem to generate a political organization sui
generis that can be understood neither as a simple intergovernmental institution nor as a regional state. From a European point of view, structural realism just seems to assume away one of the most important issues in the study
of world politics when the sovereign nation-state responding to the security
dilemma is taken as a given in world politics.

Therefore, all three fundamental assumptions of structural realism ought
to enter the analysis—as important variables instead of as given constants.
Which nation-states will in which issue areas maintain their predominance
in world politics, and which other corporate actors may play a decisive role?
Under which conditions are states able to pursue broader interests instead of
being captured by particularistic interests and national sentiments? Under
which conditions do states act in line with institutional rules instead of with
short-term interests? There is no way to answer these questions convincingly
and to decide whether the optimistic or the pessimistic outlook is more adequate unless we gain an improved understanding of how social interests regarding international issues unfold. The most fundamental questions in the
study of world politics in a period of turbulence are therefore about the determinants of societal responses to globalization and individualization.

> The man and woman in the street *know* that their world is changing and worry
> about it. Above all, unease about present or impending changes is behind the
> widespread disenchantment with political leaderships, whether in advanced in-
> dustrial nations like America, France, and Japan, in existing or recently dis-
> solved Marxist regimes, in large parts of Latin America and Africa, in the Asian
> giants of India and China, or, for that matter, in the Muslim world, where dis-
> contented youths turn to fundamentalist prescriptions. Much of this is sup-
> pressed in authoritarian states, but in both the older and the newer democracies
> the demand for political *responses* to the new challenges is immense.

This is one of the concluding remarks of Paul Kennedy's advice about how to prepare for the twenty-first century.[68] It seems fair to conclude that academics ought to be prepared to concede that the realist notion of international politics, with anarchical self-help and the security dilemma as constituting elements, is no longer sufficient to describe the fundamentals of world politics at the end of our century. The study of social change is necessary for preparing the discipline of international relations for the twenty-first century.

9

Hobbes's Dilemma and Institutional Change in World Politics: Sovereignty in International Society

ROBERT O. KEOHANE

As the editors of this volume explain in Chapter 1, any coherent attempt to understand contemporary international relations must include an analysis of the impact of two factors: long-term tendencies toward globalization—the intensification of transnational as well as interstate relations—and the more immediate effects of the end of the Cold War and the collapse of the Soviet Union. For the United States, accustomed to being both relatively autonomous and a leader of a "free world" coalition, both of these changes have immediate impact. Indeed, the very concept of world leadership is up for grabs as it has not been since World War II. Like other contributors to this volume, I do not expect the end of the Cold War to lead to a new world order, which President George Bush sought to celebrate in 1991. Voltaire is reputed to have said that the Holy Roman Empire was neither holy, nor Roman, nor an empire, and one could say about the new world order that it is neither new, nor global in scope, nor an order. A focus on the effects of the end of the Cold War, and of globalization as defined by the editors, is more fruitful.

As a result of the end of the Cold War, the United States is likely to reduce its global ambitions and be disinclined to enter into new alliances, although U.S. policymakers will continue to seek to enhance the role of NATO and U.S. leadership in it. U.S. economic rivalry with former Cold War allies will no longer be muted by the need to remain united in the face of a Soviet threat, as Joanne Gowa anticipated on theoretical grounds before the end of the Cold War.[1] Severe competitive pressures on major U.S. corporations, resulting both from the rapidity of technological change and from globalization, are combining with anxiety about rapid increases in Japanese (and more generally, East Asian) economic capabilities relative to those of the United States to increase policymakers' concern about the competitive position of the United States in the world economy. Economic strength is ultimately the basis for economic and military power, and the United States can no longer take its economic preponderance for granted. U.S. domestic policies will increasingly be oriented toward maintaining competitiveness in the world economy, which in turn requires technological leadership and may also involve further attempts to organize a trade and investment bloc, as in the North American Free Trade Agreement (NAFTA). Increasing concern in the United States about its commercial competitiveness was evident before the end of the Cold War but has been accentuated by the collapse of the Soviet Union. The Soviet collapse reduces both the U.S. need for allies against another superpower and the incentive for U.S. commercial rivals to defer to U.S. leadership.

During the early years of the Cold War, world politics was unusually hierarchical in structure. The United States was to a remarkable degree economically and militarily self-sufficient: At least for some time, it could have managed to be quite autarchic. However, U.S. policymakers viewed autarchy as unattractive, since it would have forced the United States to forgo the economic benefits of foreign trade and investment, and it could have led to the creation of a coalition against the United States that included the potential power centers of China, Japan, and Western Europe. The impact of autarchy on U.S. political institutions, Assistant Secretary of State Dean Acheson told Congress in 1945, would be severe: "If you wish to control the entire trade and income of the United States, which means the life of the people, you could probably fix it so that everything produced here would be consumed here, but that would completely change our Constitution, our relations to property, human liberty, our very conception of law."[2]

The decision by the United States in 1945 to maintain a capitalist economy with increasing openness (measured by such indicators as trade and investment as shares of gross domestic product) has been a crucial source of the globalization—the increasingly global character of social, economic, and political transactions—that we now experience. And the outward orientation of U.S. policy clearly owes a great deal to the Soviet challenge and the Cold War. Now that the Cold War is over, globalization continues apace and has implications for sovereignty that affect the United States as well as other capitalist democracies.

Yet globalization coexists with an older feature of world politics: States are independent entities with diverse interests and have no guarantees that other states will act benignly toward them or even keep their commitments. World politics is a "self-help system," as Kenneth N. Waltz has expressed it, in which states seek to maintain and insofar as feasible expand their power and in which they are concerned about their power relative to others as well as about their own welfare.[3] One of the earliest and most powerful expressions of these assumptions about human nature and human interactions was enunciated by Thomas Hobbes in the seventeenth century. Hobbes, who was thinking principally about domestic politics and civil strife but who referred also to international relations, developed an argument for unified sovereignty and authoritarian rule that led to what I will refer to as Hobbes's dilemma. Hobbes's dilemma encapsulates the existential tragedy that results when human institutions collapse and people expect the worst from each other, whether this occurs in Somalia, Bosnia, or the Corcyrean Revolution described by Thucydides: "Death thus ranged in every shape. ... There was no length to which violence did not go. ... Reckless audacity came to be considered as the courage of a loyal ally; prudent hesitation, specious cowardice; moderation was seen to be a cloak for unmanliness; ability to see all sides of a question, inaptness to act on any. ... The cause of all these evils was the lust for power arising from greed and ambition."[4]

However, Hobbes's dilemma is not a statement of immutable fact, since it can be avoided; indeed, it can be seen as an expression of the dead end to which Hobbesian assumptions can lead. Properly appreciated, it is less an insightful key to world politics than a metaphor of the "realist trap."[5] Adopting an institutionalist perspective, I suggest that one way out of the realist trap is to explore further the concept of *sovereignty*. Sovereignty is often associated with realist thinking; and globalist writers sometimes argue that its usefulness and clarity have been diminished in the modern world.[6] In contrast, I will argue that sovereign statehood is an *institution*—a set of persistent and connected rules prescribing behavioral roles, constraining activity, and shaping expectations[7]—whose rules significantly modify the Hobbesian notion of anarchy. We can understand this institution by using a rationalistic argument: Its evolution can be understood in terms of the rational interests of the elites that run powerful states, in view of the institutional constraints that they face. Our prospects for understanding the present conjuncture—globalization, the end of the Cold War, the dubious prospects for a new world order—will be enhanced if we understand the nature of sovereignty.

The first section covers Hobbes's dilemma and the failure of Hobbes's solution to it and includes a brief summary of institutionalist responses at the domestic and international levels of analysis. In the section on sovereignty under conditions of high interdependence I develop an argument about how sovereignty is changing in those areas of the world characterized by "complex interdependence," areas within which multiple channels of contact exist among pluralistic societies and between which war is excluded as a means of policy.[8] In the section on zones of peace and conflict I introduce a cautionary note by arguing that we are entering a period of great diversity in world politics, with zones of conflict as well as a zone of peace, and therefore emphasizing the limits to institutionalist solutions to Hobbes's dilemma. The section on responses to conflict is an inquiry into the relevance of institutionalist thinking in a partially Hobbesian world and returns to the theme aforementioned: the prospects for world leadership in a globalized world after the Cold War.[9] The issue of leadership, of course, is of particular relevance to the United States and of especial interest to U.S. strategists and observers.

In this chapter I do not sketch a vision of what the world should be like—if I were to do so, I would outline a Rawlsian utopia or offer a political strategy for change. Rather, as a social scientist I seek to analyze some of the actual changes in the international system from the standpoint of the United States and the institutionalist international relations theory that I have sought to develop. Rather than speculate on current events, I have sought to identify a major institution, that of sovereign statehood, and ask in light of past experience how it is changing. Hence I do not try to survey recent changes but to focus on sovereignty both as a lens through which to view the contemporary world and as a concept with implications for international relations theory. My hope is that what may appear idiosyncratic in my account will lead to some insights even if it does not command universal acceptance.

HOBBES'S DILEMMA AND THE INSTITUTIONALIST RESPONSE

We can summarize Hobbes's dilemma in two propositions:

1. *Since people are rational calculators, self-interested, seeking gain and glory, and fearful of one another, there is no security in anarchy.* Concentrated power is necessary to create order; otherwise, "the life of man [is] solitary, poor, nasty, brutish and short."[10]

2. *But precisely because people are self-interested and power-loving, unlimited power for the ruler implies a predatory, oppressive state.* Its leaders will have ex post incentives to renege on commitments; ex ante, therefore, they will find it difficult to persuade their subjects to invest for the long term, lend the state money, and otherwise create the basis for wealth and power. This is what Martin Wight calls "the Hobbesian paradox": "The classic Realist solution to the problem of anarchy is to concentrate power in the hands of a single authority and to hope that this despot will prove a partial exception to the rule that men are bad and should be regarded with distrust."[11]

Hobbes firmly grasped the authoritarian-predatory state horn of his dilemma. Partly because he regarded reason as the servant of the passions, he was pessimistic about prospects for cooperation among people not controlled by a centralized power. His solution is to establish "Leviathan," a centralized, unified state enabled "by terror ... to form the wills of them all to peace at home and mutual aid against their enemies abroad."[12] Yet

Hobbes's solution to the problem of domestic anarchy reproduces his dilemma at the international level: *The Hobbesian solution creates a "war of all against all."* Sovereigns, "because of their independency, are in continual jealousies and in the state and posture of gladiators."[13] Under neither general anarchy nor the Hobbesian solution to it can international trade or other forms of economic exchange flourish: Property rights are in both circumstances too precarious.

For Hobbes, the fact that war is reproduced at the international level is not debilitating, since by fighting each other the sovereigns "uphold the industry of their subjects." That is, the gains from international economic exchange that are blocked by warfare are dwarfed by the gains from internal economic exchange; and the "hard shell" of the nation-state, described over 30 years ago by John Herz, protects subjects from most direct depredations of international war.[14] Since it is not necessary to overcome anarchy at the international level, the contradiction inherent in the Hobbesian paradox does not pose the problems for Hobbes's approach to international relations that it poses for his solution to problems of domestic anarchy.

In much realist thought Hobbes's international solution has been reified as if it were an essential quality of the world. Yet by his own argument about the consequences of anarchy, its implications seem morally unacceptable. Only the ad hoc assumption that rulers can protect their subjects appears superficially to save his solution from condemnation by his own argument. Even in the seventeenth century, the Hobbesian external solution—anarchy tempered by the ability to defend territory—only worked for island countries such as England. The Thirty Years' War devastated much of Germany, killing a large portion of the population; the population of the state of Württemberg fell from 450,000 in 1620 to under 100,000 in 1639, and the great powers are estimated to have suffered 2,000,000 battle deaths.[15] If the result of accepting realist pessimism is inevitable military conflict among the great powers, locked into a mutually destructive competition from which they cannot escape, then rather than celebrating our awareness of tragedy, we had better look for a way out of the realist trap.

Both of Hobbes's solutions to his dilemma are deficient. Indeed, their deficiencies stem from the same cause: the lack of attention to how institutions can profoundly affect self-interested action by changing constraints and incentives. Institutions are not a substitute for self-interest, but they shape self-interest, both domestically and internationally.[16]

Hobbes's internal solution is politically vitiated by the Hobbesian paradox: It is only viable if the ruler has qualities that he cannot be expected to have given the assumptions of the theory. Otherwise, absolute rule will lead to a predatory state, whose economically self-defeating nature is well explained by the political economy literature with its origins in the thought of Adam Smith. In Smith's view, economic growth depends on an institutional framework for market exchange and the provision of public goods. Improvement in productivity results from the division of labor; the division of labor "is limited by the extent of the market"; markets are defined as areas over which transactions can take place at similar prices, which implies political action to establish money and remove barriers to exchange.[17]

Hobbesian monarchs had incentives to expand internal markets, since they would capture part of the gains from trade, but their time horizons were shorter than those of the states that they controlled; thus they had incentives to capture immediate gains at the expense of long-term growth, as the repeated defaults of the Hapsburg emperors on their debts illustrate. Furthermore, they had difficulty making credible commitments that would guarantee property rights precisely because these rulers were unconstrained by law. Their predatory states could provide some order but could not credibly commit themselves. They could not create proper incentives to produce and invest. Hence at the domestic level the Hobbesian solution is fundamentally flawed.

If predatory states cannot make credible domestic commitments, they can hardly do so internationally, where lack of enforceability of promises is compounded by the ever-present danger of war. Economically, therefore, the Hobbesian solution implies that international economic exchange will be limited to balanced trade not requiring credible commitments. Neither governments nor firms will knowingly and willingly invest in specific assets subject to opportunistic expropriation by others.[18] In the contemporary world Hobbesian states will not be able to reap the vastly expanded benefits of international scientific, technological, and economic exchange, without which no state can long remain a great power. And since they are vulnerable to the security dilemma, they may well become involved in destructive military conflicts.

Hence the Hobbesian solution in the contemporary world is self-defeating: It creates internal oppression, external strife, technological backwardness, and economic decay. Indeed, its failure is illustrated by the fate of the Soviet Union. The Soviet Union chose an essentially Hobbesian path: internally, by constructing a centralized authoritarian state and externally, by seeking autarchy and being suspicious of international cooperation and its institutionalized forms. Internally, the Soviet approach failed for similar reasons to those that neoclassical economic historians have cited for the poor growth records of absolute monarchies, although the Soviet Union compounded its commitment problem by arrogating all key property rights to the state—that is, to the Communist Party elite acting collectively—and by creating a cumbersome bureaucratic structure that did not have incentives to act efficiently or to innovate. Nevertheless, many of the Soviet Union's weaknesses were inherent in its inability to make credible internal or external commitments. The collapse of the Soviet Union suggests, although it does not demonstrate, the futility of Hobbesian thinking for modern states in the contemporary world.[19]

But Hobbes's dilemma remains: How can political order be created given the nature of human beings?

INSTITUTIONS: CONSTITUTIONAL GOVERNMENT AND SOVEREIGNTY

The historically successful answer to Hobbes's dilemma at the internal level—constitutional government—is very different from that proposed by Hobbes. Liberal thinkers have sought to resolve Hobbes's dilemma by building reliable representative institutions, with checks on the power of rulers, hence avoiding the dilemma of accepting either anarchy or a "predatory state."[20] These institutions presuppose the establishment of a monopoly of force within a given territory; hence the emphasis of realist international relations theory on the role of state power helps to explain their existence. However, regardless of institutions' dependence on state power, liberal insights are in my view important for understanding contemporary world politics. Changes in the nature of states profoundly affect international relations, and although world politics falls short of the normative standards of liberalism, it is more highly institutionalized than realists think.

For liberals, constitutional government must be combined with a framework of stable property rights that permit markets to operate in which individual incentives and social welfare are aligned with one another. "Individuals must be lured by incentives to undertake the socially desirable activities [that constitute economic growth]. Some mechanism must be devised to bring social and private rates of return into closer parity. ... A discrepancy between private and social benefits or costs means that some third party or parties, without their consent, will receive some of the benefits or incur some of the costs. Such a difference occurs when property rights are poorly defined, or are not enforced. If the private costs exceed the private benefits, individuals ordinarily will not be willing to undertake the activity even though it is socially profitable."[21]

The political argument of constitutionalism is familiar: Constitutionalism is to constrain the ruler, thus creating order without arbitrariness or predation. Economically, constitutional government created institutions that could make sovereigns' promises credible, thereby reducing uncertainty, facilitating the operation of markets, and lowering interest rates for loans to sovereigns, thus directly creating power resources for states with constitutional governments.[22] Constitutionalism involved a modification of the traditional conception of sovereignty, dating to the thought of Jean Bodin and reflected in that of Hobbes. This conception linked sovereignty to will, "the idea that there is a final and absolute authority in the political community."[23] This notion, however, was challenged by theorists such as Locke and Montesquieu, whose ideas were developed and applied by the American revolutionaries. The debates between 1763 and 1775 in the American colonies over relations with Britain "brought into question the entire concept of a unitary, concentrated, and absolute governmental sovereignty."[24] As James Madison put it in a letter of 1787 to Thomas Jefferson: "The great desideratum of Government is, so to modify the sovereignty as that it may be sufficiently neutral between different parts of the Society to control one part from invading the rights of another, and at the same time sufficiently controuled itself, from setting up an interest adverse to that of the entire Society."[25] Thus internal sovereignty became pluralized and constitutionalized in liberal polities.

Externally, Hobbes's dilemma of internal anarchy versus international anarchy was traditionally dealt with, if not resolved, by the institution of sovereignty. Internationally, formal sovereignty can be defined, as Hans J. Morgenthau did, as "the supreme legal authority of the nation to give and enforce the law within a certain territory and, in consequence, independence from the authority of any other nation and equality with it under international law."[26] This doctrine is traditionally seen as an outcome of the Peace of Westphalia, although Stephen Krasner has recently argued convincingly that this "Westphalian system" was not inherent in the treaties signed in 1648.[27] As Martin Wight and the English school of international relations have shown, the function of the concept of sovereignty changed over time: "It began as a theory to justify the king being master in his new modern kingdom, absolute internally. Only subsequently was it turned outward to become the justification of equality of such sovereigns in the international community."[28] By the eighteenth and nineteenth centuries, as Hedley Bull explains, the conception of sovereignty as reflecting equality and reciprocity had become the core principle of international society. The exchange of recognition of sovereignty had become "a basic rule of coexistence within the states system," from which could be derived corollaries such as the rule of nonintervention and the rights of states to domestic jurisdiction.[29]

This is not to imply that rulers were either altruistic or that they followed norms of international society that were in conflict with their conceptions of self-interest. On the contrary, I assume that self-interest, defined in the traditional terms of maintenance of rule, extension of power, and appropriation of wealth, constitutes the best explanatory principle for rulers' behavior. However, the institution of sovereignty served their interests by restraining intervention. Intervention naturally led to attempts to foster disunion and civil war and therefore reduced the power of monarchs vis-à-vis civil society. Hence, agreement on principles of nonintervention represented a cartel-type solution to a problem of collective action: In specific situations, the dominant strategy was to intervene, but it made sense to refrain *conditional on others' restraint.* With respect to intervention, as well as logically, sovereignty and reciprocity were closely linked. Traditional sovereign statehood was an international institution prescribing fairly clear rules of behavior. Indeed, between the late seventeenth and the mid-twentieth centuries it was the central institution of international society, and it continues to be so in much of the world. It is true that world politics was "anarchic" in the specific sense that it lacked common government and states had to rely on their own strategies and resources, rather than outside authority, to maintain their status and even, in extreme situations, their existence. But this "anarchy" was institutionalized by general acceptance of the norm of sovereignty. To infer from the lack of common government that the classical Western state system lacked accepted norms and practices is to caricature reality and to ignore what Bull and Wight referred to as international society.[30]

International institutions include organizations, formal rules (regimes), and informal conventions. The broad institutional issue to which traditional sovereignty was an appropriate response is how to preserve and extend order without having such severe demands placed on the institutions that they either collapse or produce more disorder. The key question is how well a set of institutions is adapted to underlying conditions, especially the nature and interests of the interacting units. The Westphalian system was well adapted, since the essential principle of sovereignty was consistent with the demand for freedom of action by states, relatively low levels of interdependence, and the desire of rulers to limit intervention that could jeopardize their control over their populations. As reductions in the cost of transportation increased the potential benefits from international trade, adaptations in the institution of sovereign statehood were made to permit powerful states to capture these gains. Colonialism enabled European states to capture such gains in the nineteenth century, but it was premised on the assumptions that intraimperial gains from trade would outweigh losses from interimperial barriers; that resistance by colonized peoples would be minimal; and that colonialism would retain legitimacy in the metropoles. By 1945 all of these premises were being challenged, not least in the United States. Oceanic hegemony, established first by Britain, then by the United States, constituted another response to the need for a set of enforceable rules to control opportunism, but it proved to be vulnerable to the consequences of its own success: the rapid growth of other countries and their resistance to hegemonic dominance. Yet as noted earlier, the restoration of traditional sovereignty would not create the basis for large-scale economic exchange under conditions of high interdependence. Fundamental contracting problems among sovereign states therefore generate a demand for international regimes: sets of formal and informal rules that facilitate cooperation among states.[31] Such regimes can facilitate mutually beneficial agreements—even though they fall far short of instituting rules that can guarantee the ex ante credibility of commitments.

SOVEREIGNTY UNDER CONDITIONS
OF HIGH INTERDEPENDENCE

To judge from renewed debates about the concept, traditional notions of
sovereignty seem to be undergoing quite dramatic change. On issues as diverse as ratification of the Maastricht Treaty for European integration and
the role of the United Nations in Iraq, sovereignty has once again become a
contested concept.

One way of thinking about this process has been articulated eloquently by
Alexander Wendt, who puts forward the hypothesis that interactions among
states are changing their concepts of identity and their fundamental interests.
States will "internalize sovereignty norms," and this process of socialization
will teach them that "they can afford to rely more on the institutional fabric
of international society and less on individual national means" to achieve
their objectives.[32] Georg Sørensen sees this process of socialization as breaking the neorealists' automatic link between anarchy and self-help.[33]

Wendt himself has modestly and perceptively acknowledged that the force
of his argument depends on "how important interaction among states is for
the constitution of their identities and interests."[34] Furthermore, for rational
leaders to rely more on international institutions to maintain their interests,
these institutions need to be relatively autonomous—that is, not easily manipulated by other states. Yet evidence seems plentiful that in contemporary
pluralistic democracies, state interests reflect the views of dominant *domestic* coalitions, which are constituted increasingly on the basis of common interests with respect to the world political economy.[35] And the history of the
European Community—the most fully elaborated and authoritative multilateral institution in modern history—demonstrates that states continue to
use international institutions to achieve their own interests, even at the expense of their partners.

At a more basic theoretical level, no one has yet convincingly traced the
microfoundations of a socialization argument: how and why those individuals with influence over state policy would eschew the use of the state as agent
for their specific interests in order to enable it to conform to norms that some
self-constituted authorities proclaimed to be valid. The only major attempt
in recent centuries to found an international institution on untested belief—
the League of Nations—was a tragic failure. The League could only have
succeeded if governments had genuinely believed that peace was indivisible
and that this belief was shared sufficiently by others that it would be safe to
rely "on the institutional fabric of international society." But in fact, that be-

lief was not shared by key elites, and in light of long experience with the weakness of international institutions, it is hard to blame them.[36] Idealists hope to transmute positive beliefs into reality; but the conditions for the success of this strategy are daunting indeed.

Despite the wishful thinking that seems to creep into idealistic institutionalism, its proponents usefully remind us that sovereign statehood is an institution whose meaning is not fixed but has indeed changed over time. And they have shown convincingly that sovereignty has never been simply a reflection, at the level of the state, of international anarchy, despite Kenneth Waltz's definition, which equates sovereignty with autonomy.[37] If idealistic institutionalism does not provide an answer to questions about the evolution of sovereignty, it certainly helps open the door to a discussion of these issues.

I propose a rational-institutionalist interpretation of changes in sovereignty. Just as cooperation sometimes emerges from discord, so may intensified conflict under conditions of interdependence fundamentally affect the concept of sovereignty and its functions. The concept of sovereignty that emerges, however, may be very different in different parts of the world: no linear notion of progress seems applicable here. In this section I will just sketch the argument for changes in sovereignty under conditions of complex interdependence.

Sovereignty has been most thoroughly transformed in the European Community (EC). The legal supremacy of community over national law makes the EC fundamentally different, in juridical terms, from other international organizations. Although national governments dominate the decisionmaking process in Europe, they do so within an institutional context involving the pooling and sharing of sovereignty, and in conjunction with a commission that has a certain degree of independence. As in the United States, it is difficult to identify "the sovereign institution" in the European Community: There is no single institutional expression of the EC's will. Yet unlike in the United States, the constituent parts retain the right to veto amendments to the constitutional document (in the EC case the Treaty of Rome), and there is little doubt that secession from the community would not be resisted by force. So the European Community is not by any means a sovereign state, although it is an unprecedented hybrid, for which the traditional conception of sovereignty is no longer applicable.[38]

Interdependence is characterized by continual discord within and between countries, since the interests of individuals, groups, and firms are often at odds with one another. As global economic competition among sectors continues to increase, so will policy contention. Indeed, such discord reflects the responsiveness of democracies to constituency interests. A stateless competitive world market economy, in which people as well as factors of production could move freely, would be extremely painful for many residents of rich countries: the quasi-rents they now receive as a result of their geographical location would disappear. Matters would be even worse for people not protected by powerful governments who had to face economic agents wielding concentrated power or supported by state policy. It is not surprising, therefore, that people around the world expect protective action from their governments—and in Europe from the European Community and its institutions—and that free trade is more a liberal aspiration than a reality. In a bargaining situation, concentrating resources is valuable, and only the state can solve the collective-action problem for millions of individuals. Hence as global competition intensifies with technological change and the decline of natural barriers to exchange, public institutions are likely to be used in an increasing variety of ways to provide advantages for their constituents. In most of the world, the state is the key institution: The state is by no means dead. In Europe, supranational and intergovernmental institutions play a significant role, along with states. Economic conflict between the EC and other major states, and among states (within and outside the EC) is likely to be accentuated by the end of the Cold War, which has reduced incentives to cooperate on economic issues for the sake of political solidarity.[39]

The mixture to be expected of multilateral cooperation and tough interstate bargaining is exemplified by recent patterns in international trade. During the 1980s the GATT dispute-settlement procedure was more actively employed than ever in the past; and it frequently led to the settlement of trade issues.[40] Furthermore, the Uruguay Round of GATT will subject many service sectors and agriculture to multilateral regulation to which they have not been subject previously and should thus lead to substantial liberalization of world trade. However, bilateralism appears to have grown during the 1980s with the negotiation of formal bilateral agreements by the United States as well as the maintenance of so-called voluntary export restraints and the use of bilateral agreements to resolve issues on which major countries such as the United States have taken aggressive unilateral action. Between 10 and 20 percent of OECD imports are subject to nontariff measures; in some sectors such as textiles the figures approach 50 percent. In December 1993 the Uruguay Round GATT negotiations were brought to a successful conclusion after having continued for almost three years beyond their original deadline of December 1990. But we simultaneously observe increases in globalization and in mercantilist policy.[41] Yet I expect that the OECD democracies will continue to have sufficient interest in securing the benefits of the international division of labor such that full-scale economic warfare, much less military conflict, will remain unlikely.

Under these conditions of complex interdependence, and even outside of the institutions of the EC, the meaning of sovereignty changes. Sovereignty no longer enables states to exert effective supremacy over what occurs within their territories: Decisions are made by firms on a global basis, and other states' policies have major impacts within one's own boundaries. Reversing this process would be catastrophic for investment, economic growth, and electoral success. What sovereignty does confer on states under conditions of complex interdependence is legal authority that can either be exercised to the detriment of other states' interests or be bargained away in return for influence over others' policies and therefore greater gains from exchange. Rather than connoting the exercise of supremacy within a given territory, sovereignty provides the state with a legal grip on an aspect of a transnational process, whether involving multinational investment, the world's ecology, or the movement of migrants, drug dealers, and terrorists. *Sovereignty is less a territorially defined barrier than a bargaining resource for a politics characterized by complex transnational networks.* Although this shift in the function of sovereignty is a result of interdependence, it does not necessarily reduce discord, since there are more bargaining issues between states that are linked by multiple channels of contact than between those with barriers between them. Such discord takes place within a context from which military threats are excluded as a policy option, but distributional bargaining is tough and continuous.

I suggest, therefore, that within the OECD area the principle and practice of sovereignty are being modified quite dramatically in response to changes in international interdependence and the character of international institutions. In the European Community the relevant changes in international institutions have a juridical dimension; indeed, one implication of European Community law is that bargaining away sovereignty to the EC may be effectively irreversible, since the EC takes over the authority formerly reserved to states. In other parts of the OECD area, states accept limits on their formerly sovereign authority as a result of agreeing to multilateral regimes with less organizational or legal authority than the EC; and sovereignty may therefore be easier to recapture, albeit at a cost, in the future. In the aspiring democracies of Eastern Europe, some of my colleagues have recently observed a pattern of "anticipatory adaptation," by which one of these countries unilaterally adopts "norms associated with membership in an [international] organization prior to its actually being accorded full status in that organization."[42] We can understand the pattern of often conflictual cooperation among the economically advanced democracies as one of "cooperation under anarchy" if we are very careful about what anarchy means, but it may be more useful to see it as a question of institutional change.[43] The institution of sovereign statehood, which was well adapted for the Westphalian system, is being modified, although not superseded, in response to the interests of participants in a rapidly internationalizing political economy.

ZONES OF PEACE AND CONFLICT:
A PARTIALLY HOBBESIAN WORLD

Unfortunately, the institutionalist solution to Hobbes's dilemma is difficult to implement both domestically and internationally. Although constitutional democracy was remarkably successful in Western Europe and North America, it requires demanding conditions to be realized. These conditions are not met in much of the world and are unlikely to be met during the next several decades. Many countries of the former Soviet Union, much of the Middle East and Asia, and almost all of Africa do not have good prospects of becoming constitutional democracies in this generation. They have not built up social capital in the form of practices of cooperation, norms of participation, and institutions of civil society.[44] Nor do many of them have characteristics that seem correlated with the recent "third wave" of democratization, such as broad-based economic development, the prevalence of Christianity, proximity to democratic regions, and previous experience with attempts at democratization.[45] It is indeed remarkable how much democratization has taken place since the mid-1970s, and in some parts of Latin America, Eastern Europe, and Asia democracy seems to have quite a good chance of taking root. However, in many countries democratization has been shallow. Indeed, it is quite possible that the "third wave" is already beginning to recede.

Enthusiasm for a new world order might lead some to believe that even if democratization does not spread spontaneously, powerful democratic states will act to ensure democracy worldwide. In this view, collective security will be instituted not merely against aggression but against autocracy. Democracy will be achieved not from the bottom up but from the top down. This scenario seems to me to overlook issues of incentives for the powerful states and the basis of policies in interests. Democracies may act to stop starvation or extreme abuses of human rights, as in Somalia, but they are unlikely to sacrifice significant welfare for the sake of democracy, particularly when people realize how hard it is to create democracy and how ineffective intervention often is in doing so. Reintegration of China into the world economy after 1989, Western acceptance of coups in Algeria and Peru, and weak support for Yeltsin in Russia all suggest the naïveté of the view that powerful democracies will institutionalize democracy on a global basis.

What seems more likely is that domestic and international political institutions will remain highly varied in form, strength, and function in different parts of the world. The OECD area, or much of it, will remain characterized by complex interdependence. Nationalism may be strengthened in some countries but will not threaten the status of the OECD area as a zone of peace in which pluralistic conflict management is successfully institutionalized. International regimes will continue to provide networks of rules for the management of both interstate and transnational relationships, although increased economic competition is likely to both limit the growth of these regimes and provide grounds for sharp disagreements about how their rules should be applied. The domestic institutional basis for these regimes will be provided by the maintenance of pluralist, constitutional democracies that will not fight each other, whose governments are not monolithic, and between which there is sufficient confidence that agreements can be made.[46] As argued in the previous section, sovereignty is likely, in these areas, to serve less as a justification of centralized territorial control and a barrier to intervention and more as a bargaining tool for influence over transnational networks. It will be bargained away in somewhat different ways within different contexts involving security, economic issues, arrangements for political authority, and cultural linkages among countries.[47]

In other parts of the world complex interdependence will not necessarily prevail. Some of these areas may be moving toward a situation in which force is not employed and in which the domestic conditions for democracy are emerging: This seems to be true in much of East Asia and Latin America. In others relatively stable patterns of authoritarian rule may emerge or persist. For much of the developing world, therefore, some shift toward sovereignty as a bargaining resource in transnational networks will be observable. For instance, the developing countries were able to use their ability to withhold consent to the Montreal Protocol on depletion of the ozone layer to secure a small fund to facilitate the transition to production of less harmful substitutes for chlorofluorocarbons (CFCs).[48]

In much of the former Soviet Union and in parts of Africa, the Middle East, and Asia, however, neither domestic institutions nor prospects of economic gain are likely to provide sufficient incentives for international cooperation. In these zones of conflict, military conflict will be common. The loyalties of populations of states may be divided, as in Bosnia, along ethnic or national lines, and no state may command legitimacy. Secessionist movements may prompt intervention from abroad, as in Georgia. Governments of neighboring countries may regard shifts of power in nearby states as threatening to them and be prompted therefore to intervene to prevent these changes. New balances of power and alliances, offensive as well as defensive, may emerge in a classic and often bloody search for power and order. Since traditional security risks—involving fears of cross-border attacks, civil wars, and intervention—will remain paramount, sovereignty will remain highly territorial and the evolution toward sovereignty as a bargaining resource in transnational relations that is taking place in the OECD area will be retarded. Intervention and chaos may even ensue.[49]

We do not know precisely which regions, much less countries, will be characterized by endemic strife. On the basis of past conflict or ethnic division, the Middle East, much of Africa, the southern tier of the former Soviet

Union, and parts of South Asia would seem to be in the greatest danger. In Chapter 6 in this book, Vladislav Zubok is relatively optimistic about the prospects that Russia will not disintegrate despite the stressful transition that it is now experiencing, and Gowher Rizvi, in Chapter 4, emphasizes the coherence provided to the multiethnic Indian state by its democratic institutions. To suggest that Hobbesian conflict is likely to occur in certain areas of the world is not to make a deterministic argument that all countries in those geographical regions are doomed to internal collapse and external war. Nor is this to forecast a *bifurcation* of the world: There will be a range of patterns, from highly institutionalized patterns of complex interdependence (as in Western Europe) to the conflict-ridden exercise of force. The point of referring to zones of peace and zones of conflict, however, is to emphasize that in much of the world, order cannot be taken for granted (see also Chapter 1).

RESPONSES TO CONFLICT:
IS THE UNITED STATES BOUND TO LEAD?

Threats to the rich democracies from the zones of conflict may include terrorism, unwanted migration, the proliferation of nuclear weapons, and ecological damage. The United States and other rich countries will attempt to deter or prevent such threats to their vital economic, military, or ecological interests. They will seek to isolate conflict, reduce refugee flows, keep nuclear weapons from being used, make nuclear power plants safer or shut them down, and limit wars so that large wars do not occur. Preventive diplomacy is likely to take new forms. Relations between the North and South (both increasingly differentiated) will also be affected to some extent by feelings of injustice that some Northerners have toward the blatant inequalities of contemporary world politics.[50] However, with the Cold War ended, Northerners will demand better government in the South in return for aid: As one participant commented at the meeting discussing draft chapters for this book, "We don't want to write more checks for Mobutu."

Some proponents of a new world order have suggested that intervention will become much more extensive, that unified action by the major powers under the aegis of the United Nations will enable these states, working within this international institution, to subordinate the sovereignty of smaller states to their rule. As Inis L. Claude and Martin Wight both pointed out early, the UN's founders in 1945 believed that the successful working of the United Nations would depend on great-power unanimity.[51] And consistent with their realist premises, the United Nations has been effective in peace enforcement only when the permanent members of the Security Council have been united.[52]

But sovereignty is not likely to be so easily superseded by joint action. Conflicts of interest among the permanent members of the Security Council will appear, as occurred with respect to Bosnia in spring 1993. Indeed, since the costs of intervention are specific to the intervenor but the benefits are diffuse, endemic free-rider problems will develop. These conflicts of interest are likely to be accentuated by one aspect of globalization: intense international economic competition. Insofar as policing the world draws attention and material resources away from commercial technological innovation, governments are likely to be increasingly wary of it. The combination of globalization and the end of the Cold War will, therefore, reduce the incentives for major powers to maintain order in the zones of conflict. We will observe more frequently the "after you, Alphonse," routine that was evident in Bosnia—with the United States urging more vigorous use of force on the Europeans and the Europeans suggesting that the United States first send ground troops that would be exposed to retaliation themselves.

In one sense the United States remains, in Joseph Nye's felicitous phrase, "bound to lead": As the Iraq and Bosnian crises made clear, only the United States has the combination of economic and military capabilities and political prestige and self-confidence to take decisive action in such situations.[53] As the Gulf War showed, the United States no longer has the material capabilities to lead unilaterally without the financial and political support of others. Hence it has to persuade rather than dominate; and it can only persuade when, as in the Gulf but not in Bosnia, it is willing to make a major commitment itself, putting its soldiers as well as its economy and its political prestige at risk. Yet the end of the Cold War means that the United States is no longer bound to lead in the sense of clearly having to do so in order to pursue its own self-interests. On few issues outside its borders—indeed, only on those involving either influence over major centers of manufacturing and technological power, especially Western Europe and Japan, or access to oil resources, as in the Middle East—are U.S. interests sufficiently involved that such a commitment would make sense. On other issues, U.S. leadership will tend to be hortatory; and hortatory leadership in world politics is hardly very effective.

The general point is that the *incentives* for major countries to intervene on a global scale are unlikely to be sufficient to support effective UN action on a consistent basis. Powerful democratic countries from the zone of peace will be reluctant to intervene, except where this can be done at low cost. The great powers will indeed seek to forestall threats to their security or power, as continued intervention in Iraq shows: Threat control may replace both traditional balance of power and collective security as the major principle of security. Yet maintaining peace among contentious peoples will be elusive,

even if not as utopian as instituting democracy worldwide. Western reluctance to get militarily involved in Bosnia, Armenia, Georgia, or other areas
of civil strife in the former Soviet Union make this point clear. The great-
powers are unlikely to attempt to supersede sovereignty except in highly
exceptional cases such as that of Saddam Hussein's Iraq. And even if this
great-power condominium were feasible over the long term, the Hobbesian
paradox would still bedevil attempts to solve the problem of international
political order in a broadly acceptable way through concentration of
power.[54]

Under these conditions, sovereignty in the zones of conflict may retain its
traditional role, moderating the effects of anarchy by conferring supreme authority over delimited territories and populations and, as in sixteenth- and
seventeenth-century Europe, erecting barriers to intervention and universalization of strife. Bosnia will be divided not on the basis of the legitimacy accorded to pre–civil war provincial borders by the great powers, or in line
with ethnic equity, but on the basis of the balance of military forces. The
horrors of civil war will come to an end not in a meaningful new federalism
but in a redivision of the area into sovereign states with unequal economic
and military resources and political power. The role of outside powers will
not be to dictate new lines of division, much less to invent new federal institutional arrangements, but, through credible threats of force, to limit the
ability of the winners to impose their will when the human costs are too
high. In 1993 the political will existed to save Sarajevo but not to preserve
(or rather, restore) Bosnia. In view of the conflictual conditions prevailing in
areas such as Bosnia, traditional sovereign statehood may be an appropriate
international institution. At any rate, the subordination of sovereignty to
great-power rule is both unacceptable to politically mobilized populations
and to the great powers themselves; and the concept of sovereignty as a bargaining resource in complex interdependence is premature when the conditions for complex interdependence—most notably, the political irrelevance
of military force—do not exist.

CONCLUSION

Globalization and the end of the Cold War have created a new situation in
world politics. In some ways, the new world is more like traditional world
politics than was the world from 1945 to the mid-1980s: Political alignments will become more fragmented and fluid, and economic competition
will not be muted by alliance cooperation. In other respects, however, the
new world will be very different from the world before World War II. Globalization seems irreversible with all its implications for the permeability of
borders and the transformation of sovereignty among the economically advanced democracies; and international institutions have become central to

the political and military as well as the economic policies of the major states.[55]

Yet Hobbes's dilemma cannot be ignored. Without well-developed constitutional institutions, the alternatives in many countries lie between anarchy and predation, neither of which is attractive. The extensive patterns of agreement characteristic of complex interdependence depend on pluralist democratic institutions. Less ambitious forms of world order, relatively peaceful but not necessarily so cooperative, depend on stable domestic institutions, although whether they depend on democracy is not yet entirely clear. At any rate, predatory authoritarian states are likely to become involved in international conflict, and intensely divided states are particularly prone to do so. The latter are likely targets for intervention by the former. It seems unlikely not only that democracy will sweep the world but also that all states will be governed by stable institutions, even authoritarian ones. Hence "world order" does not seem to be impending: A global security community is unlikely soon to come into existence.

Seeking to follow the Hobbesian prescription of centralized authoritarian states in an anarchic world would be disastrous: This "solution" has been shown to be deficient. Indeed, the failure of Hobbes's solution is mirrored in the misleading neorealist reification of the dichotomy between anarchy and hierarchy, as found in the work of Kenneth N. Waltz.[56] The characterization of domestic politics as hierarchic and international relations as anarchic constitutes an oversimplification that obscures crucial issues of institutional structure and choice, just as Hobbes falsely posed the issue as one of anarchy versus Leviathan. Even the Westphalian system included a degree of institutionalization in the form of a conception of sovereignty linked to reciprocity. In the short run, absent institutionalization, people may face Hobbes's dilemma; but over time, institutions help them escape it. And the growth of such institutions, international as well as domestic, has rendered obsolete the more rigid forms of realism.

The key problem of world order now is to seek to devise institutional arrangements that are consistent both with key features of international relations and the new shape of domestic politics in key countries. It will be very difficult to construct such institutions. They must be built not only by governments but by international civil society under conditions of globalization. They must be constructed not by a single hegemonic power but by several countries whose interests conflict in multiple ways. Nevertheless, among advanced democracies appropriate institutions could facilitate political and economic exchange by reducing transaction costs, providing information, and making commitments credible. The resulting benefits will accrue not only to governments but to transnational corporations and professional societies, and to some workers as well, in both developing and developed countries. But adjustment costs will be high, hence there will be losers in the short run; there may also be long-run losers, since globalization will continue to put downward pressure on wages for those workers in developed countries who can be replaced by workers in poorer parts of the world or who compete in national labor markets with such workers. Hence domestic institutions that provide retraining, that spread the costs of adjustment, and perhaps that redistribute income on a continuing basis to globally disadvantaged groups will be essential corollaries to maintaining and strengthening international institutions in an age of globalization.

Ideal institutions will never exist, but prospective gains from international agreement will continue to provide incentives for the creation of approximations to them. Hence, among the advanced democracies I expect the strengthening of international institutions over time in response to globalization, although conflicts of interest and problems of credibility will lead to reversals from time to time and will make successful institution-building difficult. The vicissitudes of the European Monetary Union (EMU) illustrate how poorly designed schemes (in this case, violating the economic principle that open capital markets, fixed exchange rates, and independent monetary and fiscal policies are incompatible with one another) can contribute to institutional crisis or temporary stagnation.

In any event, effective international institutions are inconsistent with rigid maintenance of traditional conceptions of sovereignty. Instead, they will rest on the willingness of states to give up their legal freedom of action in return for more certainty about their environments as a result of having some control over other states' actions. Thus, insofar as globalization leads to stronger international institutions with more authority and clearer rules, it implies modification of the theory or practice of sovereignty. In the zone of peace, characterized by complex interdependence, sovereignty will become more a resource to be traded off in exchange for partial authority over others' policies than a set of barriers to intervention.

The relationship between globalization and institutional change does not only work in one direction. Globalization is fundamentally a social process, not one that is technologically predetermined. Like all other social processes, it requires the underpinning of appropriate social institutions. If the sovereignty-modifying institutions essential for continued globalization do not emerge, globalization itself can slow down or even go into reverse. If the effects of global interdependence become uncertain and unmanageable, leading to high levels of domestic and international strife, governments could (at substantial costs and in varying ways in different parts of the world) cope with it through regionalization or perhaps even (in the case of the United States if no other country) through unilateral action. Globalization and international institutionalization are mutually contingent.

However, the fragmentation of political authority in much of the world, most notably within the territory of the former Soviet Union, means that in the zones of conflict, wars, international and civil, will remain common. Nation-building was a bloody 300-year process in the West and is likely to continue to be conflict-laden in the future.[57] As Robert Putnam has shown, the sources of social capital for effective civil society are often centuries old. Investments in democratic institutions, building both on interests and on previous patterns of reciprocity, can make a difference; but we should be aware that the chances for successful democracy depend to a considerable extent on previous economic, social, and political conditions.

In the zones of conflict, the traditional functions of sovereignty—to clarify boundaries, institutionalize practices of reciprocity, and limit intervention—will probably be more salient than its use as a resource in bargaining over issues involving transnational networks. Global institutions, designed to deal with the zones of conflict, will only incrementally be able to alter traditional conceptions of sovereignty, since the danger that sovereignty was invented to deal with—chronic, ideologically justified intervention—will remain prominent. Those who try to manage these institutions should recognize the limitations on international action. International institutional strategies may be crucially important at the margin, at critical moments, but the fundamental problems involve domestic institutional development, an incremental, difficult process. The United Nations should seek to act on the margin to reduce conflict and violence but should be wary about excessive ambition and institutional overload. The most fundamental problems of state-building will not be solved by international organizations.

Nevertheless, the institutionalist perspective on international relations theory remains relevant in the zones of conflict. Institutional "solutions" applicable to the zone of peace cannot simply be transferred to the zones of conflict; to escape Hobbes's dilemma, institutional change is essential. The relevant institutional strategy is likely to be modest, incremental, and long-term in nature, but crisis managers should not lose sight of the necessity to build institutions if the crisis-creating conditions of this part of the world are eventually to be superseded. In the long run, norms and values need to be modified, with shifts in the conception of sovereignty reflecting changes in domestic as well as international and transnational politics. Such processes—whether referred to as social learning or otherwise—are important to study although beyond the scope of this chapter.

Social scientists viewing the new world order should be humble on two dimensions. Our failure to foresee the end of the Cold War should make us diffident about our ability to predict the future. And the weakness of our knowledge of the conditions for constitutional democracy and for peace should make us reluctant to propose radical new plans for global democratization or peacekeeping. Nevertheless, we can go beyond the Hobbesian solution to Hobbes's dilemma of anarchy and order: We can focus on how institutions embodying the proper incentives can create order without predation within societies, and how even much weaker international institutions can moderate violence and facilitate cooperation in international relations. Strong institutions cannot be suddenly created: Both constitutional democracy and a reciprocity-laden conception of sovereignty emerged over a period of centuries. Nevertheless, it is imperative to avoid the magnitude of violence and dysfunction that occurred in the West. We should encourage the creation and maintenance of institutions, domestic and international, that provide incentives for the moderation of conflict, coherent decision-making to provide collective goods, and the promotion of economic growth. It is in such lasting institutions that our hopes for the future lie.

International Relations Theory in a World of Variation

HANS-HENRIK HOLM AND GEORG SØRENSEN

International relations (IR) theory does not provide a coherent framework for understanding the magnitude of change in the international system in the 1989–1991 period. "Well established generalizations about world politics no longer hold," claimed Robert Jervis in his recent assessment of the future of world politics.[1] We agree. The conclusion that emerges from the contributions in this book is that the changes in the international system created by globalization and the end of the Cold War have undermined much of the foundation for mainstream realist theory in international relations. Instead, less ambitious, more specific, and more context-sensitive theory must be put on the agenda, theory that is middle-range in the sense that it does not postulate one single, coherent logic or principle that is universally valid for the entire international system. At the same time, we do not support a postmodern idea of complete theoretical relativism or chaos. More specifically, we point to three areas where middle-range theory can develop a common meeting ground: (1) the changes in the role and notion of the state, (2) the dynamics and the understanding of sovereignty, (3) the structure of economics and new forms of dominance between North and South.

The problem with present theory in international relations is that there is both too much and too little of it. When students are introduced to the field, a vast array of approaches, images, and menus are presented. Yet in another sense there are very few theories in international relations. There is one dominant body of theory. It is realism with its core image of states in a system of anarchy. In the words of Kjell Goldmann, "It is not a question of a partial theory among other partial theories in international relations, but it is the Theory with a capital T."[2]

The theory of realism as developed by Kenneth Waltz in particular "holds a central place among students of international politics."[3] It is therefore only natural that it has become the focus for the debate on the relevance of international relations theory in the changed international system. For some it is as relevant as ever.[4] According to others it merely needs modification,[5] and some reject it altogether.[6] In our view, realist insights remain relevant and powerful. But realism is not the Theory (with a capital T) of international relations anymore. There are more than a few theories; there are several "big and important things" to know about international relations after the Cold War.

In other words, we do not want to embrace realism and we do not want to completely reject it. What we do reject is both the single-minded focus on system level as well as the forced theoretical choice between dichotomies supposedly applicable to the entire international system (e.g., anarchy or hierarchy, specialization or nonspecialization of units, simple or complex structures) that realism posits. Realism will have to find its place among other middle-range theories in the attempt to understand a world characterized by variation.

REALISM IN THE FACE OF CHANGE

Realism is a theory about international politics, an effort to understand the basic characteristics of the international system as well as the way in which system attributes constrain the behavior of states. "The ontological given for realism is that sovereign states are the constitutive components of the international system."[7] The system is anarchical: "The parts of international-political systems stand in relations of coordination. Formally, each is the equal of all the others. None is entitled to command; none is required to obey. International systems are decentralized and anarchic."[8] From this follows the principle of self-help. "Self-help is necessarily the principle of action in an anarchic order."[9] The behavior of states is determined by the anarchic structure of the international system and by the distribution of power among states. This accounts for the "striking sameness" of international politics "through the millennia," according to Waltz, with states engaging in power balancing in order to achieve "maximum security and freedom of action."[10] In other words, states need to be concerned with relative gains because in the anarchic system, "their security and well-being ultimately rest on their ability to mobilize their own resources against external threats."[11]

Anarchy remains a constant feature of the international realm, and the distribution of power among states changes only slowly. In this sense, the system is quite stable. Realism has its focus on the system level because it is the distribution of power at this level that is the most important factor explaining state behavior. Domestic elements are not insignificant, especially in situations where the international system is not firmly constraining. Yet the distribution of power in the anarchic system remains the decisive factor influencing state behavior.

Can realism accommodate the changes conjured by uneven globalization and the end of the Cold War? If we look first at uneven globalization, it is clear that realists have problems with all of the four dimensions of globalization spelled out in Chapter 1. Let us begin with the dimensions intensified interdependence and increased interconnectedness. The theoretical ramifications of these aspects of globalization received seminal treatment in Robert Keohane and Joseph Nye's 1977 book, *Power and Interdependence*.[12] Yet the debate about the degree to which these dynamics demand a recasting of realist understanding continues today. Prominent realist scholars in a recent contribution remain confident that realist theory needs little adjustment in the face of interdependence and interconnectedness.[13] But the dominant trend in the discipline—at least until very recently—appears to be a movement toward a merger between (neo)realism and (neo)pluralism, where realism develops in the direction of more flexibility, involving the possibility of a modified anarchy, and security communities dominated by cooperation among members. At the same time, the pluralism that in earlier days involved mostly harmony and common interests in a world of complex interdependence has developed in realist direction; pluralists are now ready to accept the influence of shades of anarchy on possibilities for international cooperation and to recognize the primary role of states.[14]

We cannot pursue this debate here.[15] In the present context, it is more important to focus on the two other dimensions of globalization, economic globalization and globalized societies, which obviously contain the most serious challenges to realism. Economic globalization means that the realist notion of states as autonomous economic units with their "own" resources behind well-defined territorial boundaries is seriously undermined. Furthermore, when the global economy dominates the national economies existing within it, states increasingly turn into "trading states" or "competition states," which means that they are less and less the undifferentiated, "like units" depicted by realism.[16] They specialize and become increasingly economically diverse in the context of a global economic system.

Finally, the notion of globalized societies changes the traditional position of states in the international system. In a globalized society, states coexist with a host of other important actors, from individuals and subnational organizations to suprastate networks of regional and global governance. States form part of a complex network of authority patterns pertaining to different levels of governance.[17] We shall argue further on that this does not necessarily imply that states are less important. Yet in such a world, the one-sided realist focus on a system level constraining the state units is insufficient. International relations consists of a variety of actors, and they need to be analyzed from a number of different yet interrelated levels.

In sum, to the extent that the qualitative change indicated in the concept of uneven globalization has actually taken place, realist analysis is no longer a useful approach to understanding international affairs. This explains why Anthony Giddens, James Rosenau, and many other scholars have sought to develop new frameworks of understanding that tend to completely reject realist perceptions.

A similar picture emerges when we turn to our other main analytical variable, the end of the Cold War. Realism can easily accommodate changes in polarity and the balance of power, and maybe even also the dimension called fragmentation and integration, although these latter processes tend to include new political forces that challenge states as we knew them during the Cold War. The important challenges are thus the two other dimensions, "end of war" and "globalized societies without war." "End of war" foresees that liberal democracies will engage in institutionalized cooperation that circumscribes anarchy in the traditional realist sense to the extent that conflicts can no longer lead to war.[18]

In the most far-reaching interpretation (globalized societies without war), we have, as described in Chapter 1, a liberal democratic world where violent struggle between competing states has disappeared and states have ceased to be repositories of the loyalties and cravings of groups of individuals. A power structure in the traditional sense can no longer be identified because power is diffused to different levels, from the individual microlevel to the global governance macrolevel. There is a wide variety of power resources, or means of influence, and concrete resources are much less fungible across issue areas. It is clear that in a world of globalized societies without war, realism is no longer a useful theoretical framework for the study of international relations. Its conception of an anarchical system consisting of state units in potential conflict is no longer valid.

In sum, with the end of the Cold War we have a world of uneven globalization where realism is still a useful guide in the analysis of some things and a not very useful guide in the analysis of a number of other things. The scholarly reactions to this state of affairs, understandably, span from attempts at saving basic realism in the face of new challenges, especially the challenge of understanding change,[19] to complete rejection of realism.[20]

We have already indicated that both of these reactions are less than satisfactory. Realist insights should not be rejected. At the same time, the changes that have taken place are, in some cases, too decisive to be contained within a basically realist framework.

We thus need to give up the idea of a single, theoretical logic or principle that is universally valid for the entire international system. In a sense, the time of the great, systemwide generalizations is over. Given the reduced importance of the structurally constraining role of the international system,

sparse assumptions leading from structure to behavior are much more difficult to set forth. Variation in the system as a result of uneven globalization
and the end of the Cold War has created a need for approaches that enable
us to comprehend both well-known issues of conflict and cooperation
among states and new and different types of international entities active on a
variety of governance levels in a system where power is multifaceted and increasingly diffused.

This is where middle-range theory comes in, as indicated in Takashi
Inoguchi's Chapter 7. In other words, there is already a large variety of
approaches and concepts in the arsenal of international relations theory that
continue to be of use in the analysis of post–Cold War international affairs.
A single approach, such as realism, should no longer be given a privileged
analytical position, acting as a term of reference for other approaches. Rele-
gation of realism to the middle range requires theoretical adaptation. As indicated earlier in this chapter, several attempts in this direction have already
been made. Our own suggestions concentrating on the development of a few
core concepts in the discipline follow.

At the same time, the idea that every possible approach is as justified and
warranted as any other because the world is replete with variation is hardly
satisfactory. Theoretical work in the discipline confronts a dilemma facing
uneven globalization and the end of the Cold War: It cannot cling to the old
dominant theory (or paradigm) of realism and it should not accept the radical postmodernist claim that every possible theoretical proposition that has
"a credible story to tell" is as important as every other theoretical proposition.

What we propose as a possible way ahead is to rethink some of the core
concepts of the discipline in such a manner that they become better equipped
to accommodate new concerns while also continuing to be able to address
old ones. Such rethinking has already taken place as regards the central concept of power.[21] In what follows we address the concepts of state and of sovereignty, believing that these core concepts of the discipline can be defined in
ways that allow us to address well-known as well as new research problems.
We also argue that the traditional focus on politics is not sufficient. Economics as well as ideology must go into the analysis. In the context of suggesting
concepts for such analysis, we also argue that new forms of dominance are
emerging in the international system.

While arguing for refined concepts, we try to demonstrate that states continue to be of special importance in international relations, perhaps even
more important than earlier. We also emphasize how changes in the concept
of sovereignty reflect a world where sovereignty is more, not less, important
than before. In both cases, this increasing importance occurs in ways different from those envisaged by realism.

THE STATE IN THE FACE OF CHANGE

The peculiarity of most realist contributions is that for all the emphasis on the state and the system of states, there is very little being offered in terms of a theoretical treatment of the state. Many realists would probably be content with the definition of *state* offered by F. S. Northedge: "A state, in the sense used in this book, is a territorial association of people recognized for purposes of law and diplomacy as a legally equal member of the system of states. It is in reality a means of organizing people for the purpose of their participation in the international system."[22] The state is regarded as an unproblematic[23] entity, a sovereign unit (i.e., a legally equal member) possessing certain assets in terms of population and other resources. But with this concept of state, realism takes parsimony too far. Indeed, "one of Waltz' most important contributions has in fact been to alert the international relations theorists among us, by the very sparseness and parsimony of his analysis, to the need of rethinking the category of the state."[24] What follows is a part of this trend.

The argument to be developed here is that it is possible to have a notion of state that plays a central role in IR theory while also allowing room for many of the critiques of the discipline's state focus.[25] For this to happen, the realist view of the state as an agglomeration of territorially organized power needs to be supplemented. We need a concept that makes a clearer distinction between state institutions and society, thus paving the way for the study of this relationship and the complex manner in which it is related to the behavior of states in the international realm.

The Weberian definition of *state* by Theda Skocpol is a relevant starting point: "a set of administrative, policing and military organizations headed, and more or less well-coordinated, by an executive authority."[26] The definition allows questions about the relationship between state and society as well as the relationship between state and nation. When *nation* is defined as "a group of people sharing a common cultural and/or ethnic heritage," it appears that specific states frequently contain societies with a variety of nations. Finally, the definition allows inquiries about relationships between state and government, "i.e. between the ensemble of administrative apparatuses and the executive personnel formally in positions of supreme control."[27]

In other words, a richer conception of the state allows us to address a number of the issues raised by uneven globalization and the end of the Cold War. Intensified interdependence and rising interconnectedness mean that state institutions and governments are increasingly both domestic and international actors, facing demands that domestic groups wish to pursue internationally and demands that international networks of institutions urge states to pursue domestically. A pioneering work in this regard is Peter

Katzenstein's analysis of how small West European states manage their relations with the global economy through democratic corporatism, which contains three elements: "an ideology of social partnership expressed at the national level; a relatively centralized and concentrated system of interest groups; and voluntary and informal coordination of conflicting objectives through continuous political bargaining between interest groups, state bureaucracies, and political parties."[28]

With the advent of economic globalization and globalized societies, individuals and groups intensify relationships across borders. National economies become parts of a global system of markets and production. The capacity of states and governments to meet various types of demands may be reduced insofar as purely national policies of welfare, culture, communication, and security become increasingly ineffective—thus the uneven denationalization process analyzed by Michael Zürn in Chapter 8. But this new context changes rather than reduces the role of states. Focusing on economic regulation, Paul Hirst and Grahame Thompson emphasize this point: "The mechanisms of national economic regulation have changed but governmental policies to sustain national economic performance retain much of their relevance, even if their nature, level, and function have changed. ... States are not like markets, they are communities of fate which tie together actors who share certain common interests in the success or failure of their national economies."[29] A similar argument can be made for a changed, but not necessarily reduced, role of states in matters of security, culture, and communication. In these areas as well, it is clear that a richer concept of state is required in order to pursue a meaningful analysis.

Another effect of uneven globalization and the end of the Cold War is processes of fragmentation and integration. At issue is the relationship between nations of ethnic and culturally based groups on the one hand and governments and state institutions on the other. Ethnic and cultural nations are demanding extended autonomy or even sovereign statehood. Often nations span across borders, involving several governments in their demands. States continue to be the fundamental units of collective identity in a globalized world. Nationalism thus creates problems both when there is too much of it and when there is too little. In the former case, it can lead to chauvinistic expansionism, as we have seen in the past. In the latter case, states fall apart when there is not enough nationalist glue to hold them together. We see this presently in the former Soviet Union and in the former Yugoslavia.

The issue of autonomy of state institutions and governments must also be addressed. With its view of states as rational and unified actors, realism supports the view that states enjoy a high degree of autonomy from the rest of society, although the matter is rarely confronted directly by realists.[30] Pluralists are more prone to see the state, or various parts of it, as more or less captured by a variety of interest groups. In the present context, we wish to pose the exact degree of state autonomy as an open question that requires fresh analysis in the face of uneven globalization and the end of the Cold War.

At a minimum, autonomy must mean that states "may formulate and pursue goals that are not simply reflective of the demands or interests of social groups, classes, or society."[31] In the view of at least some scholars, even more autonomy is conceivable. Not only is it possible for the state to fend off or insulate itself from powerful social forces, it can lead the way and impose "its own vision and goals on them."[32] Yet uneven globalization means that state autonomy is challenged by domestic groups and by international institutions and other international actors. Analysis of concrete effects upon state autonomy requires empirical investigations. On a more general level, it is clear that processes of uneven globalization set the issue of state autonomy in a new context. Current processes of democratization as well as the debates on democratizing international governance (cf. Chapter 8) is a part of this new context.

Finally, the end of the Cold War has emphasized that states pursue a number of different goals simultaneously.[33] In many regions, traditional security concerns remain high on the agenda. But the pursuit of socioeconomic development is of equal importance in many countries in the South and the East, at least seen from the people's point of view. In a number of African countries, including Somalia, Mozambique, and Angola, development has fared so badly that there is very little security in the traditional sense to defend. In the zone of peace of developed countries, welfare issues in a broad sense, including problems of unemployment and economic restructuring toward "post-Fordist" economic models, are the central concern.[34] Finally, environmental issues are of generally increasing importance in most parts of the international system.

It is of vital importance to emphasize that the relevance of the state for analyzing such issues has not decreased with uneven globalization and the end of the Cold War. The fact that states have less capacity for pursuing a number of goals in a more globalized world does not mean that states have become less important. They remain privileged actors in the global system. An unfortunate tendency has plagued the scholarly debate on this issue. Some scholars posit a false choice between the continued importance of the state in traditional realist terms and the vision of a dramatically reduced significance for the state in a globalized society.[35] Our view is that uneven globalization and the end of Cold War change rather than reduce the role of states in the system.

The argument for a continued privileged situation for states does not rest primarily on realist arguments, although we recognize the importance of traditional security and power issues in several regions. We also accept the argument that other actors are often more dependent on states than vice versa: "International organizations are created by states. Multinational corporations depend on property rights guaranteed by states. Foundations operate according to the laws of states."[36] Yet the core argument made by realists that international relations is primarily a game of power between states in an anarchical realm is less acceptable in a post–Cold War world characterized by uneven globalization.

Why, then, the continued special importance of states in such a world? Because the diffusion of power and governance brought about by uneven globalization is not a zero-sum game. Development in the South and East may depend more than ever on the international system, yet states continue to bear the prime responsibility for pushing development within their borders. Welfare and socioeconomic issues in the developed countries increasingly have an international dimension. Yet they remain the principal obligation of the single state. Vladislav Zubok vividly demonstrates in Chapter 6 the problems that emerge when, as in Russia, there is a "lack of state" to attend to these areas. Even in the environmental area, a global issue par excellence, measures taken on the international level have little significance unless implemented by state institutions in the involved countries. In other words, there is a dialectic at play that constrains the ability of states to act and simultaneously increases the demands on, and the centrality of, states in a globalized world. Finally, as already mentioned, in spite of globalization, states continue to be the fundamental units of collective identity.

DIMENSIONS OF SOVEREIGNTY IN THE FACE OF CHANGE

For realism, the "ontological given" is that "sovereign states are the constitutive components of the international system."[37] Some scholars now argue that sovereignty has "lost much of its relevance" in international relations.[38] Others claim that "de facto sovereignty has been strengthened rather than weakened."[39] Against the background of the analyses in the preceding chapters, we argue that a more nuanced notion of sovereignty is needed if we are to understand the current role of "sovereign" states in international relations.

We set forth three different dimensions of sovereignty that may serve as foundations for middle-range theory-building in the analysis of international politics: negative, positive, and operational sovereignty.

Negative sovereignty is the juridical or formal aspect of sovereign statehood. In Chapter 9, Robert Keohane defines "formal sovereignty" as "legal supremacy over all other authorities within a given territory." Alan James defines it as the constitutional independence of a state: "A territorial entity must have a constitution which is independent of other constitutions to be termed, in the specified sense, sovereign and hence able to look forward to membership in the collectivity of states."[40] States in the international system are subjects of international law. "Sovereignty is the right to sail the metaphorical ship of state on the open oceans regulated by international law without being told where to head but only how to proceed."[41]

Historically, negative sovereignty presupposed both formal acceptance by other states and a certain amount of real state power. Before the 1950s, areas that did not meet the latter criterion were not accorded formal recognition as sovereign. They were, in various forms, dependencies or colonies.

After World War II new norms of sovereignty were developed. Ex-colonies became formally accepted as sovereign states irrespective of their actual capabilities as states. They became what Robert Jackson calls quasi-states, possessing juridical statehood but not the substantive capabilities of statehood, internally or externally. This is a situation of negative sovereignty without positive sovereignty. It is a formal, legal entitlement that the international society confers upon an entity. By granting this right of (negative) sovereignty to units that could not provide for their populations, defend themselves, or maintain other central functions of positive sovereignty, the international community entered into obligations of helping these quasi-states to become fully fledged states. Negative sovereignty thus became a right in the international system, but it was accorded only to ex-colonies, not to others.[42]

Negative sovereignty is an absolute condition, a constant, not a variable. A unit either has it or does not have it. Positive sovereignty, and operational sovereignty are variables, relative and changing.

Positive sovereignty describes a state that is its own master. It is not totally independent of its surroundings, but it has the capabilities to deliver substantial goods to its citizens. A state with positive sovereignty acts in relation to others; it does not just react. "It is a substantive rather than a formal condition. ... It is the distinctive feature of a 'developed' state. ... Positive sovereignty ... is not a legal, but a political attribute if by 'political' is understood the sociological, economic, technological, psychological and similar wherewithal to declare, implement, and enforce public policy both domestically and internationally."[43] Positive sovereignty is obviously a variable. Some states possess it to a high degree, others only in small amounts. Robert Jackson's analysis focuses on the lack of positive sovereignty in African states.[44] We argue that the process of uneven globalization also affects the positive sovereignty of developed states in the North. States experience a decreasing capacity to act, to conduct effective policies, because of uneven globalization.

Operational sovereignty must be understood in this context. It indicates a situation where states choose to limit their legal freedom of action in a process of bargaining with other states. In other words, states put constraints on themselves; that is, they limit their own operational sovereignty through international agreements. This process is analyzed in Chapter 9. By limiting their operational sovereignty when establishing supranational governance, participating states hope to gain the benefits of greater influence on the policies of other states.[45]

This new aspect of the sovereignty game is an important addition to the notions of negative and positive sovereignty.[46] According to Robert Keohane in Chapter 9, it points to a situation where sovereignty "is less a territorially defined barrier than a bargaining resource for a politics characterized by complex transnational networks." Sovereign states, through international agreements, accept limits on their legal freedom of action. Cooperation among members of the European Union (formerly the European Community) is replete with different examples of this. Operational sovereignty is a necessary concept for analyzing and understanding these changes.

With these three different dimensions of the institution of sovereignty—negative sovereignty, positive sovereignty, and operational sovereignty—we are better equipped to face the debate over the increasing or decreasing importance of sovereignty. Our argument is that uneven globalization and the end of the Cold War have invoked changes that point to an increased importance for sovereignty.

First, formal, negative sovereignty is granted to more than ex-colonies. Parts of previously multinational states demand and are accorded recognition of sovereignty (i.e., the former USSR, Yugoslavia, etc). As a result, the number of quasi-states or semi-quasi-states has increased dramatically since 1989. In other words, it is easier for potential candidates for statehood to achieve formal recognition in the form of negative sovereignty than it was during the Cold War.

In particular, some quasi-states in the former Soviet Union have been readily recognized by the international community. All the same, clear criteria for recognizing new states are lacking. Some ethnic groups have been frustrated in their attempts to establish sovereignty (i.e., some of the Russian republics). Consent is required from established sovereigns, and here power politics still plays an important role (i.e., the Kurds). The criteria for acceptance of statehood by other states has become one of the crucial determinants of the future structure of the international system.

As regards positive sovereignty, the picture is mixed. On the one hand, positive sovereignty is in good shape in the sense that many states in the South have increased their capacity to act, both internally and externally. On the other hand, uneven globalization tends to undermine the positive sovereignty of states, their ability to conduct effective policies, in the South as well as in the North.

Facing uneven globalization, states must often choose some combination of two principal strategies. One is to defend positive sovereignty through protectionism and other regulation of the state's intercourse with other states. It is a defensive strategy that attempts to regain the loss of positive sovereignty by controlling or limiting intercourse with other states.

In an increasingly globalized world, such a defensive strategy is less and less feasible. The alternative strategy is increased cooperation among states, including common institution-building, employing sovereignty as a bargaining chip. This leads to the situation of limited operational sovereignty, which was described earlier.

The different dimensions of sovereignty highlighted here expose the simplicity of the sovereignty assumption in realist thinking. It is misleading to use sovereignty as the basis for maintaining a razor-sharp divide between a domestic and an international sphere. It is also misleading theoretically to posit all states as sovereign equals in the international realm. States may be equal in the formal, juridical sense covered by the concept of negative sovereignty. Yet there may be great variation in terms of positive sovereignty, as well as in the operational sovereignty, of states. Without these latter dimensions, a full analysis of how sovereignty is affected by uneven globalization and the end of the Cold War will be much more difficult.

The three dimensions of sovereignty proposed here need to be further developed conceptually, but even in the present sketchy form they (1) underline the enduringly privileged position of states in the post–Cold War international system, (2) make it possible to highlight the differences between *sovereign* states in the new international system, and (3) alert us to the fact that sovereignty has in fact become more useful as an analytical concept in international relations with the changes of uneven globalization and the end of the Cold War.

THE RETURN OF ECONOMICS AND
NEW FORMS OF DOMINANCE

The core focus of realism is power politics pursued by states. Liberalist contributions have argued for an expanded research agenda, including cooperation and regime-building among states. We argue for a further expansion of the research agenda to include the structure of economics. Uneven globalization and the end of the Cold War have brought economics more strongly into the focus of international relations. A theoretical adaptation to this situation is necessary.

Furthermore, such a focus helps us appreciate that old structures of dominance in the international system have not gone away. In other words, we cannot support the assertion made by some scholars that economic and political power has become so diffused that any overall power structure has disappeared. On the contrary, old structures of economic dominance have been supplemented by new (ideological) ones. This does not mean that we subscribe to world system analysis or other radical versions of dependency theory,[47] but the issues raised by these approaches are more relevant than ever. We briefly outline a way to address them later in this section.

The relationship between politics and economics is one of the classical debates in political science. During the Cold War, this issue was confined to specificities of West-West interdependent relations on the one hand and North-South dependency relations on the other. With the end of the Cold War, the question of politics and economics has immediate global relevance. There is a "global political economy" created by uneven globalization, and this must be acknowledged by IR theory.

For quite some time, economics and politics in IR were seen as almost totally isolated from each other, as qualitatively different activities to be studied with qualitatively different approaches. Today, advocates of the main approaches perceive a close interrelationship between politics and economics. We agree entirely with the assertion by Robert Keohane that politics and economics are two sides of the same coin.[48] Even so, there is a tendency in important contributions to either subject economics to the logic of (power) politics (e.g., realism) or vice versa and to subject politics to the logic of economics (e.g., world system analysis).[49]

In other words, the assertion that politics and economics are two sides of the same coin is less of a final solution than it is the opening of a vast problematique. The relationship between the two has only just begun to be charted, and the endeavor may proceed from several possible angles and levels.[50] There appear to be two basic strategies in present attempts to deal with the relationship. One is exemplified by Robert Gilpin's approach.[51] We may call it "Stay with your old recipe and add some flavor"; for example, if the old recipe is anarchy and power politics, the flavor is economic interdependence and the pursuit of wealth. If the old recipe is unequal development in the capitalist world economy, the flavor is competition and military rivalry among states.

The other basic strategy is "Choose any recipe from the politico-economic cookbook," or, as Susan Strange suggests, "Pick-Your-Own: or Suit Yourself."[52] Her starting point is four related dimensions of structural power,[53] namely security, production, knowledge, and finance, where "each structure affects the other, but none necessarily dominates."[54] Each of these structures can then be studied in its own right and in its relationships to the others. If this endeavor is combined with the analysis of changes in the authority-market balance for each dimension of structural power and, in addition, analyzed from the perspective not only of states but of other important actors as well (classes, firms, international organizations, etc.), we get a vast research territory where only small parts have been filled out.

We cannot complete this research puzzle here. We can merely suggest a starting point for further analysis, that is, the concept of a dialectical interplay between two equally important logics of politics and economics. At the core of politics is conflict and cooperation between states in the international system. At the core of economics is capital accumulation in a world dominated by capitalism. For a number of purposes it may be useful to further differentiate both along the economic dimension (as, for example, Susan Strange does) and along the political dimension and analyze from the perspective of many different actors, but this will not be pursued here. The point in the present context is that the economic dimension of uneven globalization needs to be studied in its own right as well as in its interplay with politics.

Some scholars argue that both economic and political power have become so diffused in the post–Cold War globalized world that unambiguous structures of dominance can no longer be identified.[55] Against the background of the analyses in this volume, we must disagree. The economic structure of center-periphery dominance analyzed by world-system theorists and others remains in place. There are still strong and weak states in the broad sense identified by Barry Buzan and others.[56] Furthermore, there is an ideological dimension involved. The international system is being divided into a group of democratic and a group of nondemocratic states. Recent policy measures of political conditionalities and new forms of interventionism indicate that the international system will be increasingly shaped by a confrontation between democratic and nondemocratic states.[57] This confrontation can take many forms, and some of them may be violent. With democracy as the dominant form of regime in the international system, it will be less acceptable internationally that some states deny their citizens democratic rights. One consequence is that domestic groups in many states will have an international audience for grievances against regimes less democratic than the accepted international norm. It will be harder to maintain nondemocratic rules and institutions. Events in Peru and Thailand in 1992 demonstrated that international pressure is present when states move away from established democratic procedures. Yet the acceptance of China into the international community shortly after the Tiananmen events show that realpolitik is still influential in setting rules of the game in the international system.

One outcome of the ideological dominance of liberal democracy in the present international system may be the establishment of a common set of regime standards that define what the international community sees as acceptable forms of governance. The standards set by the Development Assistance Committee of the OECD points in this direction.[58] Yet there are few indicators that the consolidated liberal democracies of the industrialized West will invest large resources in order to push other countries toward democracy.[59] And for reasons of national interest, be they security or economics, a number of countries (with China as the most prominent example) will be allowed to violate established democratic norms, permitting the bleak scenarios out-lined in this book by Claude Ake (Chapter 2), Osvaldo Sunkel (Chpater 3), and Gowher Rizvi (Chapter 4). A large number of weak or relatively weak countries in the developing world exhibit the surface indicators of liberal democracy demanded by donors, namely multipartyism and elections, cou-pled with a readiness to pursue market-friendly economic policies of integra-tion in the world market and support for the private sector. Yet they enjoy none of the real benefits of consolidated democracy, such as efficient and well-functioning institutions and a polity that is democratic in the sense that all major groups in society have a political voice. And market-friendly poli-cies still need to produce more tangible results for large popular groups.

This being said, the regional variation mentioned already needs to be em-phasized again. We cannot subscribe to the world-system-analysis view of seeing the development problem purely in terms of economic exploitation of the periphery by the core. It is true that the periphery is subject to more seri-ous external constraints in its development efforts than the core, but the pe-riphery is not doomed to failure. Historically informed analysis of the inter-action of economic and political forces in specific sociocultural contexts allows for a differentiation between countries and regions and for a nonreductionist, noneconomistic analysis of the interplay between different internal and external factors influencing the process of development. Fer-nando Henrique Cardoso has been a prominent exponent of this mode of analysis.[60]

In more general terms, many countries in the periphery appear to be facing two problems. On the one hand, access to the world economy is increasingly difficult, not primarily because of trade barriers but due to lack of demand. "The brutal truth," says Kari Levitt, "is that the industrialized world has de-creasing need for the countries of the periphery, either as sources of raw ma-terials, or as markets, or as cheap labour."[61] On the other hand, in order to reap maximum benefits of any world market integration, domestic political and economic reform is needed in many countries, and it may not be forth-coming. Dieter Senghaas and Ulrich Menzel have shown the decisive impor-tance of domestic preconditions for successfully facing external challenges (and seizing opportunities).[62] In an increasingly globalized world, such les-sons are acutely relevant.

In sum, the economic dimension of uneven globalization needs to be stud-ied in its own right, as well as in its interplay with politics. Focus on econom-ics in a global context helps identify old structures of dominance overlaid by new ideological elements. Together with the internal factors in specific societies, a global economical-political focus constitutes the raw material for a sensitive, historically based approach to the analysis of development prob-lems in the periphery.

CONCLUSION: INTERNATIONAL RELATIONS
THEORY FACING CHANGE

We have analyzed change as expressed by uneven globalization and the end of the Cold War. We have identified a world that is characterized neither by one particular order nor by chaos. It is a world replete with regional variation, but also with distinct patterns. Globalization sets an agenda that presents dissimilar but always urgent challenges in the regions.

These changes have made realism obsolete as the principal theory of international politics. Others have reached similar conclusions.[63] We differ from them in maintaining that the state is still the central object of analysis in international relations. The international system, with states as privileged actors, remains the backbone of international politics, but the system no longer conforms to one single ordering principle, as claimed by realism.

Therefore, it is not useful to look for a single, parsimonious theoretical approach as nominee for a replacement of realism. We have argued for a focus on middle-range theory. We have also tried to emphasize a common meeting ground for such endeavors:

1. An analysis of the changed role of states, starting from a richer concept of state than has characterized the discipline so far. This includes the issues of state autonomy, the state as repository of collective identity, and increasing difficulties for states in satisfying demands.
2. A focus on the institution of sovereignty, including its various dimensions. These include positive and negative sovereignty as well as operational sovereignty.
3. A focus on the structure of economics and its interplay with politics and ideology. On the global level this leads to identification of new patterns of dominance. On the national level it helps to highlight the continued importance of the state for economic development.

Where does this lead in terms of new theory? We started with the ambition of analyzing the combined effects of uneven globalization and the end of the Cold War as these variables were "filtered through" different geographical regions and different types of societal structures. The analyses in this book have focused mainly on different patterns of regional dynamics. But the conceptual distinctions made previously help identify another dimension, which may theoretically be the most promising. It is the interplay between systemic dynamics and different main types of societal structures. We have summarized systemic dynamics in uneven globalization and the end of the Cold War. But theorizing about present world politics requires more than the general analysis of systemic forces. The specific dynamics of different types of units, that is, different types of states, need to go into the picture. All of the contributions to the present volume focus on this interplay between systemic dynamics on the one hand and "domestic" forces of different types of states on the other. In so doing, they support a healthy trend in the discipline, which argues that

> a *comparativist* approach which distinguishes among types of societies and states and their shifting relationships to each other is needed to provide the context within which the alternative explanatory theories favored by specialists on *international* politics can be evaluated. ... Both comparativism and international relations theory need to recognize and analyze complex linkages between inter-state, trans-state, and intra-state dynamism. To recognize and understand the reasons for these variations, their global causes and consequences, requires both the international and comparativist approaches.[64]

We have focussed on the ways in which systemic dynamics affect the role of states. We have emphasized the way in which states change as a result. Let us now turn to examining how these changes affect different types of states. In other words, what are the consequences of employing the comprehensive notions of state and sovereignty outlined previously to make a distinction between different main types of state units in the present international system?

If we think in terms of ideal types, there appears to be not one but three kinds of state in the present international system. They are the premodern, the modern, and the postmodern state. Each type is characterized by specific patterns of conflict, and each confronts world politics in its own way.

The *premodern state* enjoys negative, formal sovereignty, but it has a limited degree of positive sovereignty. It is the quasi-state as identified by Robert Jackson. State institutions are weak and do not have direct, monopolized control over the means of violence. The state is also weak in economic terms, externally dependent with a low degree of industrialization. Many African countries are examples of the premodern state.

In premodern states the main conflicts are domestic (Somalia, Algeria, Angola). The processes of democratization invoked in part by uneven globalization and the end of the Cold War have stimulated new domestic conflicts between classes and groups to which democratization gave an increased voice.

The *modern state* corresponds better to the conventional IR image of the state. The state enjoys positive sovereignty. In economic terms, there is a national, industrialized economy. Anthony Giddens's definition of the nation-state applies to the modern state: "a set of institutional forms of governance maintaining an administrative monopoly over a territory with demarcated boundaries (borders), its rule being sanctioned by law and direct control over the means of internal and external violence."[65] Japan and the United States are typical examples.

Relations between modern states may fit the realist picture of power-balancing states in an anarchical realm. But relations may also be characterized by cooperation and institutionalization, which fits the liberal picture. In other words, there may be different degrees of anarchy in relationships between modern states.[66] The possible spectrum of relations is well covered by the analytical frameworks offered by (neo)realist and (neo)liberal approaches.[67]

The *postmodern* state is a different specimen. Here the most sacred principle of the modern state, that of sovereignty providing protection from outside interference, has been tampered with. Postmodern states allow outside interference in their domestic affairs because they get something in return: influence on a supranational level of governance. Why is such influence vital for postmodern states? Because previous processes of globalization have eroded actual, positive national sovereignty. In postmodern states, it is less relevant to talk about national economies.

The notion of state power loses relevance in a system of postmodern states because power is increasingly diffused to different levels, different types of resources, and different actors. Power diffusion unfolds both in an upward direction toward the supranational level and in a downward direction toward regional and local levels.

There may be no state that conforms fully with the postmodern ideal type. But it is clear that member states of the European Union are in a process of transition from modern to postmodern entities. This is no lawlike process, of course, and it may involve setbacks and crises. We cannot even know whether the postmodern ideal type of state described here will be the end result of the process.

We have argued that the use of force is irrelevant as a medium for solving disputes between postmodern states. Setting forth codified rules of behavior for conflict resolution is indeed part of the very creation of supranational governance. War in the traditional sense (i.e., between modern states) is thus out of the question in post-modern relations. Yet the truth is that beyond this we know very little about typical patterns of conflict in the postmodern world. Will the ongoing diffusion of power lead to a new kind of chaos where islands of anarchy (e.g., a mafia-dominated Sicily) and areas of order coexist within the same postmodern realm?

In sum, uneven globalization and the end of the Cold War affect existing state units, which change as a result. There have always been different types of state units in the international system. At present, the international system contains three main types of state, the premodern, the modern, and the postmodern. Patterns of conflict and cooperation vary substantially between these types. Variation in types of units and their typical relations creates the need for different theoretical cuts. This is why middle-range approaches are necessary. We need to know more about relations, both between states of a

FIGURE 10.1   System/State Unit Dynamics

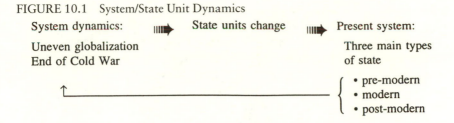

similar type and between different types of states. The analyzes in this book are a contribution to such efforts. For example, Michael Zürn's contribution (Chapter 8) can be read as an exploration of a cluster of states in transition to postmodern statehood; in Chapter 2, Claude Ake analyzes the premodern states in Africa; and Takashi Inoguchi, in Chapter 7, investigates the modern states in Pacific Asia.

Figure 10.1 summarizes the interplay between system and unit dynamics.

In a sense, this is our "theory." It conceives of a constant interplay between system and units, between domestic and international. In (neo)realist analysis, like units are treated as black-boxed billiard balls forced to respond to systemic dynamics in specific ways. The notion of like units hinges on the concept of states constituted as sovereign equals in the international system. We reject this notion of like units and the unproblematized conception of sovereignty, upon which it is based. Different main types of sovereignty point to different main types of states.

In this chapter, we have set forth more nuanced concepts of state and sovereignty, which help identify these different main types of units. A logical next step is to further analyze characteristics and typical relations of such distinct types of units, that is, to combine the system-level approach pursued here with a unit-level approach. This strategy, we think, will help provide a nuanced yet precise picture of international relations in a post–Cold War world.

Our approach is, of course, much less parsimonious than realism. It also foresees a larger and more complex research agenda than the "clash of civilizations" perspective set forth by Samuel Huntington or "the coming anarchy" argument by Richard Kaplan. Both of these latter contributions contain valuable insights, especially for our understanding of premodern states. But the thrust of their main arguments amounts to a severe underestimation of the continued importance of states combined with a tendency to reduce regional diversity to one-dimensional notions of civilizational conflict and anarchy.[68]

In sum, we believe the approach presented here contains a necessary, warranted complexity. It is premised on the belief that it is impossible "to study international relations in the absence of comparative analysis," that is, a focus on system dynamics is not enough.[69] Domestic dynamics of different types of units must have a place in the pursuit of international studies.

We have argued that in a sense IR theory is back where it started, with a focus on states, what they do, and why. But it is an agenda radically different from that of realism because the role of states has changed and so has, in important ways, the entire system. We must deal with a system that is a complex combination of old and new. The theories and concepts we employ must reflect this world of variation.

Notes

PREFACE AND ACKNOWLEDGMENTS

1. Hans-Henrik Holm and Georg Sørensen, "A New World Order: The Withering Away of Anarchy and the Triumph of Individualism? Consequences for IR-Theory," *Cooperation and Conflict* 28, no. 3 (1993): 265–301.

CHAPTER 1

1. Ferdinand Braudel, *The Structures of Everyday Life: The Limits of the Possible,* vol. 1 (New York: Harper and Row, 1981).

2. Bjorn Hettne, "Regionalism: Resurgent and Emergent," paper presented at the International Conference on the Democratization Process in South Asia, Colombo, August 19–22, 1992; Iver B. Neumann, "Regions in International Relations Theory," Norwegian Institute of International Affairs Research Report, no. 162, November 1992.

3. Robert Cooper, "Is There a New World Order?" in Seizaburo Sato and Trevor Taylor, eds., *Prospects for Global Order,* vol. 2 (London: Royal Institute of International Affairs, 1993), pp. 8–24.

4. Hedley Bull, *The Anarchical Society* (London: Macmillan, 1977), p. 8.

5. Kenneth N. Waltz, "The Emerging Structure of International Politics," *International Security* 18, no. 2 (1993): 44–79; Charles Krauthammer, "The Unipolar Moment," *Foreign Affairs* 70, no. 1 (Winter 1991): 23–33.

6. James Goldgeir and Michael McFaul, "A Tale of Two Worlds: Core and Periphery in the Post–Cold War Era," *International Organization* 46, no. 1 (Spring 1992): 467–492; Max Singer and Aaron Wildavsky, *The Real World Order, Zones of Peace/Zones of Turmoil* (Chatham, N.J.: Chatham House, 1993).

7. Goldgeir and McFaul, "A Tale of Two Worlds"; John Ravenhill, "The New Disorder in the Periphery," in Richard Leaver and James Richardson, *Charting the Post–Cold War Order* (Boulder: Westview Press, 1994), 69–80; Robert D. Kaplan, "The Coming Anarchy," *Atlantic Monthly,* February 1994, pp. 44–76.

8. Paul Hirst and Grahame Thompson, eds., "The Problem of 'Globalization': International Economic Relations, National Economic Management and the Formation of Trading Blocs," *Economy and Society* 21, no. 4 (1992): 358–359.

9. Ibid., p. 360–361.

10. Ibid., p. 199.

11. Jan Aart Scholte, "From Power Politics to Social Change: An Alternative Focus for International Studies," *Review of International Studies* 19 (1993): 8.

12. Janice E. Thompson and Stephen D. Krasner, "Global Transactions and the Consolidation of Sovereignty," in E.-O. Czempiel and James Rosenau, eds., *Global*

Changes and Theoretical Challenges: Approaches to World Politics for the 1990s (Lexington, Mass.: Lexington Books, 1989), pp. 195–220.

13. Anthony Giddens, The Consequences of Modernity (Cambridge, England: Polity Press, 1990); James Rosenau, Turbulence in World Politics: A Theory of Change and Continuity (Princeton: Princeton University Press, 1990).

14. See Dieter Senghaas, "Zwischen Globalisierung und Fragmentierung: Ein Beitrag zur Weltordnungsdebatte," Blätter für deutsche und internationale Politik, no. 1 (1993): 50–59.

15. David Held and Anthony McGrew, "Globalization and the Liberal Democratic State," Government and Opposition 28, no. 2 (1993): 263.

16. Ibid.

17. See Giddens, The Consequences of Modernity, p. 139.

18. John Lewis Gaddis, "The Cold War, the Long Peace, and the Future," in Geir Lundestad and Odd Arne Westad, eds., Beyond the Cold War: New Dimensions in International Relations (Oslo: Universitetsforlaget, 1992), pp. 7–22.

19. John J. Mearsheimer, "Back to the Future: Instability in Europe After the Cold War," International Security 15, no. 1 (1990): 5–57.

20. If the international system is no longer anarchic, the modus operandi of states is transformed. The invariant relationship between the structure of the state and the international system ceases to exist. See Barry Buzan, Charles Jones, and Richard Little, The Logic of Anarchy: Neorealism to Structural Realism (New York: Columbia University Press, 1993), pp. 165–168. Edward Kolodziej, "Renaissance in Security Studies? Caveat Lector!" International Studies Quarterly 36, no. 4 (1992): 421–438.

21. Charles Krauthammer, "The Unipolar Moment," Foreign Affairs 70, no. 1 (Winter 1991): 23–33.

22. Kenneth Waltz, "The New World Order," Millennium: Journal of International Studies 22, no. 2 (1993): 187–195.

23. See ibid.

24. Geir Lundestad, "Beyond the Cold War: New and Old Dimensions in International Relations," in Lundestad and Westad, Beyond the Cold War, pp. 245–257; Gaddis, "The Cold War, the Long Peace, and the Future."

25. Cooper, "Is There a New World Order?" p. 12.

26. Hans J. Morgenthau, Politics Among Nations: The Struggle for Power and Peace (New York: Alfred Knopf, 1966), p. 25.

27. Joseph S. Nye, Jr., Bound to Lead: The Changing Nature of American Power (New York: Basic Books, 1990), pp. 173–202.

28. Richard Falk, "The Infancy of Global Civil Society," in Lundestad and Westad, Beyond the Cold War, p. 231.

29. See Paul G. Lewis, "Superpower Rivalry and the End of the Cold War," in Anthony G. McGrew and Paul G. Lewis et al., Global Politics (Cambridge: Polity Press, 1992); Francis Fukuyama, The End of History and the Last Man (New York: Avon Books, 1992), pp. 276–286.

30. See Goldgeir and McFaul, "A Tale of Two Worlds"; and Georg Sørensen, "Kant and Processes of Democratization: Consequences for Neorealist Thought," Journal of Peace Research 29, no. 4 (1992): 397–415.

31. See Kari Levitt, "Debt, Adjustment and Development: Looking to the 1990s," Economic and Political Weekly (July 21, 1990): 1586.

CHAPTER 2

1. UNDP (United Nations Development Programme), *Human Development Report 1992* (Oxford: Oxford University Press, 1992), p. 1.

2. Ibid., p. 4.

3. World Bank, *World Development Report 1990* (Oxford: Oxford University Press, 1990).

4. Both quotes from James H. Mittelman, *Out from Underdevelopment: Prospects for the Third World* (New York: St. Martin's Press, 1988), p. 31.

5. Ibid., pp. 31–32.

6. C. Krauthammer, "The Unipolar Moment," *Foreign Affairs* 70, no. 1 (Winter 1991): 32.

7. William Pfaff, "Redefining World Power," *Foreign Affairs* 70, no. 1 (1990–1991): 30.

8. Sergei Rogov, "International Security and the Collapse of the Soviet Union," *Washington Quarterly* 15, no. 2 (Spring 1992): 21.

9. David Rothkopf, "Living Between the Wars," CEO *International Strategies* 3, no. 2 (October-November 1990): 7.

10. C. Krauthammer, "Do We Really Need a New Enemy?" *Time Magazine*, March 23, 1992, p. 76.

11. Krauthammer, "The Unipolar Moment," p. 31.

12. Peter J. Garrity and Sharon Weiner, "U.S. Defense Strategy After the Cold War," *Washington Quarterly* 15, no. 2 (Spring 1992): 58.

13. Krauthammer, "The Unipolar Moment," p. 24.

14. Ibid.

15. David Gergen, "America's Missed Opportunities," *Foreign Affairs* 71, no. 1 (1991–1992): 1–2.

16. Zbigniew Brzezinski, "Selective Global Commitment," *Foreign Affairs* 70, no. 4 (Fall 1991): 5.

17. Zbigniew Brzezinski, "Order, Disorder and U.S. Leadership," *Washington Quarterly* 15, no. 2 (Spring 1992); Brzezinski, "Selective Global Commitment," pp. 8–9.

18. Zbigniew Brzezinski, *The Grand Failure: The Birth and Death of Communism in the Twentieth Century* (New York: Scribner, 1989), p. 6.

19. Brzezinski, "Selective Global Commitment," p. 19.

20. Ibid., p. 6.

21. Pfaff, "Redefining World Power," pp. 44–45.

22. Ibid.

23. Krauthammer, "The Unipolar Movement," p. 32.

24. Pfaff, "Redefining World Power," p. 47.

25. Michael Mandelbaum, "The Bush Foreign Policy," *Foreign Affairs* 70, no. 1 (1990–1991): 5.

CHAPTER 3

1. S. Griffith-Jones and O. Sunkel, *The Latin American Debt and Development Crises: The End of an Illusion* (Oxford: Clarendon Press, 1986); O. Sunkel, "Eco-

nomic Reform in Historical Perspective," in A. Solimano, O. Sunkel, and M. Blejer, eds., *Rebuilding Capitalism: Alternative Roads After Socialism and Dirigism* (Ann Arbor: University of Michigan Press, 1994).

2. A. Maddison, *Dynamic Forces in Capitalist Development. A Long-Run Comparative View* (Oxford: Oxford University Press, 1991).

3. R. Gilpin, *The Political Economy of International Relations* (Princeton: Princeton University Press, 1987); Maddison, *Dynamic Forces in Capitalist Development.*

4. A. Shonfield, *Modern Capitalism* (Oxford: Oxford University Press, 1965).

5. O. Sunkel and P. Paz, *El subdesarrollo latinoamericano y la teoría del desarrollo* (Mexico, D.F.: Siglo XIX Editores, 1970).

6. Maddison, *Dynamic Forces in Capitalist Development: A Long-Run Comparative View* (New York: Oxford University Press, 1991), p. 168.

7. P. Armstrong, A. Glyn, and J. Harrison, *Capitalism Since 1945* (Oxford and Cambridge, Mass.: Basil Blackwell, 1991), p. 117.

8. United Nations Development Programme, *Human Development Report 1990* (New York and Oxford: Oxford University Press, 1990), p. 2.

9. V. Tokman, "Pobreza y homogeneización social: Tareas para los 90," *Pensamiento Iberoamericano: Revista de Economía Política* (Madrid) (January 1991): 82.

10. A. Maddison, *The World Economy in the Twentieth Century* (Paris: OECD, 1989).

11. C. Freeman, J. Clark, and L. Soete, *Unemployment and Technical Innovation* (London: Frances Pinter, 1982); M. Piore and C. F. Sabel, *The Second Industrial Divide: Possibilities for Prosperity* (New York: Basic Books, 1984); K. Hoffman and R. Kaplinsky, *Driving Force: The Global Restructuring of Technology, Labour and Investment in the Automobile Components Industries* (Boulder and London: Westview Press, 1988); M. Castells, *The Informational City: Information Technology, Economic Restructuring, and the Urban-Regional Process* (Oxford: Basil Blackwell, 1989); E. Rodriguez, "The Endogenization of Technological Change: A Development Challenge," in O. Sunkel, ed., *Development from Within: Toward a Neostructuralist Approach for Latin America* (Boulder and London: Lynne Rienner, 1993).

12. Bjorn Hettne, "Regionalism: Resurgent and Emergent," paper presented at the International Conference on the Democratization Process in South Asia, Colombo, August 19–22, 1992.

13. United Nations, *World Investment Report 1991: The Trial in Foreign Direct Investment* (New York: UN, 1991); United Nations, *World Investment Report: Transnational Corporations as Engines of Growth* (New York: UN, 1992); United Nations, *World Investment Report 1993: Transnational Corporations and Integrated International Production* (New York: UN, 1993); M. Mortimore, "A New International Industrial Order: Increased International Competition in a TNC-Centric World" *CEPAL Review* (Santiago), no. 48 (August 1992): 41–63.

14. O. Sunkel, "Transnational Capitalism and National Disintegration in Latin America," *Social and Economic Studies* 22, no. 1 (March 1973): 132–177; O.

Sunkel, "Transnationalization and Its National Consequences," in José A. Villamil and E. Fuenzalida, eds., *Transnational Capitalism and National Development: New Perspectives on Dependence* (Hassocks, England: Harvester Press, 1979), pp. 67–95; J. Lewis Gaddis, "Toward the Post-War World," *Foreign Affairs* 70, no. 2 (1991): 102–122.

15. O. Sunkel, "Consolidating Democracy and Development in Chile," *CEPAL Review,* no. 47 (August 1992): 37–46.

16. L. Freedman, "Order and Disorder in the New World," *Foreign Affairs* 71, no. 1 (1992): 20–37; Gaddis, "Toward the Post-War World."

17. L. Tomassini, *Estado, governabilidad y desarrollo* (Santiago: CINDE-FORO 90, 1992); J. Keane, ed., *Civil Society and the State* (London: Verso, 1988).

18. O. Bouin and C. Michalet, *Rebalancing the Public and Private Sectors* (Paris: OECD, 1991).

19. A. Lipietz, *Mirages and Miracles: The Crisis of Global Fordism* (London: Verso, 1987); J. Dunning, "Governments—Markets—Firms: Toward a New Balance?" *CTC Reporter* (New York: UN), no. 31 (Spring 1991): 2–7; S. Ostry, *Government and Corporations in a Shrinking World: Trade and Innovation Policies in the United States, Europe and Japan* (New York: Council on Foreign Relations, 1990); J. M. Salazar, "The Role of the State and the Market in Economic Development," in Sunkel, *Development from Within,* pp. 361–395; R. B. Reich, *The Work of Nations* (New York: Vintage Books, 1991).

20. M. Agosin and D. Tussie, "Globalization, Regionalization and New Dilemmas in Trade Policy for Development," *World Competition* (June 1992): 37–63.

21. P. Krugman, "Toward a Counter-Counter Revolution in Development Theory," *Proceedings of the World Bank Annual Conference on Development Economics,* Washington, D.C., 1992, pp. 15–38.

22. S. Griffith-Jones and O. Sunkel, *The Latin American Debt and Development Crises: The End of an Illusion* (Oxford: Clarendon Press, 1986).

23. S. Lal, *The Poverty of "Development Economics"* (London: Institute of Economic Affairs, 1983).

24. ECLAC, "Changing Production Patterns with Social Equity" (Santiago: UN, ECLAC, 1990), pamphlet; ECLAC, "Social Equity and Changing Production Patterns: An Integrated Approach" (Santiago: UN, ECLAC, 1992), pamphlet; C. Coldough and J. Manor, eds., *State or Markets? Neoliberalism and the Development Policy Debate* (Oxford: Clarendon Press, 1991); O. Sunkel and G. Zuleta, "Development Policy at the Crossroads: Neoliberalism vs. Neostructuralism," *CEPAL Review* (December 1990): 35–51; Sunkel, *Development from Within.*

25. A. D. Chandler, *Scale and Scope: The Dynamics of Industrial Capitalism* (Cambridge, Mass.: The Belknap Press of Harvard University Press, 1990); Ostry, *Government and Corporations.*

26. R. Wade, "State and Market Revisited. How Interventionist Should Third-World Governments Be?" *Economist* (April 4, 1992): 77.

27. A. Przeworski, "La irracionalidad del capitalismo y la inviabilidad del socialismo," *Pensamiento Iberoamericano: Revista de Economía Política* (Madrid), no. 18 (July-December 1990): 97.

CHAPTER 4

1. Barry Buzan and Gowher Rizvi, *South Asian Insecurity and the Great Powers* (London: Macmillan, 1986), see chaps. 8 and 9.

2. Ibid., chap. 9.

3. The argument that ideological differences between India and Pakistan led to India's alliance with the Soviet Union and that of Pakistan with the so-called imperialist United States does not stand up to critical test. In 1962 India went to war with a "socialist" China and received aid from the capitalist West. Pakistan, the "most allied ally" of the capitalist United States, was at the same time a close ally of China—an alliance that has stood the test of time.

4. I have developed this theme in greater detail in *South Asia in a Changing International Order* (New Delhi: Sage, 1993), chap. 3.

5. Jagat S. Mehta, a former foreign secretary of India, also made this point at a seminar on Kashmir held at Oxford on June 23–24, 1990.

6. The role of the Pakistan military, especially that of General Ayub Khan, has not yet been fully explored. Ayub was at this time scheming to capture political power in Pakistan and needed U.S. support to strengthen the armed forces. Since Pakistan public opinion was hostile to joining a Western-sponsored alliance, Ayub sought to dupe the public into believing that the 1954 U.S.-Pakistan mutual defense agreement was directed against India. In fact, the pact specifically forbade the use of weapons supplied by the United States against India. See Gowher Rizvi, "India, Pakistan, and the Kashmir Problem, 1947–1972," in Raju G.C. Thomas, ed., *Perspectives on Kashmir: The Roots of Conflict in South Asia* (Boulder: Westview Press, 1992), pp. 47–79.

7. *Dialogue* (Dhaka) April 27, p. 7, and May 4, 1990, p. 5.

8. Pran Chopra's concluding remarks at the Wilton Park conference "The Regional Balance in a Time of Shifting Super-Power Relations and Rapid Economic Development," London, March 26–30, 1990.

9. Gowher Rizvi, "South Asian Association for Regional Cooperation: Problems and Prospects," in *EC-India Perspectives in a Changing International Order* (Brussels: Centre for European Policy Studies, 1989), pp. 49–63.

10. India's rescue operation in the Maldives, following an attempted coup by foreign mercenaries, was expressly at the invitation of the government and therefore cannot be described as intervention. The Indian forces were withdrawn shortly after the coup bid was foiled.

11. See Mehtab Ali Shah, "The Linkages Between Pakistan's Domestic Politics and Its Foreign Policy: 1971–91," (Ph.D. diss., University of London, 1993).

12. S. D. Muni, *Pangs of Proximity: India and Sri Lanka's Ethnic Crisis* (New Delhi: Sage, 1993), see esp. chaps. 4 and 5.

13. Barry Buzan, "New Patterns of Global Security in the Twenty-first Century," *International Affairs* 67, no. 3 (July 1991): 431–451.

14. It has been argued that the People's Republic of China has already been co-opted. In the Security Council debates, both during the Gulf crisis and subsequently on Libya's alleged involvement in the explosion of the Pan Am flight over Lockerbie, Scotland, China did not endorse the resolutions by the Western powers but nevertheless refrained from using its veto. In the case of Saddam Hussein's aggression against Kuwait, the issues were clear-cut, and China may have found it difficult to oppose

UN sanctions against Iraq; but the issues were not so clear-cut as to prevent it from vetoing the sanctions against Libya. Indeed, it has been argued that it was Britain and the United States, rather than Libya, that may have breached international law. See Francis A. Boyle, "Libya: Double Standards," *New Statesman and Society* (April 24, 1992): 1.

15. Sat P. Limaye, "United States Relations with India, 1981–1989: The Pursuit and Limits of Accommodation" (Ph.D. diss., Oxford University, 1991).

16. Buzan and Rizvi, *South Asian Insecurity and the Great Powers,* chap. 4.

17. D. Held et al., eds., *States and Societies* (Oxford: Martin Robertson, 1983), pp. 1–55.

18. R. Sisson and L. Rose, *War and Succession in Pakistan, India and the Creation of Bangladesh* (Berkeley: University of California Press, 1990).

19. S. Tahir-Kheli, *The United States and Pakistan: The Evolution of an Influence Relationship* (New York: Praeger, 1982).

20. B. H. Farmer, *An Introduction to South Asia* (London: Methuen, 1983), chap. 1.

21. The Maldives is the seventh state in the South Asian Association for Regional Cooperation (SAARC), but because of its geographical remoteness from the subcontinent, it is not included in the analysis.

22. Robert Jackson, *South Asian Crisis: India-Pakistan-Bangladesh* (London: IISS, Chatto & Windus, 1975); G. W. Chowdhury, *India, Pakistan, Bangladesh and the Major Powers: Politics of a Divided Subcontinent* (New York: Free Press, 1975).

23. For a fuller discussion of the impact of the end of the Cold War on South Asia see Gowher Rizvi, *South Asia in a Changing World Order* (New Delhi: Sage, 1993).

24. See Endymion Wilkinson, "Asia in the Year 2000," in *EC-India Perspectives in a Changing International Order,* pp. 15–22.

25. Ibid., p. 144.

26. A recent study has suggested caution in the face of free-market triumphalism. See Robin Broad, John Cavanagh, and Walden Bello, "Development: The Market Is Not Enough," *Foreign Policy,* no. 81 (Winter 1990–1991): 144–162.

27. For a fuller discussion see my "Democracy and Development in South Asia: First Things First," in John Richardson and S.W.R. Samarasinghe, eds., *Democratization in South Asia* (forthcoming).

28. James M. Buchanan, *Liberty, Market and State: Political Economy in the 1980s* (Sussex: Wheatsheaf, 1986); Milton Friedman, "The Role of Monetary Policy," *American Economic Review* 58, no. 1 (1968): 1–17.

29. President Clinton himself has questioned some aspects of the free-market philosophy and has emphasized the role of the state in economic recovery. If the trend persists, it is quite possible that vigorous adherence to free-market dogma might yet be moderated.

30. Rehman Sobhan, ed., *The Decade of Stagnation: The State of the Bangladesh Economy in the 1980's* (Dhaka: University Press, 1991), see chap. 1.

31. Syed Nawab Haider Naqvi, *Development Economics: A New Paradigm* (New Delhi: Sage, 1993), see chap. 6.

32. Lipton, M., "The State-Market Dilemma, Civil Society and Structural Adjustment: Any Cross-Commonwealth Lessons?" *Round Table* (January 1991): 21–31.

33. Rehman Sobhan, *Rethinking the Role of the State in Development: Asian Perspective* (Dhaka: University Press, 1993), chaps. 2 and 3.

34. Atul Kohli, "Democracy and Development," in J. P. Lewis and V. Kallab, eds., *Development Strategies Reconsidered* (New Brunswick, N.J.: Transaction Books, 1986), pp. 153–182.

35. Rehman Sobhan, "Regional Economic Cooperation in South Asia: Legacy and Prospects," *Economic Bulletin for Asia and the Pacific* 30, no. 1 (June 1979): 16–23.

CHAPTER 5

1. UNDP, *Human Development Report 1992* (New York: UNDP, 1992).

2. Francis Fukuyama, "The End of History?" *National Interest,* no. 16 (Summer 1989): 3–18.

3. Charles Krauthammer, "The Unipolar Moment," *Foreign Affairs* 70, no. 1 (Winter 1991): 23–33.

4. Ted Galen Carpenter, "The New World Disorder," *Foreign Policy* 84 (Fall 1991): 24.

5. Andrei Kozyrev, "Russia: A Chance for Survival," *Foreign Affairs* 71, no. 2 (Spring 1992): 9.

6. UNDP, *Human Development Report 1992.*

7. Lester C. Thurow argues that regional integration is the intermediate step from the national economy to the world economy. Lester C. Thurow, *Head to Head—The Coming Economic Battle Among Japan, Europe and America* (New York: William Morrow, 1992).

8. *Yearbook of Chinese Statistics 1991* (Beijing: China Statistics, 1992).

9. Qiu Xiaohua, "On Chinese Economic Situation and Policy," *Outlook,* no. 28 (1993); *Xinhua News* (Beijing), pp. 4–5.

10. *Yearbook of Chinese Statistics 1991.*

11. Lu Jianren, "Dynamics of Eastern Asian Economy," *Outlook,* no. 28 (1993): 38.

12. United Nations, *World Investment Report 1993: Transnational Corporations and Integrated International Production* (New York: UN, 1993), p. 47.

13. The new optimism has emerged following a new estimation by the IMF of the Chinese economy based on domestic purchase parity; see the *Economist* (July 10, 1993): 10.

14. Samuel P. Huntington, "The Clash of Civilizations?" *Foreign Affairs* 72, no. 3 (Summer 1993): 22–49.

15. "Old Alliances, New Asia," *International Herald Tribune,* March 21, 1993, p. 1.

16. See Ian Wilson, "China and the New World Order," in Richard Leaver and James L. Richardson, eds., *Charting the Post–Cold War Order* (Boulder: Westview Press, 1993), pp. 194–209.

CHAPTER 6

1. James M. Goldgeier and Michael McFaul, "A Tale of Two Worlds: Core and Periphery in the Post–Cold War Era," *International Organization* 46, no. 1 (Spring 1992): 468–491.

2. See Andrei Kortunov, "The Soviet Legacy and Recent Foreign Policy Discussions in Russia," working paper, Luxembourg Institute for European and International Studies, April 1993, pp. 12–13.

3. Bogdan Szajkowski, "Will Russia Disintegrate into Bantustans?" *World Today*, no. 8–9 (August-September 1993): 172.

4. "The Fundamentals of Russia's Military Doctrine" (draft version), *Voennaya mysl*, special edition (May 1992): 3–9; Mary C. FitzGerald, "Chief of Russia's General Staff Academy Speaks Out on Moscow's New Military Doctrine," *Orbis*, no. 2 (Spring 1993): 282–283.

5. "The Ghosts of the Afghan War," *Newsweek*, August 9, 1993, p. 15.

6. Rowland Evans and Robert Novak, "Russia's 'Monroe Doctrine.'" *Washington Post*, February 26, 1993, p. A23.

7. Strobe Talbott, special envoy of President Bill Clinton to the CIS countries, condensed this attitude: Russia should not become a "nuclear Yugoslavia" (comments made during confirmation hearings for position of deputy secretary of state, February 8, 1994, Committee on Foreign Affairs, U.S. Congress).

8. For open advocacy of Ukrainian nuclear proliferation, see John J. Mearsheimer, "The Case for a Ukrainian Nuclear Deterrent," *Foreign Affairs* (Summer 1993): 50–66.

9. Goldgeier and McFaul, "A Tale of Two Worlds," pp. 478–479.

10. Geir Lundestad, "American Empire by Invitation," in *The Origins of the Cold War*, 3rd ed. (Lexington, Mass: Heath, 1991), pp. 11–18; Vladislav Zubok, "Tyranny of the Weak: Russia's New Foreign Policy," *World Policy Journal*, no. 2 (Winter 1992): 200–201.

11. Igor Baranovsky, "Russia May Become a World Leader in the Production and Peddling of Drugs," *Moscow News*, April 2, 1993.

12. Steve Coll, "Central Asia's High-Stakes Oil Game," *Washington Post*, May 9, 1993, p. A1; Assan A. Nougmanov, "Khazakhstan's Challenges: The Case of a Central Asian Nation in Transition," *Harvard International Review* 15, no. 3 (Spring 1993): 10–14.

13. U.S. Foreign Broadcast Information Service, FBIS Report Soviet Union, March 9, 1993, p. 5.

14. Ibid., March 24, 1993, p. 56.

15. Ibid., February 24, 1993, p. 13.

16. Ibid., March 15, 1993, p. 37; Stephen Foye, "Russian Arms Exports After the Cold War," *RFE/RL Research Report* 13 (March 26, 1993): 61–63.

17. Observation made by Dr. Wang Gungwu, vice-chancellor of the University of Hong Kong, at the Nobel Symposium, Tromso, July 31–August 4, 1993.

18. U.S. Foreign Broadcast Information Service, FBIS Report Soviet Union, "Will Turkestan Move Towards the Bosporus Beacon?" *FBIS-SOV-93-065*, April 7, 1993, p. 1.

19. Samuel P. Huntington, "The Clash of Civilizations?" *Foreign Affairs* 72, no. 3 (Summer 1993): 31.

20. Dimitry Furman, "Nasha strannaya revolutsia" (Our strange revolution), *Svobodnaya Misl*, no. 1 (January 1993): 12.

21. On this point, see Kortunov, "The Soviet Legacy," p. 13.

CHAPTER 7

1. My thinking on subjects related to this chapter can be found in Takashi Inoguchi, *Japan's International Relations* (London: Pinter; Boulder: Westview Press, 1991); Takashi Inoguchi, *Japan's Foreign Policy in an Era of Global Change* (London: Pinter, 1993); Takashi Inoguchi, "Japan's Foreign Policy in East Asia," *Current History* 91 (December 1992): 407–412; Takashi Inoguchi "The Coming Pacific Century?" *Current History* 93 (January 1994): 25–30.

2. Richard O'Brien, *Financial Integration: The End of Geography* (London: Pinter, 1992); Francis Fukuyama, *The End of History and the Last Man* (New York: Basic Books, 1991).

3. Wayne Sandholtz et al., *The Highest Stakes* (New York: Oxford University Press, 1992). Cf. Silvia Ostry, *Governments and Corporations in a Shrinking World* (New York: Council on Foreign Relations Press, 1990).

4. Cf. Robert Putnam and Nicholas Bayne, *Hanging Together,* rev. ed. (New York: Sage, 1987).

5. Ostry, *Governments and Corporations in a Shrinking World;* Henry Aaron et al., *Integrating the World Economy* (Washington, D.C.: Brookings Institution, September 1992).

6. John Coneybeare, *Trade Wars* (New York: Columbia University Press, 1987); Laura Tyson, *Who's Bashing Whom* (Washington, D.C.: Institute for International Economics, 1993); Henry Nau, *The Myth of America's Decline* (New York: Oxford University Press, 1990); Jeffrey Frankel and Miles Kahler, eds., *Rivalry and Regionalism in Pacific Asia* (Chicago: University of Chicago Press, 1994); Loukas Tsoukalis, *The New European Economy,* rev. ed. (Oxford: Oxford University Press, 1993).

7. Angus Maddison, *Phases of Capitalist Development* (Oxford: Oxford University Press); Angus Maddison, *Dynamic Forces in Capitalist Development* (New York: Oxford University Press, 1992); Samuel Huntington, *The Third Wave: Democratization in the Late Twentieth Century* (Norman: University of Oklahoma Press, 1991).

8. Takashi Inoguchi, "Asia and the Pacific Since 1945: A Japanese Perspective," in Robert H. Taylor, ed., *Handbooks to the Modern World: Asia and the Pacific* 2 (New York: Facts on File, 1991), pp. 903–920.

9. International Institute for Strategic Studies, *The Military Balance,* 1992–1993 (London: Brassey's, 1993).

10. Takashi Inoguchi, "Developments on the Korean Peninsula and Japan's Korean Policy," *Korean Journal of Defense Analysis* 5, no. 1 (Summer 1993): 27–39.

11. *Lianhe Zaopao* (Singapore), May 1, 1993.

12. Takashi Inoguchi, "Japan's Foreign Policy in East Asia," *Current History* 91 (December 1992): 407–412; also see "Japan Ties Up the Asian Market" *Economist* (April 24, 1993): 27–28. See also Robert Wade, *Governing the Market* (Princeton: Princeton University Press, 1990).

13. "China, a Confident Superpower Candidate for the Next Century," *Time,* May 10, 1993, pp. 14–45. Also see Wade, *Governing the Market.*

14. "The New Age Chaebol," *Far Eastern Economic Review* (May 13, 1993): 64–70. Also see Wade, *Governing the Market.*

15. "The Failure of Big Business," *Economist* (April 17, 1993): 11–12; also see Michael Piore and Charles Sable, *The Second Industrial Divide* (New York: Basic Books, 1984).

16. Peter Cowhey and Jonathan Aronson, *Managing the World Economy* (New York: Council on Foreign Relations Press, 1993). Cf. Ostry, *Governments and Corporations in a Shrinking World.*

17. Henry Aaron et al., *Integrating the World Economy.*

18. Bill Emmott, *Japan's Global Reach* (London: Century Business Books, 1993).

19. Takashi Inoguchi, "Children of Traditions," *Far Eastern Economic Review* (July 25, 1991): 15; David Potter, "Democratization in Asia," in David Held, ed., *Prospects for Democracy* (Cambridge: Polity Press, 1992), pp. 355–377.

20. Frank Ching, "Asian View of Human Rights Is Beginning to Take Shape," *Far Eastern Economic Review* (April 29, 1993): 27.

21. For example, Pierre Allan and Kjell Goldman, eds., *The End of the Cold War: Evaluating Theories of International Relations* (Dordrecht, Netherlands: Martin Nijhoff, 1992); Mike Bowker and Robin Brown, eds., *From Cold War to Collapse* (Cambridge: Cambridge University Press, 1993). See also R.B.J. Walker, *Inside/Outside International Relations as Political Theory* (Cambridge: Cambridge University Press, 1993); Michael Donelan, *Elements of International Political Theory* (Oxford: Clarendon Press, 1990).

22. Robert Keohane, *After Hegemony: Collaboration and Discord in World Politics* (Princeton: Princeton University Press, 1984); Robert Putnam, *Making Democracy Work* (Princeton: Princeton University Press, 1993).

23. Chalmers Johnson, *MITI and the Japanese Miracle* (Stanford: Stanford University Press, 1982); Emmott, *Japan's Global Reach.*

24. Douglass North, *Economic Change, Institutions and Institutional Change* (New York: Cambridge University Press, 1992).

CHAPTER 8

This chapter was written while I was the Thyssen Fellow for International Institutions at the Center for International Affairs, Harvard University. For the support of these institutions I want to express my gratitude. Thanks also to the contributors to this volume as well as to Emily Copeland, Wolf-Dieter Eberwein, Gunter Hellmann, Jeff Holzgraefe, Marc Levy, Thomas Risse-Kappen, and Christian Tuschhoff for helpful comments on earlier versions of this chapter.

1. Karl Polanyi, *The Great Transformation: The Political and Economic Origins of Our Time* (Boston: Beacon Press, 1957).

2. Karl W. Deutsch et al., *Political Community and the North Atlantic Area: International Organization in the Light of Historical Experience* (Princeton: Princeton University Press, 1957), p. 5.

3. As examples for this ambiguous use, see Pierre Allan and Kjell Goldmann, eds., *The End of the Cold War: Evaluating Theories of International Relations* (Dordrecht, Netherlands: Martin Nijhoff, 1992), and John Lewis Gaddis, "International Relations Theory and the End of Cold War," *International Security* 17, no. 3 (1992–1993): 5–58.

4. See James N. Rosenau, *Turbulence in World Politics: A Theory of Change and Continuity* (Princeton: Princeton University Press, 1990) for a thorough discussion of the concept of turbulence as a tool for understanding change in world politics. In contrary to Rosenau, I do not use the term as a general descriptor for postinternational politics but as limited to the realm of governance, that is, the scope and level of political regulation. For another early attempt to explore the sources and ramifications of seemingly contradictory developments, see Lothar Brock and Hans-Henrik Holm, "European Security in Transition—Overlayers and Undercurrents," unpublished paper (Aarhus and Frankfurt a.M., 1991).

5. Karl W. Deutsch, *Nationalism and Its Alternatives* (New York: Knopf, 1969), p. 99. The use of the concepts political integration and globalization heavily draws from the work of Karl Deutsch. However, contrary to Deutsch, I aim at distinguishing between political integration and social globalization. Both processes are in Deutsch's work part of the more encompassing concept of integration.

6. See Ulrich Beck, "Jenseits von Stand und Klasse? Soziale Ungleichheiten, gesellschaftliche Individualisierungsprozesse und die Entstehung von neuer sozialer Formationen und Identitäten," in Reinhard Kreckel, ed., *Soziale Ungleichheiten* (Göttingen: Schwarz, 1983), pp. 35–74.

7. See Thomas Meyer, *Modernisierung der Privatheit: Differenzierungs- und Individualisierungsprozesse des familialen Zusammenlebens* (Opladen: Westdeutscher Verlag, 1992).

8. Fred Halliday, "State and Society in International Relations," in Michael Banks and Martin Shaw, eds., *State and Society in International Relations* (New York: St. Martin's Press), p. 194; see pp. 191–209 in the same volume for a very useful discussion of the difference between the concept of the state as a national-territorial totality—which is still employed often in international relations and in politics among nations—and the sociological view of the state as governing institutions distinct from the broader social and national context.

9. For a similar periodization of fundamental transformations, which is, however, based on long-term cycles, see Chapter 3.

10. See Immanuel Wallerstein, *The Modern World System 1: Capitalist Agriculture and the Origins of the European World Economy in the Sixteenth Century* (New York: Academic Press, 1974), chap. 1; and Charles Tilly, *Coercion, Capital, and European States, AD 990–1990* (Oxford: Basil Blackwell, 1990), chap. 1.

11. A *territorial state* can be defined as an "organization with a comparative advantage in violence, extending over a geographic area whose boundaries are determined by its power to tax constituents." See Douglass C. North, *Structure and Change in Economic History* (New York: Norton, 1981), p. 249. The *nation-state* is then a special form of the territorial state, with a legitimacy based on an imagined national identity. See Benedict Anderson, *Imagined Communities*, rev. ed. (London: Verso, 1991), chap. 1, for the notion of imagined community. The *ethnic national state* is distinguished from the nation-state by its focus on a monolingual or monoethnic foundation of the imagined community.

12. See Charles Tilly, "War Making and State Making as Organized Crime," in Peter B. Evans, Dietrich Rueschemeyer, and Theda Skocpol, eds., *Bringing the State Back In* (Cambridge: Cambridge University Press, 1985), pp. 169–191; and Ekkehard Krippendorff, *Staat und Krieg* (Frankfurt am Main: Suhrkamp, 1985).

13. See David Kaiser, *Politics and War: European Conflict from Philip II to Hitler* (Cambridge, Mass.: Harvard University Press, 1990), chap. 2.

14. See Robert Gilpin, *War and Change in World Politics* (Cambridge: Cambridge University Press, 1981), p. 122. The close relationship between economic and military power throughout modern history is also demonstrated in Paul Kennedy, *The Rise and Fall of the Great Powers: Economic Change and Military Conflict from 1500 to 2000* (New York: Random House, 1987).

15. For the purpose of this historical sketch, I neglect the long-distance trade with luxury items, which had already existed for a long time. Most of these goods mainly served for luxury consumption of the aristocratic and clerical elites and thus did not play an economically decisive role. See Hartmut Elsenhans, *Nord-Süd-Beziehungen: Geschichte-Politik-Wirtschaft* (Stuttgart: Kohlhammer, 1984), chap. 2.

16. Polanyi, *The Great Transformation*, p. 70.

17. For the well-known phrase as well as for the following, see ibid., pp. 141–150.

18. For this argument see Ernest Gellner, *Nationalism and Nations* (Ithaca, N.Y.: Cornell University Press, 1983), chap. 3.

19. See Anderson, *Imagined Communities*, p. 50.

20. See Samuel P. Huntington, *The Third Wave: Democratization in the Late Twentieth Century* (Norman: University of Oklahoma Press, 1991), pp. 16–17, for a succinct account.

21. Eric A. Hobsbawm, *Nations and Nationalism Since 1870: Programme, Myths and Reality*, 2nd ed. (Cambridge, England: Canto, 1992), pp. 29–30, demonstrates this by referring to the writings of Friedrich List and Alexander Hamilton. See also Dieter Senghaas, *Von Europa lernen: Entwicklungsgeschichtliche Betrachtungen* (Frankfurt am Main: Suhrkamp, 1982).

22. See Edward L. Morse, *Modernization and the Transformation of International Relations* (New York: Free Press, 1976), p. 118.

23. See R. R. Palmer and Joel Cotton, *A History of the Modern World*, 6th ed. (New York: Alfred A. Knopf, 1984), p. 449.

24. International regimes are a subset of international institutions, as are international organizations. Whereas international organizations represent purposive entities, international regimes are only sets of norms and rules spelling out the range of admissible behavior of different kinds of actors.

25. John Gerard Ruggie, "International Regimes, Transactions and Change: Embedded Liberalism in the Postwar Economic Order," in Stephen D. Krasner, ed., *International Regimes* (Ithaca, N.Y.: Cornell University Press), p. 209.

26. See Helen V. Milner, *Resisting Protectionism: Global Industries and the Politics of International Trade* (Princeton: Princeton University Press, 1988), and Beate Kohler-Koch, "Interessen und Integration: Die Rolle organisierter Interessen im westeuropäischen Intregrationsprozeß," in Michael Kreile, ed., *Die Integration Europas*, special issue of *Politische Viertel Jahres Schrift* (Opladen: Westdeutscher Verlag), no. 23 (1992): 81–119.

27. See for instance the work of Peter Katzenstein, *Small States in World Markets: Industrial Policy in Europe* (Ithaca, N.Y.: Cornell Univerity Press, 1985).

28. Richard N. Cooper, *Economic Policy in an Interdependent World: Essays in World Economics* (Cambridge, Mass: MIT Press, 1986), chap. 4.

29. See United Nations, *World Investment Report: Transnational Corporations as Engines of Growth* (New York: UN, 1992).

30. See Robert Reich, *The Work of Nations: Preparing Ourselves for Twenty-first Century Capitalism* (New York: Vintage Books), pp. 81–153.

31. See Susan Strange, *Casino Capitalism* (Oxford: Basic Blackwell, 1986).

32. Reich, *The Work of Nations*, p. 8.

33. See Josef Esser, "Die Suche nach dem Primat der Politik: Anmerkungen zu einer Pseudodebatte über Parteien, Machtversessenheit und Machtvergessenheit," in Siegfried Unseld, ed., *Europa ohne Projekt* (Frankfurt am Main: Suhrkamp, 1993). To the contrary, Geoffrey Garrett and Peter Lange, in "Political Responses to Interdependence: What's 'Left' for the Left?" *International Organization* 45, no. 4 (1991): 539–564, still see national room for maneuver and thus an opportunity for leftist policies. In any case, there is an agreement that the instruments of effective national policies have changed and that most of the new policies cannot be generalized; they work only for one or a few countries or regions.

34. See the assessments in Graham Allison, Ashton B. Carter, Steven E. Miller, and Philip Zelikov, eds., *Cooperative Denuclearization: From Pledges to Deeds*, CSIA Studies in International Security, no. 2 (Cambridge, Mass.: Harvard University Press, 1993).

35. Robert O. Keohane, "Sovereignty, Interdependence, and International Institutions," working paper, no. 91–1, Center of International Affairs, Harvard University, p. 1.

36. See Rudolf Hrbek, "Nationalstaat und europäische Integration: Die Bedeutung der nationalstaatlichen Komponente für den EG–Integrationsprozeß," in Peter Haungs, ed., *Europäisierung Europas* (Baden-Baden: Nomos, 1989), pp. 81–108.

37. See for instance, Michael Zürn, *Interessen und Institutionen in der internationalen Politik: Eine Grundlegung des situationsstrukturellen Ansatzes* (Opladen: Leske and Budrich, 1992), chap. 2.

38. See Peter M. Haas, Robert O. Keohane, and Marc Levy, eds., *Institutions for the Earth: Sources of Effective International Environmental Protection* (Cambridge, Mass.: MIT Press, 1993); and Peter M. Haas with Jan Sundgren, "Evolving International Environmental Law: Changing Practices of National Sovereignty," in Nazli Chourzi, ed., *Global Accord: Environmental Challenges and Responses* (Cambridge, Mass: MIT Press, 1993).

39. Bernd W. Kubbig and Harald Müller, *Nuklearexport und Aufrüstung: Neue Bedrohungen und Friedensperspektiven* (Frankfurt am Main: Fischer, 1993).

40. Robert O. Keohane, *After Hegemony: Collaboration and Discord in World Politics* (Princeton: Princeton Univerity Press, 1993).

41. See *Yearbook of International Organisations 1991/92* (Munich: K. G. Saur, 1992), appendix 3. According to this source, the number of IGOs declined in 1991 to under 300; the number was highest (over 370) in the mid-1980s. These numbers look surprising and may be due partially to the breakdown of organizations in Eastern Europe and partially to a measurement error, but it is safe to assume that no growth of IGOs has taken place.

42. As to Europe, see Hartmut Kaelble, *Auf dem Wege zu einer europäischen Gesellschaft: Eine Sozialgeschichte Westeuropas* (Munich: C. H. Beck, 1987), chap. 5.

As to the United States, J. G. Williamson and P. H. Lindert, *American Inequality: A Macroeconomic History* (New York: Academic Press, 1980).

43. See "Rich Man, Poor Man," *Economist* 24, no. 7 (1993): 71. For the United States, see also Frank Levy, *Dollars and Dreams: The Changing American Income Distribution* (New York: Norton, 1988), chaps. 1, 2.

44. See Osvaldo Sunkel, "Transnationale kapitalistische Integration und nationale Disintegration," in Dieter Senghaas, ed., *Imperialismus und strukturelle Gewalt: Analysen über die abhängige Reproduktion* (Frankfurt am Main: Suhrkamp, 1972), pp. 258–315, for a related argument regarding Latin America.

45. See Meyer, *Modernisierung der Privatheit*, chap. 5.

46. See Rosenau, *Turbulence in World Politics*, chap. 6.

47. Huntington, *The Third Wave*, pp. 21–26, comes up with 29 instances. Daniel Posner, "Democratization, Ethic Conflict and Identity Formation" (unpublished paper, Harvard University, 1991), counts 62 cases of countries that had held contested elections by October 1992, mainly because he includes all former republics of the Soviet Union.

48. See Hans-Henrik Holm and Georg Sørensen, "A New World Order: The Withering Away of Anarchy and the Triumph of Individualism? Consequences for IR-Theory," *Cooperation and Conflict* 28, no. 3 (1993): 265–301.

49. See Ernst-Otto Czempiel, *Weltpolitik im Umbruch: Das internationale System nach dem Ende des Ost-West-Konfliktes* (Munich: C. H. Beck, 1991), chap. 4; Nigel Swain, "Global Technologies and Political Change in Eastern Europe," in Anthony McGraw, Paul G. Lewis, et al., *Global Politics: Globalization and the Nation State* (Cambridge, England: Polity Press, 1992), pp. 138–154, provides a balanced evaluation of this claim: For a general discussion of the causes of the third wave of democratization, see Huntington, *The Third Wave*, chap. 2, and Georg Sørensen, *Democracy and Democratization* (Boulder: Westview Press), chap. 2.

50. See Wilhelm Heitmeyer and Juliane Jacobs, eds., *Politische Sozialisation und Individualisierung* (Weinheim und Munich: Juventa, 1991).

51. See Lothar Brock, "Im Umbruch der Weltpolitik," *Leviathan* 21, no. 2 (1993): 163–173; he coined the term "identity surfing" as one feature of our turbulent period.

52. See Posner, "Democratization, Ethnic Conflict and Identity Formation," p. 2.

53. Wolf-Dieter Eberwein, "International Conflict and Domestic Regime Change 1816–1980," paper presented at the Thirty-fourth Annual Meeting of the International Studies Association, Acapulco, Mexico, March 23–27, 1993.

54. For a discussion of the characteristics of conflicts over values (as opposed to conflicts over interests and conflicts over means) in the international realm, see Volker Rittberger and Michael Zürn, "Regime Theory: Findings from the Study of 'East-West Regimes,'" *Cooperation and Conflict* 26, no. 4 (1991): 164–183.

55. See Dieter Senghaas and Eva Senghaas, "*Si vis pacem, para pacem:* Überlegungen zu einem zeitgemäßen Friedenskonzept," in *Leviathan* 20, no. 2 (1992): 230–252, who discuss the value of N. Elias's concept "process of civilization" for building peace structures.

56. For this term see Barry B. Hughes, "Delivering the Goods: European Integration and the Evolution of Complex Governance," paper presented at the Annual

Meeting of the American Political Science Association, Washington, D.C., August 1991. See also Thomas Risse-Kappen, *Cooperation Among Democracies: Norms, Transnational Relations, and the European Influence on U.S. Foreign Policy* (Princeton: Princeton University Press, forthcoming), for an interesting account of complicated networks of international governance.

57. See Joseph P. Grieco, "State Interests and International Rule Trajectories: The Politics of European Economic Monetary Union" unpublished paper, Duke University, 1992, p. 23. The *locus classicus* of structural realism, of course, is Kenneth N. Waltz, *Theory of International Politics* (Reading, Mass.: Addison-Wesley, 1979).

58. To be sure, structural realists have a strong argument about the troublesome consequences of a multipolar system as compared to the stable bipolar system. See John J. Mearsheimer, "Back to the Future: Instability in Europe After the Cold War," *International Security* 15, no. 1 (1990): 5–56. Yet the redistribution of power resources between states is only one of the consequences of social change, and arguably not even the most important one.

59. Outstanding modern representatives for such an explanation of overexpansionist policies are Hans-Ulrich Wehler, *Bismarck und der Imperialismus* (Cologne: Kiepenheuer & Wietsch, 1969); Jack Snyder, *Myths of Empire: Domestic Politics and International Ambitions* (Ithaca, N.Y: Cornell Univerity Press, 1991). Fareed Zakaria, "Realism and Domestic Politics: A Review Essay," *International Security* 17, no. 1 (1992): 177–198, demonstrates convincingly that these domesticist claims are not compatible with structural realism.

60. See inter alia Michael Doyle, "Liberalism and World Politics," *American Political Science Review* 80, no. 4 (1983): 1151–1169; and Volker Rittberger, "Zur Friedensfähigkeit von Demokratien: Betrachtungen zur politischen Theorie des Friedens," *Aus Politik und Zeitgeschichte* 44 (1987): 3–12.

61. Michael Zürn, "Bringing the Second Image (Back) In: On the Domestic Sources of Regime Formation," in Volker Rittberger, ed., *Regimes in International Relations* (Oxford: Oxford Univerity Press, 1993).

62. Theda Skocpol, "Bringing the State Back In: Strategies of Analysis in Current Research," in Evans, Rueschemeyer, and Skocpol, *Bringing the State Back In*, p. 9.

63. See the contributions in Kenneth A. Oye, ed., *Cooperation Under Anarchy* (Princeton: Princeton Univerity Press, 1986).

64. See Keohane, *After Hegemony*, chap. 7.

65. See Joseph M. Grieco, "Understanding the Problem of International Cooperation: The Limits of Neoliberal Institutionalism, and the Future of Realist Theory," in David Baldwin, ed., *Neorealism and Neoliberalism: The Contemporary Debate* (New York: Columbia Univerity Press, 1994).

66. Volker Rittberger and Michael Zürn, "Towards Regulated Anarchy in East-West Relations: Causes and Consequences of East-West Regimes," in Volker Rittberger, ed., *International Regimes in East-West Politics* (London: Pinter, 1990), pp. 9–63.

67. See Thomas M. Franck, *The Power of Legitimacy Among Nations* (Oxford: Oxford University Press, 1990).

68. Paul Kennedy, *Preparing for the Twenty-first Century* (New York: Random House, 1993), p. 344 (emphasis in original).

CHAPTER 9

I am grateful for comments on earlier versions of this paper to Stanley Hoffmann, Nannerl O. Keohane, and Jack Levy; to my fellow contributors to this volume, who met near Copenhagen on May 14–16, 1993, especially to Michael Zürn and the editors; and to participants at a seminar of the Olin Institute at the Center for International Affairs, Harvard University, March 1, 1993, especially to Tom Berger, Tom Christensen, Barbara Farnum, Yuen Khong, Lisa Martin, Celeste Wallander, and Richard Weitz. An earlier version of this chapter appeared as a working paper (May 1993) of the Center for International Affairs, Harvard University.

1. Joanne Gowa, "Bipolarity, Multipolarity and Free Trade," *American Political Science Review* 83 no. 4 (December 1989): 1245–1256.

2. U.S. House, Special Committee on Post-War Economic Policy and Planning, *Hearings* (Washington, D.C.: GPO, 1945), p. 1082. Cited in Gabriel Kolko, *The Politics of War: The World and United States Foreign Policy, 1943–1945* (New York: Vintage Books of Random House, 1968), p. 254.

3. Kenneth N. Waltz, *Theory of International Politics* (Reading, Mass.: Addison Wesley, 1979).

4. Thucydides, *The Peloponnesian War,* Book 3, paras. 81–82.

5. On the "realist trap," see Robert O. Keohane, "Theory of World Politics: Structural Realism and Beyond," in Keohane, *International Institutions and State Power: Essays in International Relations Theory* (Boulder: Westview Press, 1989), pp. 35–73, especially pp. 65–66.

6. Hans-Henrik Holm and Georg Sørensen, "A New World Order: The Withering Away of Anarchy and the Triumph of Individualism? Consequences for IR-Theory," *Cooperation and Conflict* 28, no. 3 (1993): 265–301.

7. For this definition, see Robert O. Keohane, *International Institutions and State Power,* pp. 3–7 and chap. 7.

8. Robert O. Keohane and Joseph S. Nye, Jr., *Power and Interdependence: World Politics in Transition* (Boston: Little, Brown, 1977 and 1989).

9. In terms of the paradigms discussed by Holm and Sørensen in "A New World Order," this chapter could be considered to be "pluralist" but sympathetic to realism's emphasis on the significance of conflicts of interest and interstate power competition in world politics.

10. Thomas Hobbes, *Leviathan* (Paris, 1651), Book 1, chap. 13.

11. Martin Wight, *International Theory: The Three Traditions* (New York: Holmes & Meier, 1992), p. 35.

12. *Leviathan,* Part 2, chap. 17.

13. *Leviathan,* Part 1, chap. 13.

14. John M. Herz, *International Politics in the Atomic Age* (New York: Columbia University Press, 1959).

15. Evan Luard, *War in International Society* (New Haven: Yale University Press, 1987), p. 247, says that perhaps 40 percent of the rural and town population of Germany may have died, although this estimate may be too high. On battle deaths, see Charles Tilly, *Coercion, Capital and European States, AD 990–1990* (Oxford: Basil Blackwell, 1990), p. 165.

16. Sovereign statehood in my view has helped shape states' conceptions of self-interest. For instance, great-power intervention in Africa during the Cold War was focused on helping the great power's clients gain power within unified states, rather than on promoting fragmentation. The one major attempt to change boundaries by war—Somalia's invasion of Ethiopia in the late 1970s—led to withdrawal of U.S. support for Somalian military actions and a resounding defeat. For an astute analysis, see Robert H. Jackson and Carl G. Rosberg, "Why Africa's Weak States Persist: The Empirical and the Juridical in Statehood," *World Politics* 35, no. 1 (October 1982): 1–24.

17. Adam Smith, *An Inquiry into the Nature and Causes of the Wealth of Nations* (1776), especially Volume 1, Book 1, chaps. 1, 3, 4, and Book 4. Edited by Edwin Cannan (Chicago: University of Chicago Press, 1976), p. 8.

18. Oliver Williamson, *The Economic Institutions of Capitalism* (New York: Free Press, 1985).

19. The same point applies for all authoritarian states: somehow, the state must be able to make credible commitments not to exploit members of society whose activities create wealth. Stable property rights require constitutional government, although not necessarily democracy. Hence the desire for economic growth provides a set of incentives for constitutionalism, as can be observed in Korea and Taiwan and perhaps in the future will emerge in China. But these incentives are not necessarily decisive; other favorable conditions have to apply before constitutionalism can be effectively instituted.

20. See Margaret Levi, *Of Rule and Revenue* (Berkeley: University of California Press, 1988), especially chap. 1.

21. Douglass C. North and Robert Paul Thomas, *The Rise of the Western World* (Cambridge: Cambridge University Press, 1973), pp. 2–3.

22. Charles P. Kindleberger, *A Financial History of Western Europe* (London: George Allen & Unwin, 1984); Douglass C. North and Barry R. Weingast, "Constitutions and Commitment: The Evolution of Institutions Governing Public Choice in Seventeenth-Century England," *Journal of Economic History* 49, no. 4 (December 1989): 803–832.

23. F. H. Hinsley, *Sovereignty,* 2nd ed. (Cambridge: Cambridge University Press, 1986), p. 1.

24. Bernard Bailyn, *The Ideological Origins of the American Revolution* (Cambridge: Belknap Press of Harvard University Press, 1967), pp. 201–229.

25. Madison to Jefferson, October 24, 1787. J. P. Boyd, ed., *The Papers of Thomas Jefferson* (Princeton: Princeton University Press, 1955), pp. 278–279.

26. Hans J. Morgenthau, *Politics Among Nations,* 4th ed. (New York: Knopf, 1967), p. 305.

27. Stephen D. Krasner, "Westphalia and All That," draft chapter (October 1992) for Judith Goldstein and Robert O. Keohane, eds., *Ideas and Foreign Policy: Beliefs, Institutions and Political Change* (Ithaca, N.Y.: Cornell University Press, forthcoming).

28. Wight, *International Theory,* pp. 2–3.

29. Hedley Bull, *The Anarchical Society* (New York: Columbia University Press, 1977), pp. 34–37. Martin Wight makes this connection between sovereignty and rec-

iprocity explicit by saying that "reciprocity was inherent in the Western conception of sovereignty." *Systems of States* (Leicester: Leicester University Press, 1977), p. 135.

30. One difficulty with realist characterizations of anarchy is that they conflate three different meanings of the term: (1) lack of common government; (2) insignificance of institutions; and (3) chaos, or Hobbes's "war of all against all." Only the first meaning can be shown to be true in general of international relations. For a good discussion of anarchy in international relations, see Helen V. Milner, "The Assumption of Anarchy in International Relations Theory: A Critique," *Review of International Studies* 17, no. 1 (January 1991): 67–86.

31. Robert O. Keohane, *After Hegemony: Cooperation and Discord in the World Political Economy* (Princeton: Princeton University Press, 1984); Stephen D. Krasner, ed., *International Regimes* (Ithaca, N.Y.: Cornell University Press, 1982). Note that a demand for international regimes does not create its own supply; hence a functional theory does not imply, incorrectly, that efficient institutions always emerge or that we live in the (institutionally) best of all possible worlds.

32. Alexander Wendt, "Anarchy Is What States Make of It," *International Organization* 46, no. 2 (Spring 1992): 414–415.

33. Georg Sørensen, "The Limits of Neorealism: Western Europe After the Cold War," paper presented at the Nordic International Studies Association (NISA) Inaugural Conference, Oslo, August 18–19, 1993, p. 9.

34. Wendt, "Anarchy Is What States Make of It," p. 423.

35. Peter J. Katzenstein, *Small States in World Markets* (Ithaca, N.Y.: Cornell University Press, 1984); Peter Gourevitch, *Politics in Hard Times* (Ithaca, N.Y.: Cornell University Press, 1986); Helen V. Milner, *Resisting Protectionism* (Princeton: Princeton University Press, 1988); Ronald Rogowski, *Commerce and Coalitions* (Princeton: Princeton University Press, 1989); Jeffry A. Frieden, "National Economic Policies in a World of Global Finance," *International Organization* 45, no. 4 (Autumn 1991): 425–452; Andrew Moravcsik, "Liberalism and International Relations Theory," working paper, no. 92-6, Center for International Affairs, Harvard University, October 1992.

36. See Inis L. Claude, *Power and International Relations* (New York: Random House, 1962).

37. For Waltz a sovereign state "decides for itself how it will cope with its internal and external problems." That is, sovereignty is the equivalent of self-help, which derives from anarchy. Waltz, *Theory of International Politics*, p. 96. A brilliant critique of Waltz's failure to incorporate a historical dimension in his theory is by John Gerard Ruggie, "Continuity and Transformation in the World Polity: Toward a Neorealist Synthesis," *World Politics* 35 (January 1983): 261–285. For Ruggie's chapter, other commentaries, and a reply by Waltz, see Robert O. Keohane, ed., *Neorealism and Its Critics* (New York: Columbia University Press, 1986).

38. For general discussions see Robert O. Keohane and Stanley Hoffmann, *The New European Community: Decisionmaking and Institutional Change* (Boulder: Westview Press, 1991); and Alberta M. Sbragia, ed., *Europolitics: Institutions and Policymaking in the "New" European Community* (Washington, D.C.: Brookings, 1992). On the European Court of Justice and neofunctional theory, see Anne-Marie

Burley and Walter Mattli, "Europe Before the Court: A Political Theory of Legal Integration," *International Organization* 47, no. 1 (Winter 1993): 41–76. It is not clear that the Maastricht Treaty, even if ratified, will fundamentally alter practices relating to sovereignty in the EC. On Maastricht, see Wayne Sandholtz, "Choosing Union: Monetary Politics and Maastricht," *International Organization* 47, no. 1 (Winter 1993): 1–40.

39. For a general argument about the "security externalities" of agreements to open borders to free trade, see Joanne Gowa, "Bipolarity, Multipolarity and Free Trade," *American Political Science Review* 83, no. 4 (December 1989): 1245–1256.

40. Robert E. Hudec, Daniel L. M. Kennedy, and Mark Sgarabossa, "A Statistical Profile of GATT Dispute Settlement Cases: 1948–1990," unpublished manuscript, University of Minnesota Law School, 1992.

41. See Helge Hveem, "Hegemonic Rivalry and Antagonistic Interdependence: Bilateralism and the Management of International Trade," paper presented at the First Pan-European Conference in International Studies, Heidelberg, September 16–20, 1992. His figures come from the UNCTAD database on trade control measures. On p. 16 Hveem quotes Robert Gilpin about the "complementary development" of globalization and mercantilism, citing "The Transformation of the International Political Economy," *Jean Monnet Chair Papers* (The European Policy Unit at the European University Institute, Firenze).

42. Stephan Haggard, Marc A. Levy, Andrew Moravcsik, and Kalypso Nicolaides, "Integrating the Two Halves of Europe: Theories of Interests, Bargaining and Institutions," in Robert O. Keohane, Joseph S. Nye, and Stanley Hoffmann, eds., *After the Cold War: International Institutions and State Strategies in Europe, 1989–1991* (Cambridge, Mass.: Harvard University Press, 1993), p. 182.

43. Kenneth A. Oye, ed., *Cooperation Under Anarchy* (Princeton: Princeton University Press, 1986).

44. Robert D. Putnam, with Robert Leonardi and Rafaella Nanetti, *Making Democracy Work: Civic Traditions in Modern Italy* (Princeton: Princeton University Press, 1993).

45. See Samuel P. Huntington, *The Third Wave: Democratization in the Late Twentieth Century* (Norman: Oklahoma University Press, 1991), especially chap. 2 (pp. 31–108).

46. Democratic pluralism is necessary for the multiple channels of contact between societies characteristic of complex interdependence. With respect to restraints on the use of force, it seems clear from the large literature on democracy and war that democracies have rarely, if ever (depending on one's definition), fought one another, although they vigorously fight nondemocracies. However, nondemocracies have often been at peace with one another, so democracy is certainly not necessary to peace. Furthermore, until recently democracies have been relatively few and either scattered or allied against a common enemy (or both); so the empirical evidence for the causal impact of mutual democracy is weak. Among the OECD countries peace seems ensured by a combination of mutual economic and political interests, lack of territorial conflict, and mutual democracy. On theoretical grounds, however, no one has yet succeeded in showing that mutual democracy is sufficient: to do so, one would have to develop and test a convincing theory of why democracies should not fight one another. For some of this literature, see Michael Doyle, "Kant, Liberal Legacies and

Foreign Affairs," *Philosophy and Public Affairs* 12 (1983): 205–235 and 323–353 (two-part article); Zeev Maos and Nasrin Abdolali, "Regime Types and International Conflict," *Journal of Conflict Resolution* 33 (1989): 3–35; and Georg Sørensen, "Kant and Processes of Democratization: Consequences for Neorealist Thought," *Journal of Peace Research* 29 (1992): 397–414. My thinking on this issue has been affected by a stimulating talk given at the Harvard Center for International Affairs by Professor Joanne Gowa of Princeton University on May 6, 1993, and by a just-completed Ph.D. dissertation at Harvard University by John Owen on sources of "democratic peace."

47. My characterization of emerging patterns of world politics has much in common with the stimulating discussion of "plurilateralism" offered by Philip G. Cerny in "Plurilateralism: Structural Differentiation and Functional Conflict in the Post–Cold War World Order," *Millenium: Journal of International Studies* 22 (Spring 1993): 27–52.

48. Edward A. Parson, "Protecting the Ozone Layer," in Peter M. Haas, Robert O. Keohane, and Marc A. Levy, eds., *Institutions for the Earth: Sources of Effective International Environmental Protection* (Cambridge Mass.: MIT Press, 1993), pp. 49–50.

49. For a similar argument, contrasting a liberal core and a realist periphery, see James M. Goldgeier and Michael McFaul, "A Tale of Two Worlds: Core and Periphery in the Post–Cold War Era," *International Organization* 46, no. 1 (Spring 1992): 467–492.

50. For an argument that humanitarian concerns played a key role in the provision of foreign aid, see David Halloran Lumsdaine, *Moral Vision in International Politics: The Foreign Aid Regime, 1949–1989* (Princeton: Princeton University Press, 1993).

51. Wight points out the Hobbesian premises of the charter—in the event of a lack of unanimity "the social contract will be dissolved." He sardonically remarks that "it is perhaps difficult to find the United Nations intellectually appetizing, but one of its few thrills is in seeing how the penetrating vision of a great political philosopher has this kind of prophetic quality." Martin Wight, *International Theory*, pp. 35–36. Inis L. Claude, *Power and International Relations* (New York: Random House, 1962).

52. The exception is the UN operation in Korea, which was made possible by a Soviet boycott of the Security Council and which permitted the council to approve UN action without Soviet consent. Certain peacekeeping operations of the 1950s and 1960s were also somewhat successful despite great-power disagreement.

53. Joseph S. Nye, Jr., *Bound to Lead: The Changing Nature of American Power* (New York: Basic Books, 1990).

54. The Hobbesian paradox implies that if the Security Council became effective, it would be expected to act in the interests of its dominant member and thus to become oppressive.

55. On international institutions, see Keohane, Nye, and Hoffmann, *After the Cold War.*

56. Waltz, *Theory of International Politics*, chap. 5.

57. Classic accounts include Barrington Moore, Jr., *Social Origins of Dictatorship and Democracy* (Boston: Beacon Press, 1966); Theda Skocpol, *States and Social Revolution: A Comparative Analysis of France, Russia and China* (Cambridge: Cam-

bridge University Press, 1979); Charles Tilly, ed., *The Formation of National States in Western Europe* (Princeton: Princeton University Press, 1975).

CHAPTER 10

We are grateful for comments from our fellow authors on a draft of this chapter, especially Robert Keohane and Michael Zürn.

1. Robert Jervis, "The Future of World Politics: Will It Resemble the Past?" *International Security* 16, no. 3 (1991): 39.

2. Kjell Goldmann, *Det internationella systemet: En teori och dess begränsningar* (Stockholm: Aldus/Bonniers, 1978), p. 43 (our translation from Swedish).

3. Patrick James, "Neorealism as a Research Enterprise: Toward Elaborated Structural Realism," *International Political Science Review* 14, no. 2 (1993): 123.

4. John J. Mearsheimer, "Back to the Future: Instability in Europe After the Cold War," *International Security* 15, no. 1 (1990): 5–57; Kenneth Waltz, "The New World Order," *Millennium: Journal of International Studies* 22, no. 2 (1993): 187–195.

5. Barry Buzan, Charles Jones, and Richard Little, *The Logic of Anarchy: Neorealism to Structural Realism* (New York: Columbia University Press, 1993); James, "Neorealism as a Research Enterprise."

6. Yale H. Ferguson and Richard W. Mansbach, "Between Celebration and Despair: Constructive Suggestions for Future International Theory," *International Studies Quarterly* 35, no. 4 (1991): 363–387; Philip G. Cerny, "Plurilateralism: Structural Differentiation and Functional Conflict in the Post–Cold War World Order," *Millennium: Journal of International Studies* 22, no. 1 (1993): 27–51; James Rosenau, *Turbulence in World Politics: A Theory of Change and Continuity* (Princeton: Princeton University Press, 1990).

7. Stephen D. Krasner, "Realism, Imperialism, and Democracy: A Response to Gilbert," *Political Theory* 20, no. 1 (1992): 38.

8. Kenneth Waltz, *Theory of International Politics* (Reading, Mass.: Addison-Wesley, 1979), p. 111.

9. Ibid.

10. Krasner, "Realism, Imperialism, and Democracy," p. 39.

11. Ibid., p. 39.

12. Robert O. Keohane and Joseph S. Nye, *Power and Interdependence: World Politics in Transition* (Boston: Little, Brown, 1977).

13. Robert H. Jackson and Alan James, eds., *States in a Changing World* (Oxford: Clarendon Press, 1993).

14. Robert O. Keohane, *International Institutions and State Power: Essays in International Relations Theory* (Boulder: Westview Press, 1989); Joseph Grieco, "Anarchy and the Limits of Cooperation: A Realist Critique of the Newest Liberal Institutionalism," *International Organization* 42, no. 3 (1988): 485–508.

15. The argument is developed a bit further in Hans-Henrik Holm and Georg Sørensen, "A New World Order: The Withering Away of Anarchy and the Triumph of Individualism? Consequences for IR-Theory," *Cooperation and Conflict* 28, no. 3 (1993): 265–301.

16. Philip G. Cerny, *The Changing Architecture of Politics: Structure, Agency, and the Future of the State* (London and Newbury Park, Calif.: Sage, 1990); Richard Rosecrance, *The Rise of the Trading State: Commerce and Conquest in the Modern World* (New York: Basic Books, 1986).

17. See Ferguson and Mansbach, "Between Celebration and Despair."

18. See Robert Keohane's Chapter 9 in this book and Michael Doyle's articles, "Kant, Liberal Legacies and Foreign Affairs," *Philosophy and Public Affairs* 12, no. 3 (1983): 205–235; "Kant, Liberal Legacies and Foreign Affaris, Part 2," *Philosophy and Public Affairs* 12, no. 4 (1983): 323–354. See also Georg Sørensen, "Kant and Processes of Democratization: Consequences for Neorealist Thought," *Journal of Peace Research* 29, no. 4 (1992): 397–415.

19. Buzan, Little, and Jones, *The Logic of Anarchy;* James Rosenau, "Governance, Order and Change in World Poltics," in James Rosenau, Ernst-Otto Czempiel, eds., *Governance Without Government: Order and Change in World Politics* (New York: Cambridge University Press, 1992), pp. 1–29.

20. Including, for some, the complete rejection of any kind of positivist scholarship. For an overview of various currents of postpositivism, see Pauline Rosenau, *Post-Modernism and the Social Sciences: Insights, Inroads, and Intrusions* (Princeton: Princeton University Press, 1992).

21. Joseph S. Nye, *Bound to Lead: The Changing Nature of American Power* (New York: Basic Books, 1991); James A. Caporaso and Stephen Haggard, "Power in the International Political Economy," in Richard J. Stoll and Michael D. Ward, eds., *Power in World Politics* (Boulder and London: Lynne Rienner, 1989), pp. 99–120.

22. F. S. Northedge, *The International Political System* (London: Faber and Faber, 1976), p. 15. See also Alan James, *Sovereign Statehood* (London: Allen & Unwin, 1986); and Fred Halliday, "State and Society in International Relations," pp. 191–209 in Michael Banks and Martin Shaw, eds., *State and Society in International Relations* (New York: Harvester Wheatsheaf, 1991), pp. 191–209.

23. See also Richard K. Ashley, "Political Realism and Human Interests," *International Studies Quarterly* 25, no. 2 (1984): 204–236.

24. Peter J. Katzenstein, "International Relations Theory and the Analysis of Change," in E-O. Czempiel and James Rosenau, eds., *Global Changes and Theoretical Challenges: Approaches to World Politics for the 1990s* (Lexington, Mass.: Lexington Books, 1989), p. 298.

25. For our discussion of state concepts we are indebted to Halliday, "State and Society in International Relations."

26. Theda Skocpol, *States and Social Revolutions* (Cambridge: Cambridge University Press, 1979), p. 29.

27. Halliday, "State and Society in International Relations," p. 197.

28. Peter J. Katzenstein, *Small States in World Markets: Industrial Policy in Europe* (Ithaca, N.Y.: Cornell University Press, 1985), p. 32.

29. Paul Hirst and Grahame Thompson, "The Problem of 'Globalization': International Economic Relations, National Economic Management and the Formation of Trading Blocs," *Economy and Society* 21, no. 4 (1992): 370, 373.

30. See Krasner, "Realism, Imperialism, and Democracy," p. 46.

31. Theda Skocpol, "Bringing the State Back In: Strategies of Analysis in Current Research," in Peter B. Evans et al., eds., *Bringing the State Back In* (London: Cambridge University Press, 1985), p. 9.

32. Edward S. Greenberg, "State Change: Approaches and Concepts," in E. S. Greenberg and T. F. Mayer, eds., *Changes in the State: Causes and Consequences* (Newbury Park, Calif.: Sage, 1990), p. 22. See also Stephen D. Krasner, *Defending the National Interest: Raw Materials, Investments and U.S. Foreign Policy* (Princeton: Princeton University Press, 1978); Chalmers Johnson, *Miti and the Japanese Miracle* (Tokyo: Charles E. Tuttle, 1982).

33. The point was stressed in Robert Keohane and Joseph Nye's analysis of complex interdependence, and it has been emphasized by many authors since: See, for example, Friedrich Kratochwil, "The Embarrassment of Changes: Neo-Realism as the Science of Realpolitik Without Politics," *Review of International Studies* 19 (1993): 63–80; Barry B. Hughes, *International Futures: Choices in the Creation of a New World Order* (Boulder: Westview Press, 1993). See also the debate between John Gerard Ruggie and Ethan B. Kapstein in *International Organization* 47, no. 3 (1993): 501–505.

34. See Holm and Sørensen, "A New World Order."

35. For the first view, see Kenneth N. Waltz, "The Emerging Structure of International Politics," *International Security* 18, no. 2 (1993): 44–79; for the latter view, see Ferguson and Mansbach, "Between Celebration and Despair." See also the debate between Ruggie and Kapstein in *International Organization* 47, no. 3 (see note 33).

36. Krasner, "Realism, Imperialism, and Democracy," p. 39.

37. Ibid., p. 38.

38. Ruth Lapidoth, "Sovereignty in Transition," *Journal of International Affairs* 45, no. 2 (1992): 345.

39. Stephen D. Krasner, "Economic Interdependence and Independent Statehood," in Robert H. Jackson and Alan James, eds., *States in a Changing World* (Oxford: Clarendon Press, 1993), p. 318.

40. Alan James, "System or Society?" *Review of International Studies* 19, no. 3 (1993): 285.

41. See Robert H. Jackson, *Quasi-States: Sovereignty, International Relations and the Third World* (Cambridge: Cambridge University Press, 1990), p. 39.

42. In *Quasi-States,* Robert Jackson gives an instructive account of how the principle of self-determination of the peoples, when implemented as the right to self-determination of ex-colonies, came to mean suppression instead of liberation of the peoples: "Self-determination has liberated indigenous governments in Third World states but has at the same time subjected many populations to unstable and illiberal regimes which often use their sovereign rights to deny or at least neglect human rights" (pp. 48–49).

43. Jackson, *Quasi-States,* p. 29.

44. Ibid.

45. See also Robert Keohane, "Sovereignty, Interdependence and International Institutions," in Linda B. Miller and Michael J. Smith, eds., *Ideas and Ideals: Essays on Politics in Honor of Stanley Hoffmann* (Boulder: Westview Press, 1993), pp. 91–108.

46. See the treatment of sovereignty in game terms in ibid., chap. 3.

47. As does for example, Andre Gunder Frank, *Capitalism and Underdevelopment in Latin America* (New York and London: Monthly Review Press, 1969); Immanuel Wallerstein, *The Capitalist World-Economy: Essays* (New York: Cambridge University Press, 1979); and Samir Amin, *Unequal Development: An Essay on the Social Formations of Peripheral Capitalism* (New York and London: Monthly Review Press, 1976).

48. Robert O. Keohane, *After Hegemony: Cooperation and Discord in the World Political Economy* (Princeton: Princeton University Press, 1984), pp. 18–31.

49. For an example of the realist view of economics, see Benjamin J. Cohen, *The Question of Imperialism: The Political Economy of Dominance and Dependence* (London: Macmillan, 1973). For the world-system-analysis view, see Wallerstein, *The Capitalist World-Economy*.

50. This argument is developed in detail in Georg Sørensen, "Economics and Politics in International Relations," in Helena Lindholm, ed., *Approaches to the Study of International Political Economy* (Gothenburg: Padrigu, 1992), pp. 36–60.

51. See Robert Gilpin, *The Political Economy of International Relations* (Princeton: Princeton University Press, 1987).

52. Susan Strange, *States and Markets: An Introduction to International Political Economy* (London: Frances Pinter, 1988), pp. 227–241.

53. Structural power is defined as "the power to shape and determine the structures of the global political economy within which other states, their political institutions, their economic enterprises and (not least) their scientists and other professional people have to operate," ibid., pp. 24–25.

54. Ibid., p. 27.

55. As does, for example, Philip G. Cerny, "Plurilateralism: Structural Differentiation and Functional Conflict in the Post–Cold War Order," *Millennium: Journal of International Studies* 22, no. 1 (1993): 27–53.

56. Barry Buzan, *People, States and Fear: An Agenda for International Security Studies in the Post–Cold War Era* (London: Harvester Wheatsheaf, 1991), pp. 57–112. See also Barry Buzan, "New Patterns of Global Security in the Twenty-first Century," *International Affairs* 67, no. 3 (1991): 431–451.

57. See Georg Sørensen, ed., *Political Conditionality* (London: Frank Cass, 1993).

58. OECD, *Development Cooperation, Efforts and Policies of the Members of the Development Assistance Committee, Review 1991* (Paris: OECD, 1991).

59. See also the analysis by Robert Keohane in the present volume.

60. Fernando Henrique Cardoso, "Current Theses on Latin American Development and Dependency: A Critique," paper presented to the Nordic Conference on Latin America, Bergen, May 1976; Fernando Henrique Cardoso and Enzo Faletto, *Dependency and Development in Latin America* (Berkeley: University of California Press, 1979). For a recent attempt to 'rehabilitate' this type of analysis, see David Booth, "Social Development Research: An Agenda for the 1990s," *European Journal of Development Research* 4, no. 1 (1992): 1–40. A recent contribution that emphasizes the historically bounded interplay between internal (domestic) and external (international) dynamics is Stephan Haggard, *Pathways from the Periphery: The Politics of Growth in the Newly Industrializing Countries* (Ithaca, N.Y.: Cornell University Press, 1990).

61. Kari Levitt, "Debt, Adjustment and Development: Looking to the 1990s," *Economic and Political Weekly* (July 21, 1990): 1589.

62. Dieter Senghaas, *The European Experience: A Historical Critique of Development Theory* (Leamington Spa/Dover, N.H.: Berg, 1985); Ulrich Menzel, *Auswege aus Abhängigkeit: Die entwicklungspolitische Aktualität Europas* (Frankfurt am Main: Suhrkamp, 1985).

63. Ferguson and Mansbach, "Between Celebration and Despair"; Gaddis, "International Relations Theory"; Rosenau and Czempiel, *Governance Without Government.*

64. Fred W. Riggs, "Thoughts About Neoidealism vs: Realism: Reflections on Charles Kegley's ISA Presidential Address, March 25, 1993," *International Studies Notes* 19, no. 1 (1994): 5.

65. Anthony Giddens, *The Nation State and Violence* (Cambridge: Polity Press, 1985), p. 116.

66. Alexander Wendt, "Anarchy Is What States Make of It: The Social Construction of Power Politics," *International Organization* 46, no. 2 (1992): 391–425.

67. See, for example, Robert O. Keohane, *International Institutions and State Power: Essays in International Relations Theory* (Boulder: Westview Press, 1989); Stanley Baldwin, ed., *Neorealism and Neoliberalism: The Contemporary Debate* (New York: Columbia University Press, 1993).

68. Samuel P. Huntington, "The Clash of Civilizations?" *Foreign Affairs* 72, no. 3 (1993): 22–49; Robert D. Kaplan, "The Coming Anarchy," *Atlantic Monthly,* February 1994, pp. 44–76. See also the critique of Huntington and Kaplan in Ted Robert Gurr, "Peoples Against States: Ethnopolitical Conflict and the Changing World System," presidential address, ISA Annual Meeting, Washington, D.C., April 1, 1994.

69. Charles W. Kegley, "Redirecting Realism: A Rejoinder to Riggs," *International Studies Notes* 19, no. 1 (1994): 7.

About the Book and Editors

The putative new world order, when viewed from different regions of the globe, is not really new, is hardly global in scope, and is anything but orderly in its development. In this volume, an international cast of contributors comes together to share regional perspectives on questions about peace and security, economic growth and welfare, and democracy and civil society in the post–Cold War world. They find that there has been "uneven globalization" with strong "regional variation"—two important concepts that this book brings to theory-building beyond the rhetoric of new world order thinking.

An ideal supplement for many courses in international relations, *Whose World Order?* transcends the typically Eurocentric view projected in most textbooks, combining theory and practical evidence from the different regions in innovative applications and analyses.

Hans-Henrik Holm is professor of world politics at the Danish School of Journalism. **Georg Sørensen** is senior lecturer in international politics at Aarhus University, Denmark.

About the Contributors

Claude Ake is director of the Centre for Advanced Social Science, Port Harcourt, Nigeria. His latest book is *The Political Economy of Crisis and Underdevelopment in Africa* (1989).

Hans-Henrik Holm is a professor of world politics at the Danish School of Journalism. He was formerly visiting professor at the Institute of International Studies, University of California–Berkeley. His articles have recently appeared in *Cooperation and Conflict* and *Journal of Peace Research,* and he has contributed to several books. His current research project is international relations after the Cold War (with Georg Sørensen).

Takashi Inoguchi is a professor of political science at the Institute of Oriental Culture, University of Tokyo. His most recent book is *Japan's Foreign Policy in an Era of Global Change* (1993). His most recent major article is "Japanese Politics in Transition: A Theoretical Review," *Government and Opposition* (October 1993). Currently he is researching U.S.-Japanese relations and international institutions after the Cold War.

Robert O. Keohane is Stanfield professor of international peace, Harvard University, Cambridge, Massachusetts. He is the author of *After Hegemony: Cooperation and Discord in the World Political Economy* (1984) and *International Institutions and State Power* (Westview, 1989) and coeditor with Judith Goldstein of *Ideas and Foreign Policy* (1993). He is currently studying contested commitments in the history of U.S. foreign policy.

Gowher Rizvi is a fellow in international relations at Nuffield College, Oxford. His most recent publications include *South Asia in a Changing International Order* (1993), and he is currently working on *The Third World and the International System: A Self-Induced Dependence.*

Georg Sørensen, doctor of political science, is a senior lecturer in international politics at the Department of Political Science, Aarhus University, in Denmark. He is the author of *Democracy and Democratization: Processes and Prospects in a Changing World* (Westview, 1993) and the editor of *Political Conditionality* (1993). His current research project is international relations after the Cold War (with Hans-Henrik Holm).

Osvaldo Sunkel, a Chilean, holds a degree in economics and business administration from the Universidad de Chile and the London School of Economics. He has been a visiting professor at several Latin American, U.S., and European universities and was a professorial fellow at the Institute of Development Studies, Sussex University. Currently he is a Bacardi Family Eminent Scholar in Latin American Studies at the University of Florida. His most recent book is *Development from Within: A*

Neostructuralist Approach for Latin America (1993). At present, he holds the post of special adviser to the executive secretary of ECLAC, Chile.

Zhang Yunling is the director, Institute of Pacific Asian Studies, Chinese Academy of Social Sciences. He has published books and articles on Euro-Chinese relations. Recent work in English includes "National Economic Policies in China," in D. Salvatore, ed., *National Economic Policies* (1991). His present research focus is relations in Pacific Asia.

Vladislav M. Zubok is senior fellow of the Norwegian Nobel Institute, 1993–1994. His publications include "Tyranny of the Weak: Russia's Future Foreign Policy," *World Policy Journal* (Spring 1992) and (with K. Pleshakov) *Shades of Darkness: Soviet Cold Warriors from Stalin to Khrushchev* (1995). He is currently working on the history of the Berlin crisis, 1958–1962.

Michael Zürn is a professor of international politics at the University of Bremen. He received his doctorate from the University of Tübingen, where he was an assistant professor at the Center for International Relations/Peace and Conflict Studies until 1994. In 1992–1993 he was Thyssen Fellow at the Center for International Affairs, Harvard University, and in 1991, visiting professor at the Graduate School for International Studies, University of Denver. He is the author of *Gerechte internationale Regime* (1987) and *Interessen und Institutionen in der internationalen Politik* (1992).

Index